IS A STATE OF MIND

White

IS A STATE OF MIND

A Memoir

MELBA PATTILLO BEALS

G. P. Putnam's Sons

New York

G. P. Putnam's Sons
Publishers Since 1838
a member of
Penguin Putnam Inc.
375 Hudson Street
New York, New York 10014

Library of Congress Cataloging-in-Publication Data
Beals, Melba.
White is a state of mind : a memoir / Melba Pattillo Beals.
p.   cm.
ISBN 0-399-14464-1
1. School integration—Arkansas—Little Rock—History—
20th century. 2. Central High School (Little Rock, Ark.)—
History. 3. Beals, Melba. 4. Afro-American students—
Arkansas—Little Rock—Biography. I. Title.
LC214.23.L56B47 1999   98-40768 CIP
379.2'63'0976773—dc21

Printed in the United States of America

1   3   5   7   9   10   8   6   4   2

This book is printed on acid-free paper. ∞

Book design by Judith Stagnitto Abbate

Acknowledgments

I'd like to thank:

my mother, Dr. Lois Pattillo, who endowed me with the words to describe the visions I chronicle;

my grandmother, India Anette Payton, who planted seeds of confidence in my soul;

Dr. George McCabe and Carol McCabe, who by their parenting process made my dream and hope real, that freedom is always mine to claim;

Dori, Rick, Joan and Judy McCabe, who share their parents with me;

Kellie, Evan and Matthew, my children, the lights of my life;

Conrad Pattillo, my brother, Joyce, my sister-in-law, and Conrad Jr., who have always been loving and kind;

Jane McNally and Dana Durst Lawrence—sisters—white doves of peace;

Maria Picard, a dear one whose spirit hovers and inspires;

Catherine and Sanford Rosen and family;

Jean Jefferds, Jenny, Jeanie and Vincent;

John, Nick and Olivia Vos;

Babette Wurtz;

Sarah Blanchard;

Alaister and Consie Smith.

A special thanks to Dr. David Geisinger.

To Kellie Joy Beals, my darling daughter, the angel sent to accompany me on my path and to ease my journey. I cannot imagine my life without you.

Thank you for allowing me to be your mother.

ALTHOUGH MY STORY IS TRUE, I have changed some names and some places in order not to infringe on the privacy of innocent people who still live and treasure their anonymity.

M.B.

IS A STATE OF MIND

Chapter 1

IT WAS A MUGGY, STEAMY AUGUST NIGHT, the kind that forced people like us living in Little Rock, Arkansas, to leave our windows open if we wanted to breathe. But for my family and me it was different. We were concerned about much more than breathing—we were trying to save our lives—racing from room to room, slamming our windows shut and locking them as fast as we could. We were frightened out of our wits by the men banging on our front door and shouting. They said they were gonna get rid of us. My heart was pounding in my ears because I knew it was me they were after. I was only sixteen and not at all ready to die.

"Get that Melba out here right now!" one voice shouted. "Schoolin' with white folks ain't worth starving to death or gettin' skinned alive."

Once again my family was suffering because of my being one of the nine teenagers to integrate the all-white Central High in 1957. Now, as the September 1958 school term was about to begin, I was hoping to return to Central for my senior year. But lots of people—even our own—didn't approve of our going back. The angry men shouting and banging on our porch were serious about their disapproval.

There we stood—Grandma India, Mother Lois, my younger brother Conrad and me—our knees quivering, huddled together in the front hall, next to the rubber tree plant.

"We're locked down good and tight," Grandma said. "Now we wait and pray."

How could they know already that I was home? I had come back from Cleveland only hours before. Besides, I couldn't understand why these men were up in arms. They must not be reading the newspaper. There was little chance that we Negro students would be going back to attend Central High. United States District Judge Harry J. Lemley of Hope, Arkansas, had made a decision two months before, back in June, to suspend integration for two and a half years. The NAACP was filing all sorts of lawsuits to prevent delay, but it appeared we would be tough out of luck. Governor Faubus had vowed he would do whatever was necessary to keep us out. "Little Rock school integration is over forever," he said.

The yelling started again. "We know she's in there. You ain't foolin' us! She's done come back from the North this very afternoon," the deep, angry voice growled once more through the door.

All the fracas started about 9:00 P.M. when we had just laid our heads down and begun hugging our pillows. Awful banging crashed through our sleepy peace and silence. At first we thought it was segregationists come to punish me for wanting to go to school with their children. They had come to our house before, or shot their bullets through our windows late in the night. They had called on the telephone threatening to come and bomb us or take me away. But this time, one voice shouting louder than the others sounded familiar. I struggled to put a name to it. Was it one of my people?

"We ain't waitin' all night for you womenfolk to make up your minds. We gonna ride that girl outta here on a rail before daylight!" The shouts came again.

Beads of perspiration stood on Grandma's upper lip and Mama's forehead. I could hear our panic-stricken breathing over our silent waiting. "Grandma, what's gonna happen to us?" Conrad cried out. I felt really sorry for my younger brother. This kind of terror at night was enough to frighten an eleven-year-old out of his wits, except I noticed Conrad was kind of enjoying it. Every now and then he'd say it was like Hopalong Cassidy fighting off the bad guys. The hallway felt tight and hot. I could feel myself growing desperate for a breath of fresh air. I tugged at the collar of my pajama top to pull it away from my throat.

"Rupert Vogel," Grandma whispered with the excitement of sudden recall. "I'd swear one of those varmints is Rupert."

"Rupert Vogel." I couldn't help repeating his name aloud. He was someone my family had known — a neighbor, a Negro, one of my own people who occasionally helped Grandma India with yard work. He had never behaved this way before.

Once more he shouted. "The white folks is gonna choke the life out of all of us if you all don't keep to our own colored schools."

Grandma picked up a wooden straight-back chair and propped it beneath the knob of the front door. "No telling what he'll do this time," she mumbled.

"This time?" I whispered, as I looked into her huge, almond-shaped eyes for an answer and saw the cloud of sadness there. Avoiding my inquiry, she lowered her gaze to the floor. He must have been taunting them all the while I was up North this summer. While I was being feted with a tour of the White House, attending press conferences and being treated like a star, my folks must have been fending off Rupert.

Since the summer of '57 Grandma had borne up well under the unrelenting phone calls laced with harsh death threats, the shadowy intruders who parked in front of our house and followed us back and forth, and even through the hail of gunshots fired through our window. All this time we, especially Grandma, had let go of counting on any safety even in our own home. But these days I was noticing a difference in her. She neither walked nor talked nor smiled the same. Sometimes she behaved as if she were living in slow motion.

She was tall, strong and queenly in her bearing, but her bright eyes had dimmed just a bit and her smile was not as full. Now, here we were facing more trouble that would no doubt take more out of Grandma.

"We want to talk to your gal eyeball to eyeball, right now!" Mr.

Vogel's ear-shattering voice blasted us as he pounded his fist on the door. Or was it a piece of wood he was using? The door rattled on its hinges. Pretty soon, not even the heavy bolt lock, put there by the church members to keep out the Ku Klux Klan night riders who threatened to hang us, could hold the door.

"Don't you fool with me. *Now!* We want her *now!*" he insisted. His voice must be echoing through the whole neighborhood. Why didn't anyone come to our rescue? Were all our neighbors against us? A sense of helplessness was taking me over.

It was the same feeling I had during my gut-wrenching year at Central High. Memories were rushing into my head. I tried to push away the horrifying pictures of gun-toting mobs with twisted white faces, their mouths shouting hurtful words; moments inside Central High's halls filled with hateful students spitting at me and calling me "nigger"; the hopeful sight of the 101st Airborne soldiers whisking us past those who would keep us out. Helicopters had roared overhead. The spark of hope brought by the military was dashed, as school officials stood in silence, permitting—sometimes even encouraging— students to harm us. The soldiers had been instructed that they could only intervene in life-threatening situations.

For a few magical weeks of summer, we toured the country—to speak of our experiences before audiences of appreciative people. As I visited up North with those who had gone with me to Central High, I blanketed myself in all the praise, the picture-taking, the news reporters' questions. I had let myself feel safe and normal and pretty during our travels. A reporter in New York described me in a story as pretty, with a dimpled face and a well-developed hourglass figure like a model. Another in Cleveland carried a picture of me on the front page of its Living Section with the headline "The Fox Is in Town."

I had mostly thought of myself as big-boned like my father, taller than most of my friends and not as pretty as Mother Lois. People often mistook her for being Hawaiian or Italian. She was fair and petite with sharp features and long, flowing hair, and I figured I could never measure up to her. Instead, I had Grandma's chocolate complexion, her huge, almond-shaped eyes and high cheekbones. Mother would point to me and say, "You're too big-boned, you look like your dad. Thank God you've got my brains and long hair." But with the newspaper compliments, I looked into the mirror and actually smiled back at myself. My hair was long and wavy, my waist was thin and I was full-breasted, which was now in style. Jayne Mansfield's popularity as a movie star had done me a favor.

During that sixteenth summer of mine, when we were on tour, I was once again giggling aloud and thinking about the things other teenagers thought about, like Johnny Mathis's songs, dancing with boys and having all the clothes on the pages of *Seventeen* magazine. But now I was back in Little Rock and right back in the middle of the integration storm. My happy thoughts vanished, replaced by worrying about survival, just finding comfort and safety for me and my family. A cold fist tightened around my stomach.

"Melba, girl, do you hear me talking to you? Help me move this hutch to block the front door." Grandma India's voice brought me back into our current crisis. Mr. Vogel's shouting voice spewed garbled words as Grandma strained to be heard over his yelling. "Quickly now," she commanded.

Each of us squared off to take a corner of the heavy old relic. Grandma India was Mother Lois's mother, but she was tall and big-boned, like me. So even though Mother Lois and Conrad would make an effort, it was really Grandma India and I who would bear most of the weight. On the count of three, we hoisted the hutch and with a mighty effort we lifted the monstrosity toward the front door. After only a few steps, we had to stop and set the piece down. Perspiration dripped down Grandma's face. I wiped away the drops trickling down my own temples.

"If you all don't open this door, we're gonna kick it in." Rupert Vogel's shouts speeded our struggle to move the clunky, unbearably heavy piece. "Let's just push it," Grandma India ordered. In unison, we each drew a deep breath and shoved the hutch into place. Still panting, Grandma whispered, "Even if he breaks the lock, this will give us time to escape out the back way."

This was one of many times when I wished my father and mother had not divorced. If Papa Will was with us those menfolk wouldn't treat us like this. My father was well known in our community. He was six feet four inches, and his muscular good looks, cocoa brown skin, huge dark eyes, dimples and curly hair made some of

Mother's women friends refer to their divorce as her loss. Tonight, his absence was indeed our loss. If he was here he would have sent those men running in an instant.

"Oh my goodness," Mother Lois grimaced with fear. I thought to myself that it must be these repeated incidents that were putting lines in her beautiful forehead. "Listen! Footsteps," she whispered. "Many more voices and footsteps. Who can we call for help?" We knew the police wouldn't respond to a Negro's call for aid.

Frozen in my tracks, I strained to hear. Had more men come to join those taunting us? Now they would have the strength to break down the door and even get past the hutch. Panic-stricken expressions on the faces of Mother and Grandmother reflected what I felt inside. Nobody moved. Outside, footsteps scrambled and quickened. Voices tried to shout over each other—and then there was a lull in the activity. We dared not even draw a breath.

"Are you all all right in there, ladies?" It was Pastor Nelson from down the street. He must have heard the ruckus and come to help us.

"Praise God," Mother whispered as we all moved closer to the door.

"Oh Lord, we don't deserve your sweet love," Grandma sang gleefully. "Do you hear? The Lord has sent his messenger to rescue us."

A shadow lifted from Mother Lois's face as she spoke softly, "And it sounds like Deacon Wilder and Elder Lloyd."

"Don't open the door, ladies. We don't want to disturb you any more. We just happened to be holding prayer meeting at my house this evening when we heard the commotion. We're gonna hold a moment of prayer with the rambunctious gentlemen who came a-calling, if that's all right with you." The minister spoke in a take-charge voice.

We bowed our heads and listened in silence as the church men first chided Mr. Vogel and whoever was with him for disturbing womenfolk. Then the minister led them in a prayer asking for forgiveness for their sins.

"You ladies have a good night now," the reverend yelled to us as we listened to footsteps scuffling down the front steps.

"Thank you so much—thank you." We all spoke at once and then drew a collective sigh of relief and turned to force a smile at one another.

"I'll bet that Rupert guy was the one who put the pipe bomb under Mother's car," Conrad said. Pipe bomb! What was he talking about?

"Ah ah ah . . ." Mother Lois cautioned him.

"You hush your mouth right now, boy," Grandma India said, "and use your strength to help move the chest back to its place." Grandma turned to click off the porch light as she began humming a tune in order to pretend that nothing unusual had happened.

"Pipe bomb?" I couldn't believe my ears. "Pipe bomb—when?"

"Well, Rupert could'a been the one," Conrad said, as once again we prepared to lift the hutch. Suddenly Grandma India signaled us to halt.

"You don't need to speak the devil's piece, boy," Grandma said, as her smile faded with a deepening furrow of her brow.

"Mama was so scared. We almost didn't see it, but we smelled something awful and then . . ." Conrad pressed on with his story as if compelled to do so despite the adults' objections. He just couldn't keep quiet.

"If you can't keep your mouth shut, boy . . . Tell you what— we'll let the hutch rest here for the night and take care of it with the morning's strength. Good night all," Grandma said suddenly, and then she pointed at Conrad. "You get on your knees and say your prayers before you get in bed. And ask God to seal your mouth."

"I'm not sleepy," Conrad complained.

"I wanna know about the pipe bomb," I pleaded.

"Well, last week, uh, Thursday . . . It wasn't big. The police came. Daddy was really angry and . . ." As Conrad continued to explain, his face lit up and his breathless words spilled out even faster. But all of a sudden, Grandma India interrupted him with her no-nonsense voice.

"It was just a bunch of folks acting crazy. No need to give it any more thought. Sweet dreams." She snatched my brother's arm and dragged him toward his bedroom.

I was glad that my little brother spoke up, despite Grandma's objections. I needed to know, even though I couldn't bear the thought of my family suffering because of me.

Back in bed for the night, I snuggled beneath the dutch-girl quilt Grandma had sewn for me. Although my room was as hot as a wood-burning furnace, I pulled the quilt over my head, wishing it could fend off the outside world. But as I lay quiet, I couldn't push back the gushing memories forcing their way into my mind, spilling more pictures of the past that I longed to forget.

I tossed and turned for hours as I relived that incredible September day the year before when I and the eight others tried to enter Central High for the first time. Mother and I were stunned by the angry mob that greeted us as we approached the school. Throngs of white people were shouting, waving their fists, bumping and crowding into each other and into us as we stood directly in front of the school. We had plowed our way through the human sea of rage, trying to link up with the others who would attend Central with me. The plan had been for all of the integrating students to meet at one end of the school and enter together. None of us had discussed the possibility of all these people. It was like a football game or rodeo. Where had they all come from, and what did they want? They seemed more angry than any adults I'd ever seen before.

The angry mass seemed to stretch the entire two-block length of the front of the castle-like building that was Central High. I wondered how we would ever find the other integrating students. How would we connect and get across the street and up those many front stairs into the door of the school? The crowd didn't at all seem ready to let us through.

Suddenly, the voices rose even louder, as if the fire of hate had been stoked and now burned even hotter. Mother Lois and I tried to see what was causing an explosive ruckus nearby. What could possibly be happening that could enrage hundreds of people even more than they already were? And then we saw: My petite schoolmate, Elizabeth Eckford, was across the street from us, standing all alone, surrounded by shouting white people. Soldiers and state police were blocking her repeated attempts to step onto the pathway that led to the front door of Central High.

What was she doing there by herself, separated from us and the others? She must not have gotten word of the appointed meeting place. Dazed and disoriented, Mother and I stood there, our attention riveted on Elizabeth, trying frantically to search for a way to help her. Why weren't the police or the National Guard rescuing her? We realized that we could do nothing, we were helpless.

"We got us a nigger right here!" shouted a red-faced man with a rope slung over his shoulder. He was pointing at Mama and me. That's when we realized that we were in real trouble too. Men, women and children were shouting and gushing about us like the whirling winds of a tornado. We had to save ourselves, but how? We were trapped by human bodies clustered around us, hissing and screeching. In an instant they had made us their prey. They waved sticks and ropes and fists at us as their piercing, outraged voices yelled, "You ain't gonna sit beside our children! You gonna die, nigger, right here, right now, you gonna die."

"Melba, move now, fast," Mother whispered. We were backing away, turning sideways until we hit up against the people forming a barrier behind us. Scowling faces surrounded us so close that they seemed to smother me. Panic rose in my throat as I watched more overall-wearing men moving toward us, their hands groping for the ropes looped over their shoulders and under their arms.

Suddenly, my mother and I sensed the grave danger surrounding us. She urged me to run as fast as I could, but I couldn't leave her. We turned and headed back to the car, desperately trying not to be noticed. One of the men was so close that when he reached out to grab for Mama he tore her blouse, but still I had to stay with my mother, had to disobey her breathless, frantic cries for me to save myself. They chased us through the streets and as we ran I prayed aloud for God's help. Only by the miracle of a fallen branch in the path of our predators, which tripped the leaders of the pack and sent the followers sprawling, did Mother Lois and I reach the safety of our car. I jammed the gears into reverse, racing backward with my foot pressing hard on the gas pedal. And we made it. We got home with our shattered dreams, broken hearts and aching bodies.

After three weeks of waiting behind locked doors and windows in a violent war zone that had once been our home, a federal court ruling decreed that the troops must stop blocking our entry to Central. We hoped and prayed that even the most outraged segregationists would want to obey the law and end this hideous circus. But on our second trip to Central High we encountered the same howling mob outside.

Only a twist of fate got the nine of us past their treacherous gauntlet and into school. At the instant we passed, the mob's eyes and attention were suddenly drawn to news reporters being beaten in the front yard. We scampered undetected into a side door, and into the hallways of Central High. It was a place we and our ancestors had only dreamed of being, but we were really there amid crowds of white students shouting, "The niggers are getting in! Get the niggers!"

I felt as if I was being rushed to the center of a churning tornado where I had no time to admit my fear. I had to keep moving. I made my legs move forward, to outrun the angry insults, to leave behind the menacing crowd, to start my first day at Central High and grasp our hard-won victory.

By noon, our experience as Central High students was abruptly halted. By 11:45 the mob was out of control as it rampaged toward the school. The police said they couldn't protect us anymore. Some were throwing down their badges and joining the mob. Others said they had to get us out in order to save our lives and the lives of other teachers and students inside the school. One of the officers suggested they might have to distract the mob by allowing them to hang one of us while they got the other eight out. For the first time, I realized the crowd could kill me and that some of the group, including police, would let them. But one man prevailed, insisting that he could not live with "killing a child, even a Negro child."

We were spirited out through an underground garage, through the raging mob, with hundreds of hands grabbing at the rolled-up windows of the two Little Rock police cars that ferried us to safety.

Forty-eight hours later, President Eisenhower sent uniformed and armed World War II heroes of the 101st Airborne to stop the mob that would not cease their unlawful rampaging, even at his command. When those starched and armed combat-ready soldiers of the 101st escorted us through the front door of Central High, once more we hoped and prayed that this would be the end to the danger we faced. But it was only the beginning of even more horror than we could have imagined.

The days and weeks turned into months of torture at the hands of our angry and intolerant classmates. The really hostile laid down their unwelcome mat by kicking, spitting and throwing lighted pieces of paper at us. They were organized and tenacious in their physical torture, walking on my heels day after day, calling me unspeakable names, and dousing me with bowls of raw eggs. They had even sprayed acid in my eyes, an incident I survived with my sight only because the 101st soldier who guarded me had the presence of mind to jam my face beneath the water fountain and drench my eyes. And all the while I was trying to do my homework and pretend I wasn't more lonely and frightened than I thought I ever could be.

"Something the matter with you, honey? I heard you call out and then make an odd noise." Grandma India's voice and her soft touch on my cheek interrupted the flow of my nightmare.

"Just a bad dream," I explained. She left only after I promised that I would go to her room if I needed her. My body was wet with perspiration and my heart was still beating fast when I closed my eyes and tried to get back to sleep. I couldn't stop myself from twisting and turning in the covers as I fought to keep from thinking about what had been the most un-Merry Christmas of my life—Christmas of 1957.

By that time I had lived through almost four months of punches to my back and stomach, being tripped up and pushed down flights of stairs, and having acid sprayed in my eyes. My cruel classmates sang "White Christmas" to torment us. I had never felt such unrelenting hatred.

The segregationists urged Central High's student leaders to antagonize and taunt us until we responded in a way what would get us suspended or expelled. The other students tortured us relentlessly, but it was Millijean who got expelled. First, they accused her of intentionally dumping chili on a white boy's head without provocation, and she was suspended. My friends and I witnessed the incident and believe she was indeed provoked. When Minnijean returned to school after her suspension she became their prime target. She was kicked and knocked about repeatedly. Eventually, Minnijean fought back and was expelled. We were now eight integrating students among two thousand.

Meanwhile, day by day we were watching our people's jobs, the food on their tables, their rents, their house payments being wrestled away. All of the parents of those who had integrated were being threatened with losing their jobs. Mother had overcome the first big threat to her job and our security. But we didn't have any assurance that it wouldn't happen again.

Our once-strong community of businesses and church organi-

zations was being attacked one by one, systematically, by segregationists. Both white advertisers and businessmen from our own community were withdrawing their support from our only newspaper,
The State Press. The president of the local NAACP, Mrs. Daisy Bates,
and her husband were the owners. She had been the target because
her home had become one of the headquarters for organizing the integration of Central High. She had been one of the people who escorted us to school on that first day. Her home had been fire-bombed
and bricks were tossed through her windows. Now, segregationists
were strangling the newspaper her husband had founded. It was our
voice, a vehicle for rallying our people.

My own father was against my participation in the integration
of Central High. Although Daddy's fearless manner and willingness
to serve often led him to defend helpless folks who were being
taunted for no reason, now he was the one being taunted. Because
of my part in the integration turmoil, he was being beaten down by
the constant harassment from the white men on his job. Most of all,
he didn't want to lose his position as a hostler's helper with the Missouri Pacific Railroad. Negro men didn't come by those kinds of jobs
easily.

Nevertheless, we eight survived the year and even survived our
senior member's graduation from Central. Ernest Green risked life
and limb, walking alone into the history books as the first of our
people to wear the cap and gown and hold the diploma of Central
High School.

During the summer of '58 we were labeled heroes and heroines
and treated as "stars." Touring in the luxury of long, shiny black limousines and spending our nights in ritzy hotels, we strutted on stages
and pranced into crowds of admirers, signing autographs. Only an
occasional memory intruded to make me face the pain I tried to shed
that summer. There were awards and compliments from my folks, as
well as from many whites, and in some cities parades of mostly white
people welcomed us. For a time, I had stopped shrinking back and
biting my nails when white people moved toward me. I also stopped
having nightmares.

But with this night and Mr. Vogel's ugly behavior, I realized
those nightmares lay just beneath the surface. Like a panther
crouched to strike unsuspecting prey, these memories had once again

taken over my mind and body, making me feel as though I had never been away. I turned my face into my pillow and sobbed until dawn's light brought a quiet peace.

I didn't know how to tell my mother that I was beginning to think it would be best for me to give up attending Central High and leave town. How could I tell her what was really in my heart—how weary I felt and how disappointed I was at the thought of giving up my senior year for integration? All through junior high I had thought about what it would be like to become an ordinary, almighty senior with all the privileges and parties and fun involved. If I missed that, how was I ever going to make up for it?

I just wanted to be a normal sixteen-year-old with a date for the senior prom. I wanted to slow dance to Johnny Mathis's romantic songs, or swing to Elvis's "Don't Be Cruel." I wanted to date some cute boy as all my girlfriends looked on with envy. I wanted to giggle and talk about boys all night at a silly pajama party. I wanted to be free to go to the library or walk the halls without being called names. Most of all, I just wanted to feel safe. I wanted angry people to stop focusing their attention on me and causing me pain.

The added burden of knowing that integrating Central was hurting not just my family but so many of our people preyed on my mind. I continued reading the newspaper each day, wondering what would become of all of us. Would we once again be swallowed up by the storm caused by that word "integration," the storm that had taken us over the year before and turned my life into something I no longer recognized? That night I wrote in my diary:

Oh, God, please help me find my way. I don't want to disappoint anyone. Don't I deserve to have a senior year? Can't we have integration but not have me participate? This is such a big problem, only You can figure it out. Thy will be done.

Please—give me courage.

Chapter 2

LEMLEY RULING UPSET;
FAUBUS QUIET ON PLAN
The Arkansas Gazette, August 19, 1958

The next day there came the headline that I considered God's answer to my request for guidance. I held my breath as I read the article below the headline. The first line said, "The United States Eighth Circuit Court of Appeals today set aside a District Judge's Order suspending integration in Little Rock Central High School." I supposed that to mean we'd be going back to Central. I was both joyful and saddened.

The 6–1 decision reversed the ruling of Judge Lemley. At the school board's request, he had issued an order suspending integration at Central High School for two and a half years to allow for what he called a "cooling-off period."

The article pointed out that the decision setting aside the delay could have a far-reaching effect on the South. Other southern districts could now be forced to move ahead with school integration. The article said that while Governor Faubus had "no comment" on the Appeals Court decision, Capitol sources were expecting a legislative call at any moment, probably to convene Monday.

We knew the legislators getting together meant they would be looking for ways to get around the new Court of Appeals' ruling reinstating integration. The school board was loud and clear in its intentions. In that same article the members announced that they would take "any and all" measures to hold off integration for the two and a half years Judge Lemley had decreed.

Grandma said she was mighty suspicious that Faubus was so silent when he must really dislike the court's decision. That meant for certain he was planning to "do evil" against us—anything he figured would stop integration.

I sank into the cozy green velvet chair just inside the living room where I could be alone and read every word. The chair sat near the front door beside the walnut end table with the Tiffany lamp. It was the perfect spot in the front of the house where I could see out through the bay window. But most important, I could sink down and feel as though I was being comforted and hugged in the folds of its lush surface. It had been in our family forever.

I continued to read the article. Justice Matthews wrote: "We say that the time has not yet come in these United States when an order of a federal court must be whittled away, watered down or shamefully withdrawn in the face of violent and unlawful acts of individual citizens. Delay of integration of Central High School would amount to an 'open invitation' in other school districts to oppose integration with violence."

Even though I was weary and fearful of going back to Central, I took heart in the fact that maybe all my suffering, all the pain we had endured the year before was not in vain. But a queasy feeling crept into my stomach. It was as though something was tugging me in opposite directions, pulling me apart. I felt a real obligation to continue going to Central if the courts said so. But I still felt terribly sad and resentful at being cheated out of my senior year.

I had discussed going back to Central with some of those who had survived that same torment of the year before—Thelma Mothershed, Carlotta Walls, Jefferson Thomas and Elizabeth Eckford. Their thoughts seemed to be the same as my own. We would now be only five among two thousand mostly vindictive whites. Our number had been reduced by four. Minnijean had been the first to go. In early August, two students decided not to return because of the danger and uncertainty; Terrence Roberts, slated to be a senior, and Gloria Ray, set to be a junior, had changed their minds. Terry's family had moved to Los Angeles, while Gloria and her mother sought safety with her uncle in Kansas City, Missouri. And of course, Ernie Green wouldn't be returning; he had graduated triumphantly in June.

I thought about what a treat it would be to go to a town where I was unknown and start anew with no one looking at me with either expectation or hatred. Going back to Central was like going back to prison. No friends, no social life, and I would most likely hold hands with fear every moment of my school day. The more I thought about it, the more anger I felt. "Why me, God?" I whispered aloud. "Why not someone else?"

"Because the Almighty knows you are strong enough to make this sacrifice." Grandma India's starched dress crackled as she crossed the threshold into the living room, sat on the arm of the chair and snuggled up close to me. The dab of vanilla flavoring she often placed behind her ear as her favorite perfume gave off a comforting aroma. Her hair was pulled back to the nape of her neck to form a cluster of curls. She peered at me through her wire-rimmed spectacles with her huge, piercing eyes that always saw what was really true in my heart.

"I guess it's hard for a girl to ponder giving up all the fun she imagines she could have if things were different?" She looked me right in the eye.

"Yes, ma'am. I feel so sad when I think of being at Central and missing all my friends and the fun we were gonna have as seniors."

"But there are some good things about going."

"Like what?"

"Well, the experience helps you know the Lord better because you have to trust Him more. I don't doubt you'll be quite a special adult with insight and understanding."

"Maybe I'm not ready to grow up."

"Melba, most folks don't get a chance at such a speedy spiritual journey. And if they do, it's when they're much older. At Central you've learned that you can turn the other cheek and survive. You've learned to trust God and yourself, and child, this experience has put a core of steel in your spine that will make you strong forever."

"I just want to be me and have some fun with my friends."

"No turnin' back now."

"Why not?" I asked.

"Because this integration task seems to be your fate," Grandma India said, turning to look me in the eye once more with an emphatic expression as though I dare not question what she said. "You're not going there to socialize. You're cutting a pathway through their dense forest to opportunity. Our folks need access and this could give them more open doors to college, to jobs, to God's abundance."

"Central High is my fate?" I looked away, not wanting to see the certainty she seemed to have about my future. As she continued talking, I began to resign myself. Maybe I had no choice but to return to that school. I told myself it would only be one more year out of my life. One more awful, lonely year without friends or fun. I asked myself, "Can I make it if I keep in mind that I am doing it to please God?"

IN THE DAYS that followed, folks on the radio, on the television and everywhere else talked about Governor Faubus and his big plans. He was calling a special session for the purpose of instituting the laws he had created to take over public schools. These laws would allow him to do anything he wanted with the schools—including keeping us out. One morning as I sat chewing my nails, Grandma India was mumbling and grumbling as she sat in her wine-colored velvet rocking chair in the dining room. She was reading aloud an article that reported the details of Faubus's anti-integration program.

"That just ain't right," she said, suddenly crumpling the paper up in her hand.

"What?" I moved closer to console her. She seemed upset. Her lips smiled up at me but her eyebrows knitted a frown.

"Those six bills give Mr. Faubus the power to close public schools and use our tax money to set up private schools for white kids while he leaves our kids on the streets."

"What will we do if me and my friends don't have a school to go to?" I said.

"Well, the Supreme Court hasn't had a final say yet. They're mighty powerful men! They can erase all of Mr. Faubus's fancy laws if they see fit to do so." Grandma sat there for a long time rereading every word of that article and continued mumbling to herself.

To avoid thinking and fretting about integration and Mr. Faubus, I busied myself preparing for the first day of school as though it would be ordinary. I was to be a senior no matter which school I attended. I vowed to look the part. I thumbed through my *Seventeen* magazine, a special fall issue filled with pretty new school clothes I couldn't afford; I hoped I might be able to sew similar garments. With help from Mother and Grandma, I launched into sewing the absolute best wardrobe I could afford using the few dollars I had saved from my allowance. When I ran out, Grandma India sneaked me a few dollars from the change in her cookie jar that she saved for her dream, to buy her own land. It was sacred money and I knew she must really love me to spend it on fabric for my school clothes.

The August 30th newspaper told us that the 61st General Assembly adjourned after arming Governor Faubus with all the legislation he had demanded in order to do battle with federal judges over schools. This legislation gave him the power to call for and sign any of his bills at a moment's notice. Each bill included an emergency clause which allowed it to become law as soon as he signed. Once those laws were instigated, he could halt all integration and legally shut us out. Meanwhile, the school board met and changed the opening date of Little Rock's high schools from September 2nd to September 8th.

The week before Faubus's August 30th legislative victory, President Eisenhower had finally made his long-awaited statement about integration. It wasn't at all what we had hoped for, but rather mumbles about the need to delay integration. NAACP chief counsel Thurgood Marshall was furious and expressed his anger several times in print. I was just plain hurt and disappointed.

HIGH SCHOOL TERMS DELAYED BY BOARD
UNTIL SEPTEMBER 15
The Arkansas Gazette, September 2, 1958

Early September had always been a time when I leafed through textbooks with shiny new pages, relishing the scent of fresh paper and ink. Even when I was a toddler, Mother had permitted me to press open the pages of her new textbooks as she worked on her graduate degree or taught night classes. I would climb up on a chair and she would carefully place the book in my lap. Slowly I would caress each page to absorb what was pictured or written, even when I could only pick out a few letters of the alphabet.

On the morning of September 3, 1958, Conrad gathered his textbooks for his sixth-grade class. He would soon be a twelve-year-old. I wondered if he'd have the same awful high-school turmoil I did. I watched as Mother packed her textbooks in her satchel resting on the dining-room table. She was wearing her crisp forest-green linen suit with the white collar, dressed all spiffy to teach her seventh-grade English class at Jones High in North Little Rock. "This is a temporary setback, sweetheart," she said with a smile. Her words did not lift my spirits. I was overcome with melancholy. I didn't have new textbooks or a school to attend. All I had was a faint flicker of hope that the governor might change his mind.

After Mother and Conrad left, the house was very silent. I went back to my room, closed the door, got into bed and pulled the covers over my head. I don't know how long I had been under there feeling sorry for myself when I heard familiar footsteps.

"Idle hands are the devil's workshop," Grandma India said as she tugged at the covers. "You've got twenty minutes to get up, do morning prayer, get dressed and meet me in the kitchen."

"My spirits are down, that's all," I said, climbing slowly out of bed.

"It's not over yet," she snapped. "There's plenty of time for God to bring about a solution that will serve everybody."

Grandma immediately began fluffing my pillows and straightening my sheets, letting me know I dared not crawl back under the covers. She was perky and cheerful in her blue print dress with the pale blue apron. A flowered scarf covered her head indicating it was time for her to dye her gray hair as she had done every two weeks for the last few years. Her expression was pleasant and her eyes sparkled through her spectacles. I always hoped that when I got to her age I would have that same magical energy she displayed.

For most of the morning, she and I canned and baked as though we were preparing to enter a competition at the county fair. When it was time to take a break, I picked up the newspaper and read about the governor putting more pressure on frantic Arkansas school board members to ask the Supreme Court to stop our going back to Central High. He wanted the Eighth Circuit Court of Appeals' ruling in favor of our entry to be set aside.

Realizing my fate was being decided by some of the same white men who voted yes to the 1954 *Brown v. Board of Education of Topeka, Kansas*, decision made me feel hopeful. Against all odds, they were the men who had voted that separate was not equal, overturning a law passed in the 1890s, *Plessy v. Ferguson*, which decreed that Negroes could be kept separate because separate was equal. Their vote had knocked down the apartheid laws of the South—the legal measures which allowed whites to have separate bathrooms, water fountains, schools and eating places and to enforce every indignity that defined my way of life as I grew up. *Plessy v. Ferguson* had made it legal to keep my people separate and oppressed by inadequate education, facilities and opportunities. If those justices could turn all that around, how could they allow our governor to reverse the progress they had decreed? How could they allow Governor Faubus to shut the doors they said should be open to Central High?

I read the newspapers each day as soon as they arrived. I combed their text for even one word of what was going on. I spent a significant amount of time listening to radio news and watching television. Grandma thought television was a waste of time, but I had convinced her that news-watching was a worthwhile project, like studying civics.

I was upset by one of the articles I read in *Newsweek* magazine, which once more reported that President Eisenhower said he was in favor of a slower approach to integration. When asked to confirm that statement, his response, as printed in the magazine, was confusing at best. He said, "It might have been that I said something about 'slower,' but I do believe that we should—because I do say, as I did yesterday or last week, we have to have reason and sense and education and a lot of other developments that go hand-in-hand with this process—if this process is going to have any real acceptance in the United States."

I had never counted on Eisenhower as a barnstorming integrationist; yet I had assumed he was a fair man who believed in equality. He had, after all, dispatched the 101st Airborne troops to enforce integration and hold back the hooligans who challenged it. I hoped after investing all that energy and money, he wouldn't change his mind.

Still, one large pocket of fear outweighed all the others lingering at the back of my mind. Radical segregationists and states-rights advocates vowed that no matter what, there would be no more use of marshals or troops as enforcers of integration. If they got their way, we would once again be on our own, surrounded and far outnumbered by antagonists inside Central. I knew that meant taking more physical punishment. I couldn't take the same kind of pain I had endured the year before. Even though it had been three months since I survived the last attack by a Central High student, I still suffered. Sometimes my heels still hurt from the persistent heel-walkers who had dogged my trail daily pounding at my Achilles tendon. My eyes occasionally stung from the acid they had sprayed in them. I continued to see the eye doctor on a regular basis for treatment. I savored Grandmother's words: "God never gives us more than we can bear." I hoped she was right.

As days passed, I noticed a difference in the way the grown-ups around me behaved. Ever-optimistic NAACP leaders, attorney Wiley Branton, Mother Lois and all our parents, who had always been hopeful, now began wearing strained expressions. Their conversations showed their fear and doubt.

On the afternoon of September 12th, the day before Conrad's birthday, Mother Lois came rushing into the kitchen after school. "Melba, it's all right," she said, breathlessly. "It's on the car radio. They've decided . . . the Supreme Court says there will be no further delay in integration."

Waving her hands in the air and shouting "Hallelujah," Grandma tossed her pot holder up to the ceiling and said, "Soooooo, you see, young lady, you'll be going to school after all. Now get those saddle shoes polished and let's spruce up so that you look like you're ready to present yourself as a proper Central High School senior."

For most of the night before school was to open I lay awake wondering what it would be like to go back to Central. Had the white students become more sympathetic toward us? Were any of my prayers answered? I was so anxious that all I could do was pray my way through the night.

The next morning I found myself caught up in the usual first-day-of-school hustle, trying to find everything and make myself pretty in time to get breakfast down and run out the door.

"Up jumped the devil," Grandma said as I entered the kitchen. "Mr. Faubus has done it again."

I hurried myself to settle at the table, looking at my watch and all the while eyeballing the warm biscuits and mixed fruit. I didn't even pause to give my full attention to what she was saying until I noticed the anguished expression on her face and heard the sad tone in her voice as she spoke.

"Our governor has ordered all high schools closed."

"Even Horace Mann—the Negro school?" I gasped.

"Horace Mann, as well as the white high schools. Hall High and Central are closing tight as a drum."

"Oh my Lord," Mother Lois said, "that leaves almost four thousand high school students on the streets."

Chapter 3

THE THUD OF THE FRONT DOOR CLOSING echoed as once again I was left behind while Mother and Conrad went off to their schools. With Governor Faubus's closing our high schools, life would become just like it was the year before when the integration storm in Little Rock was the biggest news event in the country. There would be more reporters, more interviews and more national debates. How could the governor make such a spectacle of all of us?

"Just a temporary setback," Grandma India said, as she served the mixed fruit and warmed the biscuits for me. "Things aren't over—not yet." She winked and smiled. She behaved as though all was well.

But by the end of our meal, four phone calls had come from the newspapers, from school officials, and from a nosy neighbor. An NAACP representative phoned to urge us to be patient because their lawyers would be fighting to open the schools. I exchanged the spiffy yellow sailcloth dress that we had sewn for my first day as a senior for my dreary cotton house dress and settled down on the living-room couch.

"Tell you what. Get that pattern. I'll find you a brand-new piece of fabric in my trunk." I knew Grandma was appeasing me because of how sad I felt. Taking fabric from her trunk was reserved for very special occasions, like Easter and Christmas, weddings and funerals.

Just as we got the lush blue velvet fabric laid out on the dining-room table and the pattern pinned to it, the telephone rang. Grandma put the leftover pins back into the frog-shaped, green velvet cushion. I watched as she answered the phone, then smiled and handed the receiver to me.

"It's Marsha. You haven't heard from her in a long time." Grandma chuckled with delight as she handed me the phone.

Great, I thought to myself. *Maybe we could get together.* Marsha was a friend from Horace Mann, the Negro school I left to go to Central.

"I'll sharpen the shears." Grandma India moved toward the kitchen.

Already feeling a happy giggle deep down inside, I said, "Marsha, hi, I, uh . . ." She cut me off.

"What's gonna happen to us now? Who do you think you are?" she snapped at me from the other end of the line. Sniffing and spewing anger at me, she was barely able to catch her breath. "I'm not gonna get to be a senior this year, and it's all your fault."

"But . . ." I protested. She cut me off.

"This means we won't have a senior day, senior picnic or a senior prom," she growled. "How can we have anything with our schools closed?" Her voice was angry, her words rude and loud enough to hurt my ears.

"Well, uh, no," I sputtered. My mind raced for something to say that would make her feel better. But what could I say? Besides, she wouldn't let me get a word in edgewise.

"We've already elected our senior-events committee, our senior student body president, and I've already picked out my prom dress. And for what?"

"Look, Marsha—" The sound of her receiver slamming into the phone cradle jolted me. Tears brimmed my eyes. I slowly hung up my phone.

"Please, child, you don't want to make the pattern wet with your precious tears, do you?" Grandma smiled as she teased me, but I couldn't make myself smile back at her.

"Oh, Grandma, Marsha's so angry at me."

"Don't bring wrath down on your head for no good reason. The fact is, Marsha's angry about the situation and that's her problem."

As we cut out the dress pattern, the phone rang several more times with disgruntled voices on the other end sounding just like Marsha. Most of them began the conversation saying they were my former friends from my old high school and they were stuck home today because of me. Many of the adults in our community wasted no time in letting us know they too were very angry. With each additional vicious phone call, I felt myself trapped and growing more heartsick.

I knew they were weary of trying to survive all the penalties segregationists had dished out to them for supporting us. They blamed those of us who had integrated Central High for all of their hardship and now school was closed. That meant more hardship, more disappointment, more inconveniences.

When Mother Lois came home after school, I was still distraught over the wrath that was directed at me from my own people. I understood their anger, because they were losing so much. But why didn't they see that our going to Central High would help our people in the long run? Why was their blame so harsh?

"You can't allow anger to stop your doing what you know is right," Mother Lois said, setting her briefcase down on the dining-room table. "Like Grandmother India says, you're opening a door at Central for Marsha and all other Negroes."

Mother Lois sat down as she continued, "When I'd get discouraged about my schoolwork Grandma India would say to me, 'I work hard for my dollar, scrubbing, sweating. I know there's a better life and no one else is going to be a dollar-a-day maid in this family.'"

Despite Mother Lois's confidence in my actions, in the days that followed I felt increasingly lost. I didn't really belong to any group of friends, and now my own people, as well as the white students, hated me. I just wanted to hide in my room and come out when I knew only good things would happen to me. But Grandma would have none of that.

"God rests in action. Your mama and I have made up a schedule for you. The mornings will be for schoolwork, the afternoons for chores."

Mother Lois had left behind a full set of books and homework assignments. She had created lesson plans designed to keep me up to the senior grade level. She warned that she would be giving me exams and marking grades on my English papers and book reports.

I knew I had to apply myself and take interest in my schoolwork. Mother Lois would accept nothing less. She had walked ten miles each day, sometimes on cardboard-soled shoes, to get her college education. She was loving and kind, but she would accept no excuses for sloppy schoolwork.

Despite all the efforts Mother and Grandmother exerted to make things appear okay, I was still dispirited. To cheer me up, Mother relented and allowed me to spend an occasional afternoon with friends, but only if there was an adult available to accompany me. It saddened me that Mother feared even our own neighbors might strike out at me. The effort at integration was taking jobs and money from our community. Nearly every one of us depended on white people for survival—for work, for credit and for holiday handouts. Our attempt at integration had reduced that benevolent stream to a trickle.

Dunbar Community Center had become the gathering place for all of us out of school. A few of my afternoons were spent there playing cards, chatting and listening to Johnny Mathis and James Brown blasting from the stereo.

It would have felt almost normal except for the adult "babysitter" and the Horace Mann students who, for the most part, ignored us five Central High integrating students. We often found ourselves huddled in a corner together, but at least we were in the same room, listening to the same music, and that made me feel so good.

Most afternoons, Grandma India kept me busy. She taught me to make pie crust that didn't harden into concrete and to water the four o'clock flower plants only after the sun had moved to a place that left them in shadows. During our late afternoon breaks, we would sit in her room and read the Bible to each other. She would tell me of her childhood and of what she wanted for her future. She wanted her own place—a small farm with the space to raise a big flower garden and vegetables.

When Grandpa had died, she wasn't able to keep her land on what she earned as a maid. That was her big dream, owning land. "When a body's got a piece of the earth to call their own, they're closer to God because the earth belongs to Him." She folded her hands in a prayer position and smiled her sweet smile. "That's my prayer," she said, "and I know the Lord's hearing me."

As the days passed and we spent more time together, I noticed Grandma was dozing off in the middle of our conversations. Occasionally, I found her fast asleep in a chair, and sometimes she even sneaked off to take an afternoon nap. She had always said it was a sin to lie down in daylight. "A body must keep busy doing the Lord's work."

But for the first time in my life she had stopped abiding by her own words. She would never do such a thing unless something was terribly wrong. She grew more pale and weary with each passing day. I asked myself what I could do to cheer her up, to help her regain her magic energy that had sustained us all our lives.

"Please, Grandma India, let's tell Mother Lois to take you to the doctor," I pleaded one chilly, cloudy afternoon. I had found her leaning across the ironing board, drenched in perspiration.

"No, no, child, let's not bother her. You know I don't have insurance. I ain't got much money. I'm trying to get in my work time so I can get my Social Security money."

Grandmother had for most of her life worked in white ladies' kitchens as a maid, earning a dollar a day. Before becoming eligible for Social Security, she had no provision for retirement or sick leave. For her, it was no work, no pay. Later, in her late sixties, when she became eligible, she went back to work to earn the right to Social Security. But until then, she relied on Mother Lois's teaching salary and what little money she could save from her extra house-cleaning jobs.

"But Grandma, I know your throat is hurting," I protested. "Sometimes you can barely speak." She no longer read aloud to me, not even Shakespeare or her Bible.

"It'll be fine soon, child, just a little pesky cold hanging on." She quickly turned away from me and began folding the sheets she had pressed which were resting across the back of the dining-room chairs. "Besides, your mama has just started to pay back the loan she made to keep us through the summer. We can't add this burden on her shoulders."

I knew she was right. Sometimes during September we almost didn't have money for food because Mother Lois, who was only paid for the nine months she taught, had to begin paying back what she borrowed to feed us through the summer. Further, I had read articles in the paper about how teachers in our community earned really low salaries, not nearly as much as the white teachers—who weren't making all that much themselves. She also had to get us going in school with new pairs of saddle shoes, underwear and at least one new outfit. Still, I knew if Mother had known about Grandma India's condition, she would have sacrificed everything to see that she got the proper care.

Each day I fretted about telling Mother Lois of Grandmother's illness. I hoped she would notice it herself, but Mother had begun night classes. She would work all day and go directly to graduate school. At 9:30 in the evening when she arrived home weary, she would go to Grandmother's bedroom and they would talk to each other for only a moment, sometimes in the dark. They rushed past each other in the morning tizzy, so what chance did Mother have to see how ill Grandma India really was?

Grandma India and I continued sharing our special time together. Just after lunch, when we had cleared up and put dinner on the stove, she would invite me to her bedroom. That magical chamber was filled with colors and textures that always warmed my heart. There were the deep wine and forest-green velvet throws, the mahogany rocking chair with its new violet cushion and always her Tiffany lamp collection sitting on her white ruffled doilies. The room smelled of lilac and vanilla.

Crocheted pillows lay all around me. It was a special treat to use them and be alone and quiet with her. Now, more than not, she wore head scarfs that matched her crisply starched dresses. She had such pride in her appearance, and it was so unlike her to let her hair go undyed, but it was getting more and more gray. How I loved sitting beside her, stroking her hand. But now her smile had a dimmer glow and she moved more slowly.

On a muggy, overcast mid-September day, I found her staring off into the distance through her bedroom window with a vacant look in her eyes and sadness in her expression. To lift her spirits, I offered to make her a cool glass of chilled lemonade. When I returned with the glass, she smiled up at me and said, "Remember that time when you were a little bitty thing and you talked on and on about how our bodies and spirits are separate?"

"Yes, ma'am." As I drew near her to sit at her feet I could see her brow was furrowed and the energy was draining from her face.

"You were such a funny little girl, kinda like an old woman hidden inside a child. You said people's bodies were like suits of clothing and that our souls are the hangers which hold them up whenever they walk on earth." Her expression turned more serious.

"You told me I had to keep my secret and write that secret in my diary," I laughed.

"Yes, but I never said you were wrong. You were so right when you said the soul lives on forever while the Lord changes the suits. Each time we return, we're here to learn our lessons until we understand that all there is, is God, good and service."

As we continued our exchanges, it seemed to me that she wanted to make certain I learned more about how life worked. Often she peered deep into my eyes, sharing her wisdom and her deepest thoughts with me, then repeating herself until she was certain I understood. I felt an urgency to write things down. Somehow it struck me that I must remember every word of those precious conversations. The light in her room would turn to shadows as the afternoon became evening. As always, it was the sound of Conrad's voice calling out his arrival after play which ended these precious visits. But I couldn't stop thinking about her words way into the night.

HALL STUDENTS ASK IMMEDIATE SCHOOL OPENING
The Arkansas Gazette, September 20, 1958

"65 Meet at Church, Adopt Resolution Deploring Closing"

These few white students were the only ones among thousands who publicly objected to Governor Faubus's decision to close all high

schools in order to halt integration. I was stunned when I saw they
were speaking out, knowing they must be enduring wrath from their
own people who supported the decision. As time passed and the reality of what it meant to have no schools became apparent, even more
white people spoke up.

The governor's reply was that sixty-five students didn't seem
like many to him. He was en route to the southern Governors' Con-
ference where newspapers reported that he was met with kudos and
applause for his renegade attitude in defying the law.

I glanced at headlines in passing now; no longer did I rush
breathlessly to be the first one to retrieve the newspaper from the
front porch and read each and every word. I could think of nothing
else except that Grandma India, the person I loved most in the world,
was getting increasingly sick every day.

As September turned into early October, Mother Lois finally
noticed Grandma's failing health. She began nagging Grandma India
to go to the doctor, and finally after a week had passed, Mother summoned Uncle Charlie and Auntie Mae, Mother's brother and sister.
Together, they pressed Grandmother with questions about her health,
but Grandmother refused to go to the doctor's office. It was decided
that a doctor would be called to the house whether Grandmother
wanted it or not. Mother arranged for one of the special doctors from
the University of Arkansas, where she had studied, to come to our
house. It was a big deal because usually a white doctor would never
visit our neighborhood and certainly not someone's home.

Meanwhile, most of the news reporters had left town to go back
to their far-away news bureaus, saying that we had reached a stale-
mate. The few reporters that remained interviewed me every now
and then to ask how it felt to live without the fanfare of being a
celebrity. I had thought it would feel wonderful, but my whole world
was twisted into unrecognizable coils.

Segregationists continued to make threatening calls, saying they
would do whatever was necessary to halt our return to Central High.
I still could not go away from our house by myself because it was un-
safe. I had no friends, really, except the remaining members of the
"Little Rock Nine."

I was so lonely for the companionship of people my own age, for a normal teenage life, that whenever the phone rang I raced to grab the receiver, even though I knew an angry voice could be on the other end.

"Hi, it's me. Did you think I forgot you?"

"Who?"

"Link. How are you?"

Link had been the one white boy at Central High who had earned my trust by risking his life to save mine. When hooligans chased me down, he had tossed me the keys to his car so that I could escape to the safety of my home.

It happened in early March 1958. Without thinking, I had gone to the more dangerous, isolated, 16th Street side of Central High School to await my ride home. There were fewer teachers there, and seldom did any of our parents congregate to pick us up. Suddenly, a gang of white boys descended on me, threatening to get their final revenge. Their knife-wielding leader, Andy, with his growling threats and foul mouth, had become my special enemy, dogging my path for many months.

I was paralyzed with fear, feeling doomed because there seemed to be no escape. Suddenly, Link had stepped forward and offered me his car keys. When I balked and revealed my fear that he was one of the gang that was attacking me, he insisted that I take the keys and run. From that time on he had been my guardian angel even though his folks were staunch segregationists. Finally, although we had become good friends, talking on the phone almost every night during those last two months of school, I stopped returning his phone calls because I feared an unspoken attraction developing in him for me. He had begun asking me to come with him to the North, where he would be attending college, although I always made it clear that I didn't even consider dating white boys. He protested, saying that it was not a date he wanted but just to have me safe so he could stop worrying about me. When I refused, he became so angry that I had thought he would never speak to me again. But here he was on the phone and I so desperately needed someone to talk with.

"How's that fancy northern college?" I asked.

"It's great. But I called about you. Now you have no excuse. You have to come here because your school is closed."

Hearing his voice, I had to admit I missed him terribly. I didn't know what I should say to his invitation now. Today, for just an instant, I actually thought to say, "Yes—I'll come."

But instead I said, "I'll be fine. Schools will open soon."

"You can't wait around forever. Come here. It's already integrated. We could do things together. Even go out and dance together. Nobody would stare or call us names."

I ignored his romantic overtures and tried to dissuade him with facts. "The NAACP people say my leaving town could jeopardize the integration case."

"So what? Haven't you had enough?"

"I can't leave, not now," I said, as tears filled my eyes and a lump rose in my throat. "Grandma India is real sick." My voice quivered, because by now I had grown nervous waiting for the white special doctor to come to the house and tell us what was really wrong. Grandma India was fading so fast. Even though only a few days had passed since Mother Lois had contacted the doctor, it seemed like forever.

"What's wrong with her?"

"She says it's a sore throat, but I can tell it's more—much worse."

"Probably just a bad cold. Miss Peyton would never get sick. She's too busy taking care of you," he laughed.

"Something's really wrong. Our family doctor came and went away telling Mother that Grandma needs a specialist."

"Well, a specialist just makes you better quicker. Stop worrying! Call if you need anything. Promise?"

"Sure, goodbye."

"I think about you every day," he said quietly. "I miss you." There was a long pause while I said nothing, and then he said, "I hope Miss India gets better real soon. I'll call later to check on you all."

"I'm praying hard that she gets better soon too."

I held onto the receiver for a long moment after I replaced it in its cradle. For an instant, I allowed myself to daydream about what it would be like to run away—to be free, to be with Link. We had had more than fifty long and deep phone conversations over the past year, laughing, lamenting and arguing. Could we be pals in the North?

I knew I was losing my hold on reality even to ponder the question. Even though he spoke of race-mixing couples actually holding hands at his college, I knew such behavior was unthinkable. I knew more than one Negro boy who was beaten to a pulp for even looking at a white girl in the eye, let alone showing any visible signs of admiration. How could I even think of going away with a white friend—a boy at that—in this year of our Lord 1958. Impossible! Besides, how could I leave Grandma India until she was completely well and strong and happy?

Chapter 4

THE NEXT AFTERNOON, AS GRANDMA INDIA lay taking a nap, a white doctor, a throat specialist from the University of Arkansas, knocked on the door. After Mother explained about Grandma's throat and how listless she seemed to be, he entered her room to examine her. I peeked through the crack in the door as he introduced himself, saying he'd heard about her stubborn cold and came to halt it before she infected all of us. I was pleased that he took a moment to tease Grandma, because that meant he saw her as a person. He smiled at her. He laughed with her and when he laughed, he had kind eyes. And he called her Miss India, not "Auntie" or by her first name, as most white people did when they wanted to show disrespect for her age.

The doctor continued chit-chatting with Grandma, charming her into allowing his examination. I satisfied myself that he seemed to be a nice man and would care for her, so I stepped into the living room to wait with Mother and Conrad. None of us spoke. I could hear the clock ticking the minutes away and after a long while my stomach grew queasy and my heart started pounding in my ear. I could almost hear the anxiousness that was taking us over.

When Dr. Roth called Mother into the front hall, I rushed to stand by her side, but the expression on his face was so serious that I couldn't make myself stay to hear what he had to say. Instead, I ran out of the back door in tears and seated myself on the steps.

"You better get inside," Conrad said, when he came out to get me after what felt like an eternity. "Something's wrong."

Mother Lois appeared pale and drawn. Her hands were shaking as she entered the living room. She was silent as she slumped down into the big green velvet chair.

"How long will it take her to get well?" Conrad asked.

"What's the matter with her?" I asked.

"It's leukemia," Mother whispered and stared at me with the most awful look in her eyes.

"Leukemia?" I didn't know that word. "What do we have to do to make her well?"

"Pray, Melba, pray."

As Conrad and I fell to our knees and put our heads in Mama's lap, our tears began to flow uncontrollably. I thought the three of us would cry ourselves a river.

After a time, Mother offered us handkerchiefs and instructed us that we could never let Grandma India see us cry. We had to cook and care for her as she had always cared for us—cheerfully, with a smile.

A week later, Grandma completely lost her sweet gentle voice that had so many times whispered "I love you" as she tucked me into bed. She could only write notes to me on paper. "Smile," she would write. "Smile because God is loving you and me both at this very moment."

Day after day, I sat at the end of her bed reading the Twenty-Third and Ninety-First Psalms to her. On October 17th, the ambulance carried her off to the hospital. We walked those shadowy, stark white halls as nurses in starched uniforms rustled back and forth. Whenever I entered her room, she forced a smile and pulled the head scarf down over the two-inch-wide band of gray hair that framed her weary face. The light in her eyes was dimming. On October 24th, just before dawn, we were called to the hospital. An unfamiliar stoic-faced white doctor gathered us in a sterile, shiny and windowless room to say the awful words — Grandmother India had expired.

"Expired — what does that mean?" Conrad asked.

"Died," the doctor said with no emotion in his voice.

Suddenly, Conrad broke away and ran down the hallway toward her room, shouting her name at the top of his lungs.

At that moment I felt all life drain from my body. I stood frozen. It felt like the walls, the floor, Mother, the doctor standing in front of me, all fell away from me. I could neither hear, see, or feel anything around me. I couldn't catch my breath. It was utterly silent in the room. Had I died with her?

I don't remember how we gathered up Conrad and got home, but I found myself sitting on the back stairs. There was nothing inside me telling me what I should do next. Grandma had been with me all of my life. She was my playmate as a toddler, my home teacher as a preschooler, and always my friend whenever I needed her. She had taught me to read using the Bible, to grow plants, to clean toilets, to iron shirt collars.

Grandma India had tucked me into bed almost every night of my sixteen years on earth. She had gotten down on her knees beside me to help me make God my friend. Each morning she opened my bedroom drapes and welcomed the light to start my day. She was the safety in my darkness. She was music, all my Sunday picnics, my Christmases, Easters and birthdays. She was everything right and good that I knew of life. Without her beside me, I was certain the sky would fall and there would be no tomorrow. Surely the sun would cease to shine. She was the hope and strength that had carried me through my year at Central High. How could I go on without her?

Only the chill of dusk drove me inside. In the front of the house I heard people coming and going; some of them brushed past or spoke to me, but I could not discern their words or speak back to them. I went directly to the bathroom, slammed the door and stared into the mirror wondering how my reflection could be there with Grandma India gone.

Later that evening, Mother Lois collapsed and had to be given a sedative and put to bed. Conrad whimpered endlessly. I sat paralyzed and silent in the green chair that no longer felt like a cozy friend hugging me.

Church people had come to take care of us. All their hot plates of food, tears and talk about Grandma's wonderful character did not make my hurt go away. I felt empty and cold inside even when I stood by the fire. I would never feel her hug or love again. When bedtime came, I lay down to sleep on top of the covers with all my clothes on and prayed that Grandma India would come to tuck me into bed. When she hadn't come by dawn, I stood and went back to the green chair to sit. In my diary I wrote:

India Anette Peyton, India Anette Peyton, India Anette Peyton, India Anette Peyton, India Anette Peyton . . .

over and over again, until I filled two pages. Then I wrote:

God, I'm so angry at you. How could you take away the person I love most on the earth? India Anette Peyton.

I didn't move, not to eat or even to go to the bathroom, until late that afternoon when the pastor's wife dragged me up to wash my face.

"Cleanliness is next to Godliness," she said, sounding like Grandma India.

Early the next morning, the third day without Grandma, Mother Lois, Conrad and I found ourselves alone, sitting in the living room without the well-meaning friends. The house was in disarray, something Grandma India would never have tolerated. I stared at the mess, wondering who would come along and organize things. I could hear her melodic voice echo in my head: "Get off your 'sit-down' and show that you can get started doing His will. That's all God requires of you and He will do the rest." I got up and started humming the spiritual I had heard her hum all my life, "On the Battlefield for My Lord," as I tidied up and put things away in the places she always had.

I made breakfast the way I had seen her do a million mornings, with napkins and placemats and silverware sparkling. As the toaster purred, I was careful to follow Grandmother's instructions about fallen egg yolks. Mine stood like soldiers on parade. She would be proud of me, I thought, as I called Conrad and Mother Lois into the kitchen. They were surprised and pleased. As we took our seats around the table we all stared at the empty fourth chair—her chair. We couldn't hold back the tears. I could just hear Grandma laughing as she teased us, "Tear-soaked eggs and toast, you ought to be ashamed." Despite the fact that I didn't remember ever having a family meal without her, we got through that first meal somehow. I stared at her empty chair and the unused place setting as though wishing would bring her back.

Then a conversation with my father made me feel as though someone had unplugged my heart. I don't know why I had expected him to behave differently. He had let us down during my year at Central High by not protecting us against the violence and threats that came from my people and the white people who tried to invade our home at night, even when we pleaded with him. I would have given the moon if he'd just sat in the house with us some nights during all the violence we suffered.

Although he and Mother had been divorced for years, he had behaved as though he loved Grandma, and I called him for some much-needed sympathy. He told me how sorry he was about her death and said, "She wouldn't want you to waste a lot of time crying tears over her 'cause she was a go-gettum kind of lady. I had a lot of respect for Miss India." And then he said, "Say 'Congratulations,' I'm gettin' married," and told me that he was going off to Memphis in a couple of days for the nuptials and wouldn't even be able to attend the funeral. I shouted into the phone so loud it hurt my ears, "I'll never ever speak to you again! You're not my father!" When I slammed down the receiver my whole body was shaking with anger.

Papa Will and I had not had a whole bunch of kind words and smiles for each other since he and Mother divorced. I missed him so much when he first left, but when he refused to visit regularly, I began to wonder about him. Did he really love me? Then, when he didn't help me when I needed him most, when my very life was threatened, I stopped loving him so much. By not standing by us when Grandma India was gone, he took away more of my love for him.

I finally decided to telephone Link. I didn't know who else I could really talk with. Mother Lois was barely coherent. The only thing that seemed to bring her out of her fog was cutting out the pattern and sewing up the white wool dress she would wear to the funeral. She was in no shape to explain things or make me feel better. I hadn't been able to reach Minnijean, who'd been my dear friend when we attended Central High together. With few exceptions, friends from my old high school and my church only spoke to me with anger, blaming me and the other members of the "Nine" for causing their school closure. I had to dial somebody and Link was at least available. Link's words and the sound of his voice would be a comfort to me.

"Hey, what a great surprise." Link sounded so happy.

"Link, you were wrong. Grandma . . . she . . . uh . . . expired."

"Expired? You mean Miss India died?" His voice was so pained that just for an instant I knew he felt my loss. "I'll be there tomorrow."

"No, no . . . even if you came, you know you couldn't come here to the house. Your father would kill me and you'd be in real trouble." His father was still a staunch segregationist, an organizer who contributed money and time to keep Central High all white.

"Then what can I do to help?" he said. "Money, do you need money?" I heard tears in his voice.

"I just want to talk."

Link went on and on about coming home and taking me back with him, but I had only called him because I desperately needed to talk about my sadness. We stayed on the phone for twenty minutes. I felt a little better but nothing really changed.

The next morning, the day of Grandma India's funeral, I got up very early to clean and scrub the house—even the toilets—to make certain everything was just as Grandma would have it. I was sweeping off the front steps when long, black shiny limousines, just like the limousines I had ridden in while we were in New York, pulled up in front of the house. I didn't want to see them. I ran inside and slammed the front door.

I knew I should be getting dressed for Grandma India's funeral, but something inside was holding me back. I couldn't make myself go with Mother, Conrad and the other relatives and church members to do that awful thing: to sit in church looking at Grandma India stiff and cold, lying so still in a wooden box, and then to bury her. While neighbors and friends arrived in their Sunday clothing, I wore jeans, a loose shirt and uncombed hair. People stared at me but I said nothing.

I would come out from my room to see what was going on, then duck back in and slam the door. Hard. Then I snuck down the hall to Mama Lois's bedroom to watch the sisters from Grandma's church in North Little Rock help dress her in the white wool dress she had made.

My aunt Mae came and banged on the door to my room. "You better come out here, girl, you better get yourself together," said Miss Lula Brown. "You look a might undone in them jeans." I just glanced at her and then I turned and walked back through the door. I could hear the chatter in the living room where the minister was gathered with other people, starting to say a prayer. I stepped down the hall to pause and look at them. At that moment, they hushed up and stared at me as if I was some awful figure, some freak. Once again, several of the women came towards me with their hands outstretched, saying how much Grandma loved me—as if I didn't already know that.

"I don't know what you're doing, Melba Joy, but you know you gotta get dressed. Now you hurry. You can't hold up everything," Auntie Mae said, standing there in her Sunday white. "You've got to walk this last mile with your grandmother."

I walked down the hall toward the living room, thinking for an instant, Maybe they're all right; if I went with them to bury Grandma, it might not be so bad. But then I felt something shaking deep inside. I closed my eyes tight and put my hands over my ears. I stood stock-still in the hallway with my aunt behind me, trying to push me forward. Some man whom I didn't even know was telling me what to do. He kept saying my grandma was dead. *Shut up*, I thought to myself. *Grandma India would never, never die and leave me.* I felt my whole body start to tremble, a trembling that got stronger and stronger as I fought against it.

That's when a voice screamed so loud it hurt my throat and my ears, "Grandma is not dead!" It was an angry voice that sounded much like my own.

"It's all right, Melba . . . I understand." Mother Lois stood over me speaking in a calm voice.

"Never mind, I'll tend to her." I heard the familiar tones of our family doctor, then a needle prick in my arm. The shot did its job—all of me softened in an indefinable drift to nowhere. When I became conscious again, I was sitting in the green chair in the living room. There was only silence around me. The house seemed empty. I folded my arms against the chill. Then I heard two church ladies' voices in the kitchen, but it still felt as if I were all alone.

I walked into Grandma India's room where she kept all her personal belongings, the items she called her "dibbies." I reached out to stroke her embroidered pillow that read "God is love." Then I drew my hand back as though she would catch me. It had been one of her "untouchables." Now I could touch them all I wanted because she wasn't there to say no.

I would have given anything to have her slap my hand as I picked up her green music box with the ivory cameo on top and held it to my chest. It was her favorite possession. When I lifted the lid, it played "Stardust." The tinny music filled the air as I opened the door to her closet. There hung all her clothes. I could smell the scent of vanilla flavoring she had made her special perfume. I touched her blue crepe dress with the buttons down the front. All her shawls hung across hangers, waiting for her to choose one. I nuzzled among her clothes and hugged a bunch of her dresses. It made me feel as though she were hugging me. I didn't know where it came from but a voice seemed to say to me that she loved me just the same, even though I could no longer see her.

FTER A WEEK'S recuperation, Mother Lois and Conrad went back to their schools, but I still had no place to go to. Governor Faubus had won this round. Neither the Supreme Court justices, nor the president, nor the NAACP, nor anybody else could stop him. So I was left alone in that house with Grandma's memories all around me. At first I thought I would lose my mind. I wanted more than anything to see her as she was, alive and well, to speak with her just once more. But I was frightened that she might reappear as a ghost and what then? Just as clear as a bell, one afternoon, I heard Grandma's voice remind me that I couldn't lose my mind because God is my mind. From that moment on, I was no longer afraid of seeing her, because I felt such love from her that I knew even if she were a ghost she would never hurt me.

Days melted into one another the way they do when you don't have a place you belong or a work routine. I didn't follow any pattern in eating, or bathing, or dressing, or any of the other tasks I had to do to live. I just did them when I was forced to. I felt numb and cold, like a statue. It was as though I lived behind a big piece of glass that separated me from all other living people.

One night, Grandma India came to me in a dream that was so real I felt as though I could reach out and touch her. She was robust and smiling. "Life is such a precious gift—a cherished grant only to those who use it to its fullest each day," she said as she hugged me and smiled. I felt so good.

The next morning, I sat upright, feeling as though she were nearby. Then I remembered she couldn't be. Still, I felt a rush of new energy. I knew I had to resume my morning studies and afternoon housework. I felt her watching me. So with television playing in the background to lessen my loneliness, I began doing all the household chores. I discovered that the busier I kept myself, the better I felt.

Although Mother was teaching and pretended things were okay, I could see that by Thanksgiving, a month later, she was nowhere near being herself. Since someone had to shop and prepare the Thanksgiving dinner as Grandma India had done, I made a list and went shopping. Perhaps it wouldn't be the best Thanksgiving meal we'd ever have, but still I smiled as I basted the turkey to keep it moist. I knew somehow that Grandma was proud of me, because I had followed her instructions. I was proud as I stepped back and surveyed the table I set, and pleased at the comfort it brought to Mother and Conrad.

On December 7th, my birthday, no one came to my bedroom early in the morning to pull the covers down and sing "Happy Birthday," as Grandma India had always done. No one baked me a chocolate cake, or lit candles or sang to me. I didn't mention it because I didn't want to bother Mother Lois. Mother had been so strong, re-

minding us that Grandma would want us to do our best. But I could
see this was taking its toll on her. I loved her and felt so sad that she
seemed to be very frail, barely holding herself together. My birthday
was important, but her getting okay again was more important.

Conrad was missing Grandma India too. He still rocketed
through the house, but I'd catch him sitting at the kitchen table staring into space with a sad expression on his face. When I touched him
on the shoulder and told him it was going to be all right, he said it
was never going to be all right, because he missed the aroma of
Grandma's magic, fresh-baked gingerbread; he missed her warm
words of comfort; he missed holding on to her dress tail when all the
rest of the world seemed to be rejecting him. When he asked me to
play Monopoly I had to say yes, otherwise he would sit there for almost an hour staring across the board as if Grandma were sitting
there with him.

As the school year rolled deeper into winter, the governor's closing of our schools continued to go unchallenged by U.S. authority. At
first President Eisenhower expressed hope that public sentiment
would force the governor to reopen schools. But with the creation of
private schools based on a charter grant, whites were indeed able to
run their private schools with our tax money. The NAACP continued
telling the five of us who remained to integrate Central High to wait,
that the case hinged on our not registering in another school. So wait
we did, while newspapers reported that the segregationists were hoping that we'd register in another school.

Every day I studied my textbooks and Mother Lois checked my
homework. Sometimes we five would meet to work with a teacher or
just to do our homework together. Always, our conversations were of
what we would do if school started.

Those annoying, threatening night-time phone calls continued.
But with the emotional paralysis that came from losing Grandma
India, we just answered them, said mean things back, and slammed
the phone down. I no longer feared the callers because the pain of her
loss dulled everything else. Life seemed to be happening as though
we were on automatic pilot.

The approach of Christmas gave me an opportunity to make
myself very busy. Mother Lois had little time to shop and cook and
decorate. Somehow, I felt obligated to keep the house running the

way Grandma wanted it to. I found myself taking on her role, becoming more and more like her every day. Once again, I made a list of all the things I remembered she had done in holiday seasons past, and then completed everything on that list. Listening to carols and decorating the Christmas tree, we even laughed when Conrad did his Santa routine. Still, there were no gingerbread men with jellybean eyes or double butter cakes because none of us knew the secret recipes.

Worst of all, we forgot to hang stockings. Grandma India had always hung the stockings and filled them with tiny goodies from Santa, like a bracelet and toothpaste and warm socks that she had knitted. On Christmas Day I sat alone, trying to remember just what it was like to have her present. All our family members had gathered as usual. Except for Mother, they laughed louder and sang louder, pretending everything was joyous. They never even asked why I sat alone staring out the window.

GRANDMA INDIA HAD always said that if a body had faith, even if it was only the size of a mustard seed, the promise of spring is to renew all things, and so it was with me. I felt her energy driving me to be a part of the rebirth. By March of 1959, I actually began enjoying my days filled with housework, studying and watching soap operas. *As the World Turns* was my favorite. I loved the Nancy character, because her mannerisms and tone of voice reminded me of Grandma. She also kept her house immaculate and gave the same advice that Grandma might have. Chris, her husband, was strong and wonderful like the father I wished I'd had.

There, on my television each day, was the active, happy and complete family I would have liked to have been a part of. Never mind that they were white people on a TV screen; they provided comfort and companionship. Besides, watching the way they were with each other taught me a lot about being a family member. Sometimes I pretended I was in their family, burying myself deeply in their joys and their problems. I could hardly let a day go by without watching.

By early April, the segregationists' threats had increased. We realized we were being watched by a car of white hooligans who parked in front of our house each night. I was under orders from Mother Lois not to go out of the house by myself. I especially hated that I had to stop going to the community center to listen to music and play card games with Carlotta, Jeff and Thelma.

Meanwhile, the NAACP continued its court battle to force Faubus to open the schools by trying to have the courts declare the school closing unconstitutional. Governor Faubus's power and popularity grew because he had succeeded in preventing integration and maintaining segregated schools for most of the white students while shutting down our community high schools.

Just after Easter, I caught myself laughing out loud at *I Love Lucy* on television as I vacuumed the living-room rug. I hadn't laughed in a long while because I felt as though I was betraying Grandma by laughing when she couldn't be there. But I was doing such a good job of house cleaning that I figured she wouldn't mind so much.

As spring brought warm weather, I consulted Grandma India's almanac. I had gone past the time to plant the flower seeds. Nevertheless, I couldn't face summer without her four o'clock flower bed. I had never known a summer without it. Besides, she wouldn't have approved of my not turning over the soil and planting in the spring.

Hour after hour, I dug into the ground, ruining my fingernails, and developing calluses in the palms of my hands. I watered the seeds and resurrected the bulbs at the prescribed times. I learned gardening was hard work, but after a while my aching muscles became badges of honor. By June, the seeds had turned into wonderful flowering plants. Our summer was filled with rows of blooming four o'clocks, daisies and forget-me-nots, almost as though Grandma had been there to plant them.

Summer came and the long, hot and muggy days followed one after the other. Mother wasn't teaching so, as usual, she had to borrow money to keep food on the table. She seemed to be gaining her strength back, though, and that was a relief. We talked a little more about Grandma India, commenting if we were eating her favorite foods at dinner, or wondering what she'd say about the neighbor's yappy new dog. Little things, but it felt good, as if Grandma were still a part of our everyday life. And once again, on Sundays, Conrad was making the banana pancakes that Grandma India had taught him from her secret recipe.

One late afternoon, as September drew near, I found myself sobbing as I lay face down on the ground beside the flower bed, as though being there in the dirt made me closer to Grandma India. But I wiped away the tears, noticed all the weeds and reached out to pull them up. Grandma absolutely hated untidy gardens. *She must be looking down from the heavens and applauding me,* I thought. Pulling myself up to my knees, I giggled.

One day, after I completed my gardening and entered the back door, I was stunned to hear Mother Lois talking on the telephone to her cousin Griffin. He would not risk calling unless something was terribly wrong. He lived in a distant southern city where he passed for white. He had a white wife and five children who thought they were all white. White skin and blue eyes sustained him in his charade as a prominent member of the Klan.

Griffin's maternal grandfather had been a fair-skinned, green-eyed Negro and his maternal grandmother was a white woman. Griffin's mother, Grandma India's sister, was very light-skinned and she'd married an equally light-skinned Negro. Griffin bore no resemblance to any relative we'd ever seen. We always teased him about being lost "in our woodpile."

Cousin Griffin had met a white woman on his first day of college at a northern campus and had fallen madly in love with her at first sight. From her patter and descriptions of her Alabama family, not to mention the state of race relationships in 1944, he knew she would not marry him if she discovered that he was a Negro. That's when he called home and told his mother, Auntie Grace, what he would do—that he was going to live his life as a white man.

Family folklore said Auntie Grace objected and tried to dissuade him because she knew it meant her son wouldn't be a part of her life anymore. My family was familiar with the routine of "passing." There were at least four other relatives in the immediate family who had done it. When a person decided to "pass" it meant you didn't call them, you didn't write to them and if you saw them downtown you acted like you didn't recognize them. You waited for them to contact you. After Griffin made his decision he established himself on campus as a white person and married his true love.

Now he was the sheriff of a small southern town by day and donned a white sheet by night to "stalk niggers." He had always said he was forced to keep his high place in the Klan in order to keep his high place among the city fathers. Twice a year he came home to visit Auntie Grace. That was the only time we saw him. It was a firm rule that we never phoned each other except in an emergency.

I walked over to Mother in order to listen to her anguished conversation. Her face was ashen. When she rested the receiver in the cradle, I saw awful fear in her eyes. "Griffin says the Klan is willing to kill all five of you to keep you out of Central forever. They're especially angry with you. Remember how they targeted you and Minnijean in the beginning because you were tall, visible and verbal? Well, they're wanting to get you as an example to frighten the others. They're posting signs in all their secret places — $10,000 if you're captured and killed and $5,000 if turned over to them alive." She started to walk away but her words trailed behind her.

"That's a whole lotta money in Arkansas in these tight times, baby."

Chapter 5

"HURRY NOW. YOU CAN'T MISS YOUR PLANE." Mother's voice broke and tears filled her eyes as she pushed me away. "Our people from the Santa Rosa NAACP will meet you. I just know they're good folks—people you can trust. You'll be just fine."

My heart pounded in my chest as I strained to hear Mother's voice over the whirring engines of the huge passenger plane. So much had happened in the last forty-eight hours that I could hardly believe it was real. I was flying away to live in California—forever!

I was leaving behind the family and friends I had known for all of my seventeen years. Like all the other girls I knew, I had figured I would only be leaving home at age twenty-two to get married. Mother had preached, "Good girls don't get married and even think of children before they are twenty-one years old, the age of maturity." After hearing the whole family debate my situation again and again, I now accepted the fact that I had no choice. I had to leave to save my life. Still, that didn't make going any easier.

I felt as though sacks of bricks were hanging from my shoulders, weighing me down as I climbed each metal stair that led to the narrow door of the plane. Here I was, leaving my mother and brother in peril. It was my fault that their lives were at risk while I ran for safety. What if the Klan people hurt or even killed them? At the same time, I was leaving all that was familiar to me, all that was dear, the only life and family I loved. What would become of me? What if I had gone to all this trouble and the Klan was following me to kill me? Thoughts were swirling around in my mind.

As the stewardess smiled and beckoned me to move through the narrow metal door, I could smell the fuel coming from the roaring engines of nearby planes in motion. I turned to wave one last time. I could hardly see my mother and brother through my tears. "Come with me," I wanted to shout. "Please, let's all run away to California." But I knew there was no use. Over and over again, I had pleaded. But Mother Lois said she couldn't let go of her teaching job.

I took a deep breath and tried not to whimper aloud. I felt so torn apart inside—relieved to be getting away from the threats of death that hung like a cloud above my days and nights, but at the same time terrified by the thought of leaving behind everything else as well. I had no idea what my new life would be like, with whom I would be living or what school I would attend. It felt to me as though I were stepping off into space, with no map or sense of direction.

As we crowded into the aisle of the airplane, the other passengers and I were crushed into the sardine-like confines. Everyone was searching for their seats and trying to place luggage in overhead compartments. The other passengers were all white and they looked me over with curiosity. I was glad I had only one suitcase and Grandma's trunk, which I checked, and no extra bags to store away.

The smell of stale cigarette smoke, perfume and strangers' body odors used up the fresh air. It felt like an eternal wait to get seated. As I moved past a window in first class, I bent down hoping to see Mother and Conrad. I had no idea when I'd be seeing them again. I knew very well that the plane fare to California was more money than Mother could afford. A bubble of sadness caught in my throat as I was shoved through the aisle much too quickly to ever get that last glimpse of them. I finally reached my seat as the announcement came to buckle up.

As the plane taxied along the runway, I looked out the window and read a huge sign on a billboard: "ARKANSAS—THE LAND OF OPPORTUNITY." Not for me and my people, I thought. For me it had been the land to battle folks for a glimpse of their opportunity. Still, I would have given anything not to be forced into leaving this way.

I had to keep repeating in my mind, "California. I am going to California to make a new life." As the plane took off, I gripped the arms of my seat. The cabin rattled and shook just like my own insides. In an effort to avoid the queasy sensations in the pit of my stomach as we lifted off, I burrowed deep into my thoughts. I asked myself what California life would be like for me. How did my people live there and how would I fit in to their way of doing things?

By the time the pilot announced that we were flying at a high altitude and leaving the state, my seatmate, Ron, was already becoming a real nuisance. He was an over-friendly young white man who insisted on describing in detail his duties as a soldier in the Presidio army base of San Francisco. He had been home to Little Rock and was returning to duty. He was suspiciously nice and anxious to make nonstop chitchat.

I put up a shield of silence to fend him off. When that didn't work, I determined to show my disinterest by asking for a pillow and blanket. As I closed my eyes, I couldn't stop myself from reliving those last hours before I boarded the plane. The frantic effort had begun just after Mother said goodbye to Uncle Griffin and decided to take his warning to heart. Should I leave immediately, we pondered, or did I have time to pack my things? Where could I go? Should I tell the other students I was abandoning them and the integration of Central High?

Mother had telephoned our local NAACP representative. Maybe they could help. We had been told they had a contingency plan for us. They had already put the word out that they needed safe houses in case the students who integrated Central needed to make a sudden getaway.

An exchange of phone calls revealed that Thelma, Elizabeth, Gloria, Jeff and Carlotta were also leaving town because of what they considered reliable evidence that we were in danger and because they wanted to continue their education. Their families were already seeking schools for them elsewhere. They were headed for different cities across the United States to live with families of strangers and to start new lives. None of us would enter Central that semester.

Mother had commenced sorting my clothes as I asked what she had in mind. "You're getting out of this town as quick as possible. I don't know what I've been thinking about." From that moment, until the time we left for the airport, I wasn't allowed to go out of the house.

And so began the frenzied washing, ironing and sewing of my clothing. Mother went to what had become the spare room since Grandmother India's death and pulled out the familiar old trunk— the one Grandma India had used for her precious fabrics. She shifted the remaining linens, velvets and cotton yardage to her chest of drawers and began stuffing all my belongings into the trunk.

Meanwhile, the nonstop phone calls began. The threatening ones continued, but they had much less opportunity to get through since my mother was always on the phone making travel arrangements and consulting with the NAACP and a few of the older relatives. On the two nights before I was to leave, she invited our kinfolk to come for open house. She even invited Papa Will because by this time they had begun speaking civilly to each other. I felt uncomfortable with him then because I still held it against him that he had married someone else—and on the day of Grandma India's funeral. Mother Lois said having all the people around would be for both fun and protection. But I noticed she didn't tell all of them I was leaving or where I was going. "Words travel to the wrong listening ears sometimes," she winked.

The night before I left, I couldn't sleep at all. Mother's sewing machine wheezed and clanked all night long as she patched my worn clothes and made one new California outfit for me. Weary from lack of sleep, we stumbled through the next day collecting the remainder of my things and saying goodbye. A few close relatives had gathered as the menfolk loaded my trunk and suitcase into the car. After Uncle Charlie, Mother's brother, said a brief prayer, we climbed into our green 1954 Pontiac and headed for the airport.

"Don't look at this as a defeat," NAACP attorney Wiley Branton had said. "It is just a recess to build our strength for the battle ahead. We will continue pressing the courts and you'll be back in a few months. You are a heroine. Your hard-won victory was the year you remained in that school and nobody can take that away from you."

Despite his reassurance, I didn't feel much like a heroine leaving in victory. I felt as though the segregationists were the winners by taking what was most precious away from me—my family and the only life I had known for all the years I had been on Earth. What else was there to give up?

"Don't you want to see the mighty Pacific?" Ron drawled from his window seat, rousing me from my cave of thought. I had never seen the Pacific Ocean before. I leaned into the window to see the magical body of water beneath us. The glimmering sheet of azure satin stretched into forever and the direction of our flight seemed to draw us nearer to it with each passing moment. Golden sunlight sprayed its rays from the heavens down to the white-capped waves, flickering like sparklers on the Fourth of July.

Seeing that vast and beautiful body of water made me feel hopeful and closer to God because only He could create this extraordinary picture. I tried to memorize every detail. For an instant, negative thoughts washed away and I began to smile. It was the first time I had ever witnessed such splendor. It made me feel brand new. A wonderful thought occurred to me. *This day really could be the beginning of a new life for me.* I sat back as the tension drained from my shoulders and my stomach warmed as though I had swallowed a spoonful of the sunlight that surrounded me.

Maybe the time had finally arrived when I could become a regular, everyday teenager, having fun and dating and just plain living. Something inside me giggled at that notion. What would it be like to allow the real Melba to be seen? I wasn't certain I knew any longer who that really was. Had I forgotten how to behave like an ordinary teenager?

We continued our descent, coming so close to the water it seemed as though we were skimming it with the plane's belly. My heart raced in my chest. What did the pilot have in mind? Where would he land? And then I saw the concrete runway rising up out of the middle of the waves.

With his radio newscaster's voice, the pilot announced we should prepare to land at the San Francisco International Airport.

He promised we would enjoy the pleasant weather. Ron said to keep in mind that September was summer in San Francisco. Summer, what summer? *This is certainly not a Little Rock summer,* I thought, folding my arms against the chill as I deplaned and was hustled along by the throng of humanity that conveniently separated me from Ron.

The San Francisco airport was much larger than the Little Rock airport. It resembled the fairway at the rodeo, with all its bright lights, concession stands, voices announcing planes, and people everywhere talking, laughing and running to and fro. There were boards posted all around announcing what must be hundreds of arrivals and departures. But most of all there were all these white people who didn't seem to notice I was there. No one cast a hostile glance at me. Instead, they brushed past me to greet their loved ones. I wished I had someone familiar to greet me with a hug and a kiss.

Craning my neck to look around me, I tried to find some point of reference, something or someone familiar to me. I looked around for the people from the Santa Rosa NAACP. I drew a deep breath as my eyes searched for some of my people. They should be easy to spot in this crowd. But there were just two of my people to be seen: one man dressed in a suit whisked past with a determined look on his face, and a lady was making a purchase at a counter far in the distance. But we were only three among hundreds. To quiet my fears, I told myself that the Santa Rosa NAACP delegation would surely be a large group of my people. Where were they?

All at once, I started feeling uncomfortable. I couldn't account for it, but that sickish feeling of anxiety was definitely developing in my tummy. Was I in danger? Was I being stared at? I looked around to see ten smiling white faces rush toward me, clamoring their greetings. Had I done something wrong? I swallowed the panic in my throat. Did I need to call for help? What did they want with me? I looked behind me—surely I was standing in front of the person they sought. I stepped aside.

Now they were even closer, in my face. They all spoke at once. Their accents were different, but their faces were the ones I had just escaped in Little Rock. No, there was a difference, they were smiling, reaching out their hands to me. And then one woman stepped forward and put her arms around my shoulders to hug me. "Welcome, Melba, we've been looking forward to your arrival."

I jumped backward, away from her grasp, and prepared to do battle with her. But her kind expression made me hesitate. I quaked as they all chorused at once, "We're the Santa Rosa NAACP. Welcome to San Francisco."

They grinned and extended their hands for me to shake. Encircling me with examining eyes, they behaved as though I were some newfangled gadget they had just purchased. Were they Klan members come to trap me? My heart pounded in my ears and I clutched at my purse. Panic-stricken, I looked for an escape route. But even if I got away, where would I go? How would I find my way in this unfamiliar town? I didn't know a single soul. Now what?

"Melba, dear, did you hear me?" The small, meticulously groomed woman dressed in hues of brown and tan, was tugging at me. How did she know my name? "I'm Sarah and I'm so pleased to be your sponsor." She extended her hand to me.

"Miss—uh —? My sponsor?" The words leapt out of my mouth in my surprise.

"Just call me Sarah."

I had to take her extended hand, which dangled in the air. She smiled as I shook it gently. How could I call her Sarah? Mother would never approve. Adults were all Miss or Mrs.—but once more she insisted.

"My sponsor." I repeated her words aloud once more and it jogged my memory. Yes, Mother had said NAACP branches around the country were sponsoring passage to safe houses for each of us who had integrated Central High. I smiled politely. "Thank you," I said, as another woman stepped from the ranks to offer me two beautifully wrapped boxes.

"Just a moment, Miss Pattillo, could you look this way?" And there it was, that bright flash that hurt my eyes. Reporters and photographers, two of each, were joining us. Sarah made a pleasant introduction and I answered three questions: Why had I decided on California? Was I angry at President Eisenhower for not making Governor Faubus obey the law? Did I feel betrayed?

I felt free to vent my real feelings because I was far away from home. Still, I knew I should show some restraint because I was surrounded by white people I didn't know. Yes, I was angry with the president for not standing up to the governor and making him open the schools. Why did he not finish what he had started? I had to take a deep breath to calm myself. I didn't want to display anger.

I turned away from the reporters and focused my attention on the gifts I had received. "Why don't you open them when we get to the car," Sarah instructed.

"Thank you." I felt myself squeeze out words as I pretended I wasn't frightened. Then I had no more time to think. Everyone, not just the reporters, started asking more questions. How was my plane trip? How were things in Little Rock? How was Mother? What grade would I enter in high school? Did I have a luggage ticket? Did I have much luggage?

A man wearing a gray visor cap that covered his eyes requested that I give him my luggage ticket and he would get my bags. We moved forward in a makeshift but almost synchronized ballet: me, with the NAACP members and reporters encircling, asking nonstop questions. Although my mind was churning with frightening thoughts, for the moment, I had no choice but to go with them. I had to be polite. After all, the NAACP folks wouldn't lie to the press, would they? Unless maybe they were Klan members working undercover like secret agents on television crime shows. But if they were the Klan, they wouldn't have summoned the press saying they were NAACP. Why would white folks identify themselves that way and have their pictures taken? I determined that I had to cooperate with them until I collected more evidence.

Finally we were at the curb outside the airport and they insisted I climb into a huge, shiny, beige vehicle that resembled a small school bus. It was bigger than the station wagons I had seen, taller and wider, with three rows of three seats.

"But shouldn't I wait for the family I'll be living with?" What I really wanted was to wait for at least one of my own people to join us. How could I allow myself to be trapped in a car with only white strangers? I had no idea where they were taking me or if, in fact, they were who they said they were. They could drive off, murder me, destroy my body and no one would know.

Nonsense, another voice inside my head said. *Their voices and faces seem kind and loving. They keep touching me and smiling — genuine smiles.*

"Well, no. You're coming with us for right now." Sarah motioned me to get in. I hesitated and then decided I had no choice.

"We'll be going about an hour outside of San Francisco, up to Santa Rosa," she said, as if to reassure me. "You'll enjoy the ride through the beautiful countryside." The others crammed into the vehicle. What was going on? I was certain Mother Lois had said I would be met at the airport by the family I'd be living with, as well as the NAACP.

I sat quietly in the car, squeezed into the middle row in a seat next to the window. There were people chatting all around me. One woman in the front row of seats turned frequently to point out San Francisco's landmarks as though she was a tour guide. The streets and neighborhoods looked like someone had cleaned them just for me. The area they called the Marina, near the bay, was most beautiful with houses that stood side by side like soldiers at attention. Amid a light flow of traffic, we cruised onto the Golden Gate Bridge. "It's or-ange—no, rust-colored, not gold," I said aloud in astonishment. I was breathless as I tried to take in the grandeur of it all—the bay, the ma-jestic cliffs that rose above the blue waters and that incredible bridge.

How could I have been on earth for seventeen years and not seen this? For that instant it didn't matter who I was or what I wanted or where I had come from. Only what lay before me had any significance. I felt tiny and insignificant, like a grain of sand. For the moment, all my questions and tears and doubts melted into wanting to see and worship the wonders of the sights before me.

"How far is it from here to the home I'll be living in?" I asked, as the highway curved beyond the bridge and past vast, golden hillsides. I was hoping it would be close enough for me to make my way to the Golden Gate Bridge at least once a day.

"Uh, well," Sarah cleared her throat as the expression on her face changed from pleasant to anxious and then to red flush embar-rassed. I wondered what could be causing her such consternation.

"You see, honey, the family, the Denizens, they have changed their minds about having you come to live with them."

Changed their minds? Why didn't somebody tell me before I left home? I felt a hot rush to my head, pounding drums flooded my ears.

"It happened only this morning and we thought it too late to say you shouldn't come at the last minute."

"We're absolutely certain there will be another home for you," a woman wearing a green hat and horn-rimmed glasses chimed in from the back seat.

"Oh yes, there's no doubt we'll be able to find you a home," Sarah said.

I felt apprehension creeping back into my chest. Nevertheless, I had to ask the question. Could the family have been white?

"Why the last-minute change? Is someone ill or did they get another house guest?"

"Well no, not exactly." Sarah hemmed and hawed for a long moment. "Well, it's really nothing for you to be concerned about. It's plain ignorance, that's what it is."

"Ignorance?"

"Yes, several of the neighbors got together and objected after an article appeared in the paper announcing your arrival. They said they feared the consequence of having you come to live in their neighborhood," said a man's voice from the back seat.

"Feared the consequence," I repeated. "What do they think, that I would march and integrate or do something like that?"

"Something like that," Sarah smiled nervously. "But never mind, just open your gifts."

Frustrated and even a bit angry at the thought that the woman must be holding something back, I did as Mother had always instructed; I obeyed my elders and dug deep into my bag to find the boxes. Inside the smallest box wrapped in white tissue with a gold ribbon was a cross, a gold cross with a shiny stone at the center. "It's real," Sarah said. "It's a real diamond."

I couldn't help smiling at the beautiful necklace. I had never, ever owned something so precious. I carefully replaced it in the velvet box, closed the latch and put it back into my bag to keep it safe. Inside the second package was a white Bible with gold letters on it. "Family Bible," it read. It had a gold zipper. I caressed it. It made me want to cry because Bibles always reminded me of Grandmother India and she would have especially liked this one.

"These gifts are from the mayor of Santa Rosa and his wife," Sarah said. "They welcome you."

"Thank you," I said. In my silence, I pondered how the mayor knew I was there. It made me feel special that someone so important was welcoming me. Still, it didn't make up for the neighborhood that had not wanted me without even getting to know me. The news of their rejection was especially hard to take because I figured they must be my own people, but obviously they had not been.

Soon we were in the countryside where there were small clusters of stores and houses. Signs promised that we would reach Santa Rosa in forty miles. We drove through flat land where precisely patterned rows of crops extended farther than the eye could follow. Green pastures stretched for miles up to the steep golden hillsides where lazy cows stood grazing beneath the sun. Had there not been so many hills and modern buildings in the towns, I could have just as easily been riding with Mama and Conrad along a road outside Little Rock.

We reached Santa Rosa in due time and began driving past houses that looked unlike any I had ever seen in Little Rock or anywhere else. They were very modern: A-frame shapes, some with brown shingles, some of natural wood with peaked roofs and stained glass windows. Some stood in neat rows, set further apart than those in San Francisco, but with the same meticulously arranged patches of flowers. Some stood on hillsides, with space between them and generous lawns, while others stood close by each other in rows on flat land.

"Here we are."

"Where?" I asked.

"It's my house," Sarah said cheerfully. "You'll be staying with me for now." She leaped out of her seat and invited me to climb out of the car. I hesitated before following her up the walkway to the fawn-colored house. It was made of birch wood and shaped like a series of interconnected triangles. I had never seen any house like it.

After settling me down in the living room, the other NAACP folks bade me goodbye. I called Mother Lois to tell her I had arrived safely but I didn't tell her I had a problem. What could I tell her about my circumstances now? I hardly knew anything myself. I couldn't risk frightening her. I knew what her response would be. "Come home, now," she would say. But I still held out hope—I couldn't give up so soon. A chill settled over the house and pierced my bones. I sought my sweater among the few neatly folded possessions in the top of my trunk.

"Here," Sarah said, returning to the room and reaching for my overnight kit. "Let me show you where you'll be sleeping." Sleeping, I thought. It dawned on me that I was going to be sleeping overnight in a white person's home. This would be the first time. I wondered if there would be any different expectations of me than I'd find in a Negro family's home. What if they suddenly changed their minds about having a Negro as a house guest? Would they kick me out in the middle of the night? Would they hurt me? *Nonsense, that's all silly, Melba,* I scolded myself, as Sarah continued to move toward the front hall giving me a tour of her house.

"Since I didn't know you were coming, I didn't have a chance to clean my son's room. I'll change the sheets after dinner."

It was a small narrow room near the front door, about the size of two guest bathrooms back to back. It was a jumble of baseball mitts, two bats, a basketball, posters of jocks playing various sports and sneakers . . . smelly sneakers. The musty smell wafted up, almost smothering me. We put my things down and then Sarah led me to the bright, yellow kitchen.

"Do you like borscht?" Sarah asked, smiling at me with a very pleasant expression and pointing to the steaming hot pot.

"Borscht?" I tried to pronounce the word.

"Here, taste it," she said. Just for an instant, as she held out the spoon to me with her hand beneath it to prevent the dripping, I felt her genuineness—her warmth. Her eyes held mine as though she were checking my response to her desperate efforts to make me feel welcome.

"Interesting," I said with my mouth half full. It was a strange taste, but the spicy liquid warmed my tummy.

Just before dinner, she introduced me to her teenage son, Cliff, who had been at school. Sarah's husband, Tom, joined us at the table after arriving home from his engineering job. The tall, lanky, salt-and-pepper-haired man made no pretense about his feelings. He was decidedly cold, and so unlike Sarah. I could tell he wasn't as pleased with my surprise visit to their home.

"The night, you say, she's staying the night?" He muddled through his borscht.

"Uh, yes, things got a little tangled up," Sarah explained. "Melba will be with us just a few days while we find her a new home."

"Oh, I see," he said, glaring at me and then looking down for a long time at the bread he was buttering. The pasty white skin on his forehead crinkled all the way up to his hairline. He peered at me once more above his wire-rimmed glasses.

His stare made me shiver and feel unwelcome. By the time dinner had ended and the strained conversation had trailed off, I just wanted to put my head on a pillow. Sarah did her best to make me feel at home; she ushered me into her son's bedroom with a friendly "Sleep well." It looked and smelled the same even though she had opened the windows and changed the sheets. This time I noticed a cage containing something hairy with eyes that I didn't want to get close to.

As the boy came to fetch his pajamas he mumbled, "Good night" and he stomped out the door heading for the couch. I could tell his lukewarm welcome was changing to resentment. Reaching once more into the neatly folded stack in my trunk, I found my pajamas and asked where the bathroom was so I could brush my teeth.

Snuggling down onto the narrow mattress—decidedly not my own bed—shivering against a cold, damp September evening, I felt painfully alone and claustrophobic in the dinky room. Even after a day of isolation at Central, I had my home and family to go to. Now I had to find comfort among a nest of white strangers. Although bone tired, I couldn't sleep.

Flipping through the stations on the radio next to the bed, I was drawn to the sound of beautifully blended voices singing a capella the call letters of the station, "KSFO—San Francisco." There was the sound of foghorns and the clang of cable car bells. And then a man's deep, soothing voice caught my attention—Frank Johnstone was the announcer's name. And then the choir voices once more. To hold back the tears that lay just below the surface, I amused myself by trying to identify the notes they sang. In the bass clef—F natural, A natural, C sharp—E natural in the treble clef. And then they sang, "The sound of the city . . . the city, the sound of KSFO in San Francisco."

Their a cappella sound reminded me of the church choir at my Sunday services in Little Rock at Bethel AME Church. Far into the night I lay awake, waiting for those voices to come once more. It was the only familiar thing I had to hold on to in a place where everything was so strange. As the clock struck 4:00 A.M. I wrote in my diary:

Dear Diary,
I have to count on you, Lord, to take care of Mother Lois and Con-
rad. Please let them be content and not suffer even one bit at the
hands of segregationists.

I must remember what Grandma India always said. God has a
place for everybody. There is never a time when you are lost to Him.
Please God, let me find the school and the home You have picked out
for me. Help me not to be lost in California.

Chapter 6

FIVE DAYS AFTER MY ARRIVAL IN CALIFORNIA, I still had no promise of a home or a school. The only good news was that I had discovered that a few Negroes did, indeed, make up the core of the Santa Rosa NAACP. I wondered when Sarah was going to take me to a neighborhood where lots more of my own folks lived. I thought they would be much more willing and able to help me find a place to stay. I was becoming a bit suspicious of Sarah because even though she was a member of the NAACP, she had very few nonwhite friends. I gathered my nerve and asked where the Negro people and churches were. She told me there was no Negro church nearby because there were few people of color around.

"You can count the Negroes that live up here on one hand," she said.

"So there is no neighborhood?"

"There aren't any in Santa Rosa or Montgomery proper. Just the few people we know—the ones in the NAACP, the Greys and such."

I didn't know what to make of that information. No Negro neighborhood? Where had I landed? To quiet my nerves I sat quietly, reading *The New York Times*, fascinated by the news of Khrushchev's arrival in Washington. I reasoned that if President Eisenhower were preoccupied with Mr. Khrushchev's visit, he would have little time to even consider enforcing the laws that would integrate Central High and bring me back home to Little Rock.

Sipping yet another cup of the aromatic spice tea Sarah had introduced me to, I sat staring off into the distance. I was exhausted from trying to be invisible in that home where I knew I wasn't wanted. Her teenage son, whose room I had squeezed into, was definitely showing signs of resenting my presence, as was his father, so we all played the game: Melba isn't here. Those two pretended I was not there as hard as I tried to make it so. Sarah always brought us back to reality. She would ask her husband or son to explain something about the city to me or she would sit me between them at dinner.

I felt calmer during the day when only Sarah and I were in the house. I had come to like her, even to feel a bit relaxed in her presence. Her soft voice, easy manner, ready smile and perky manner made her nonthreatening. She was the only white lady I had ever spent that much time alone with.

Sarah spent a lot of time on the phone. I could hear her in the next room, discussing my need for a home. Sometimes, it made me feel as though I were an orphan child, a homeless beggar. But I knew that having a home was the only way I could remain in California. She didn't know I had heard her dialing call after call, searching for a family that would take me. The confidence with which she sought a home for me gave me hope that she could work a miracle. Nevertheless, I felt like a balloon floating in the air, attached to nothing. Was there no place for me?

Mother Lois called every evening, asking what had happened to the family I should have been living with. She didn't mince words. If I didn't get settled soon, she would insist I ask the NAACP for another location, another safe house.

"I'm just fine, Mama." I hoped raising my voice and making nonstop cheerful chatter about California people and places would veil my anxiety. "Mama, it's so different here. Grown-ups want me to call them by their first name."

"Mind your manners, girl. Look to getting settled and putting yourself all the way into your schoolwork."

"I'm waiting for the family I'll live with to return from their emergency trip." I felt I had to lie to her. How could I tell her I had not even the prospect of a family? She would certainly make me come home if she knew that.

"You're falling behind in school."

"Soon, Mama, soon I'll have a school and a family." I did it again. I lied to her.

"They're letting you eat at the table with the family, aren't they? They're not treating you like a servant, are they?" She would ask those same questions at the end of each phone call.

"Oh, yes, ma'am. They've treated me like a real guest. Every time I offer to wash or dry dishes, Sarah takes the towel away."

"Indeed. That's as it should be. You're a guest. Make certain you behave like one, with dignity and self-respect."

"Don't you worry, Mother. You should stop spending your money on these telephone calls." Choosing words that would comfort Mama was not easy.

I was also trying really hard to present a happy face to Sarah. I didn't want to let her know how frightened I had become about not having a place to go. I wanted her to understand that I was grateful for her help. I hoped she would continue to believe in me because I needed her help to survive in California. On those chilly late September evenings, while praying to God for a family to take me in, I fell asleep listening to the radio sounds of the a cappella choir singing the station's call letters—KSFO. "Please God, make some way for me to stay in California," I whispered over and over again into my pillow.

ELL, YOUNG LADY, I've got some news." Just before lunch on the sixth day, I turned from staring out of the living-room window to see Sarah enter the room wearing a smile that revealed something good was happening. "I've found a wonderful family for you. You'll be living with the McCabes. They're very nice people," she continued, her expression animated, her hands fluttering in the air.

"Now that I think about it, they're just perfect. He's a professor at San Francisco State College. Psychology, I believe. At any rate, he heads the Santa Rosa branch of San Francisco State Teachers College. Carol, his wife, is a real political activist involved in a lot of community projects. They have four youngsters, two are about your age and two are much younger."

"Do they live nearby?" I asked, anxious to meet people who sounded so neat.

"Only about twenty or so minutes away, just outside Montgomery Village."

"Are we going there now?"

"No, they've just learned of your arrival. Let's give them a chance to make room for you."

I imagined that the neighborhood resembled Sarah's—only there would be a few more Negro people. Maybe the McCabes would even live in the same kind of A-frame house with stained-glass windows. Maybe they would be surrounded by magnificent lawns and pretty inlaid stone driveways.

Hmm, I thought to myself—McCabe—that was an odd name. I had never heard it in my Little Rock community. I hoped they would cook the foods Grandmother and Mother had fixed: collard greens and oven-baked chicken and cornbread. And that there would be music—my kind of music: Johnny Mathis and Nat King Cole. It felt so good just to think about being with a family of my own people who wanted me.

"I hope you'll come back and visit," Sarah said as I marched off to her son's room to try and organize my belongings.

"Sure I will." The words just fell out of my mouth. The truth was that I'd never been invited on casual visits to white people's houses. I thought that maybe I should have said no. Oh well, I would figure it all out later. That night I wrote in my diary:

Thank you God. I'm not lost at all. You've found me my right place with my own people. Thank you for the new people.

You've also taught me an important lesson. This is the first time I've ever seen the inside of a white home up close. I can't believe it. It's all the same. Just like when I went into the white ladies' bath-

room and found all the ladies preening and peeing when I was five years old.

The white people in this home are living just like we live. Their food tastes different, because they eat borscht, but the rooms look the same and they do mostly the same things that we do.

Why does everyone think my people are so different just because our color is different? I thought I'd learn some big secret if I stayed in a white home and got to see everything, but I don't think there are any secrets.

That night, I once again listened to KSFO and the choir voices, but I wasn't praying and crying into my pillow. I wasn't feeling lost any more. Instead, I imagined what it would be like to live with the wonderful family of a college professor. He must know other teachers with families that read the same books, spoke the same language and harbored the same dreams, like Mother's friends back home in Little Rock. Finally, the blessing was here. I drew in a deep breath down to my tummy and let it out slowly.

The next afternoon, some of the same NAACP members who had greeted me at the airport joined Sarah and me for the journey to my new home. Only this time, I was thrilled to greet three of my own people along with the white members; there was a couple who had started the Santa Rosa branch of the NAACP and a man who was high up in the organization.

After several miles along a rural road, the asphalt turned to gravel and I felt a sinking feeling in my stomach. Along the roadside, there were only a few rustic farm houses. Is this how the McCabes lived? Occasionally there was an estate with a beautiful home like Sarah's. Did the McCabes own one of these? The questions rumbled in my mind. I told myself that if I were really a Christian, I'd be grateful for whatever home God had chosen for me. Still, there was just the tiniest part of me that wanted to live in a really nice house. Surely college professors had nice houses with a library and a huge yard and the amenities I had seen in movies.

"We're here," the driver said.

"Where?" I said aloud. It was a desolate area with only one house in sight. "Where are we?"

We had pulled up onto a gravel lane that ran alongside a large, white, two-story farmhouse. As the station wagon slowed, I noticed that our tires started to make even louder crunching noises. I looked out the window to see that walnuts lay on the ground—walnut shells were everywhere.

"This is exciting, isn't it? I'm pleased this all worked out so you can stay with us here in California." Sarah grinned with pride. I realized she thought she had done a splendid job, but I was beginning to question her choice.

Except for the walnut trees that surrounded it, the farmhouse reminded me of Rock Hudson's house in the movie *Giant,* only it was much, much smaller. It was isolated, set in the middle of a vast piece of land and with no neighborhood houses in sight. It didn't have a California-style look. It might just as well have been transplanted from one of the white neighborhoods in Little Rock, were it not for the huge hills that loomed in the distance behind it.

As we got out of the car, a petite, brown-haired woman emerged from the front door of the house. Oh, my goodness—she was white. Maybe she was just another NAACP person. She wore bangs that covered her forehead and had a pageboy haircut cropped just beneath her ears, emphasizing her sculptured cheekbones and pointed chin. Both her hands remained in the pockets of her denim dress as she moved past the front porch swing, down the stairs and along a narrow concrete walkway that led around the circular stone pond. A scruffy little black-and-white dog with long shaggy ears scampered in front of her, barking nonstop.

As she came closer, I could see the pleasant smile on her face and the huge, piercing brown eyes that peered through brown-framed spectacles. "I'm Carol McCabe. Call me Kay," she shouted over the loud barks and then looked down at the source. "And this is Rags. He'll settle down in a moment. Welcome home!"

"Mrs. McCabe?" I whispered aloud. I could hardly speak. Sarah expected me to make my home with a white family? Mrs. McCabe was extending her hand to me, beckoning me to follow her.

"Uh, hello," I said, smiling, hesitant to extend my hand for fear she wouldn't want to touch me.

"Oh," she said. "Please call me Kay. We're pleased you've come to be with us." Her words were slow and measured. In the tone of her voice I heard kindness and strength. When I extended my hand, she never flinched. She took it and pulled me closer to her, then put her arm through mine and guided me toward the front door. She behaved as though I were an old family friend come for a long-awaited visit. Still I couldn't call her Kay—it would be impolite, a disrespect for a kind adult. But like Sarah, she insisted.

"Will you sit and visit for a moment? I have the teakettle on." Kay extended her invite to Sarah and the others to come in. They trailed behind me, helping to carry my belongings.

"How about the living room? I've got a fire going. It's chilly today, don't you think?" Kay chatted as she seated Sarah and the others on the brown couch and tan chair in a room decorated with chintz curtains, paintings of landscapes and flowers and pottery pieces that could have just as well belonged to my aunt Mae.

"Melba, why don't you come and give me a hand," she said.

She was already inviting me to help her in the kitchen. Was this the first step in training me to be a servant? Why me? Why not one of the adults she knew so well? I cringed at the thought of disobeying an adult. But did my folks mean white adults—would I also go to hell for disobeying white adults?

She smiled encouragingly and tugged at my sleeve. Rags trailed behind me. I followed her to the large, inviting kitchen where she showed me around in a friendly fashion.

At the center of the room was a huge, round mahogany table with straight-backed chairs that reminded me of the tables and chairs in Little Rock kitchens. The aroma of cinnamon from the baking cookie dough filled the air. There was a pot-bellied stove with a tea kettle sitting on the burner the same way Grandma India's copper kettle rested in our own kitchen.

"What time is it?" She glanced at the clock over the kitchen doorway. "It's about time for George to be coming home. The girls, Joanie and Judy, should be getting home from school soon too. Then we'll have a big family meeting so we can get to know you." As she prepared the tea, she explained that Dori was seven, Ricky almost three, Joanie was fourteen, and Judy was my age. She took out the tray that would hold the cream, sugar and cups, continuing to talk about my "new family."

Walking to the back door, I pulled aside the curtain to look out. A few feet away there was a big brick-red barn. "Is this a working farm?" I asked. "It's huge."

"We live on a hundred and twenty-five acres. But it doesn't all belong to us. Some of it's irrigated acreage that belongs to the state."

"Oh," I said, looking about, trying to visualize the size of 125 acres.

My attention was then drawn to the tree stump that hung over the stove, with hooks that held several pots and pans. Homemade crafts all around showed what Grandma India had called a sense of home. Woven pot holders, hand-painted frames with children's artwork in them, homemade candles and clay-dough gingerbread men figures filled the room with love. I also noticed the dust and the clutter on some of her shelves. I had almost stumbled over the fire truck on the floor.

"Here, will you help me? Please take the napkins." Kay's eyes searched mine for an instant. I wondered what would happen if I refused and insisted on being treated like a guest. But that nagging voice in the back of my head made me reach my hand out to take the napkins.

"Sure," I said, thinking that Grandma India would have deemed paper inappropriate, not fit for guests. But maybe this was California style, I thought, as we collected our trays. After all, I had a lot to learn about California white people.

If I decided to remain with the McCabes I would have to convince Mother Lois that it was okay to do so. I wondered what she would think. I had to admit I was desperate for a place to stay. Maybe living with these white people wouldn't be as bad as going back to Little Rock.

In the living room, Mr. Winston, the driver, Mrs. Lawford, the pleasant, slender woman with the bun at the nape of her neck, and the stylish J.P., as she called herself, continued to talk with Sarah about what the group had planned for NAACP activities in the fall.

"Oh, we'll be calling on you," J.P. said to me. I smiled, but I didn't know what to say. Calling on me? What did that mean?

After some more polite chatter and tea, the NAACP folks wished me well and made their departure. As I said my goodbyes to Sarah, I wanted to ask her if she didn't have a family of my own people I could stay with. But I knew all too well how hard she had worked to find the McCabes. Was it my fate to choose between this white family and returning home to my old life of isolation and fear?

As I heard the car engine start up and the tires grind backward on the walnut shells and gravel in the driveway, panic rose in my throat. Now I was alone, out in nowheresville with these strangers, these white people. I ran to the front porch and down the walkway. I had the urge to call out to Sarah to remain behind for a few hours to ease me into my new home. My body shuddered as I tried to control tears rising up. I was so frightened.

"Come along, dear," Kay called to me. "Let's get you settled."

Reluctantly, I turned to walk back to the house.

"You can put your things in here," Kay said. I followed her into the hallway that led past stairs climbing to the second level. "You'll be bunking in here with the girls. They've decided to make one of their bedrooms a sleeping room for all of you and the second bedroom will be a study room." She paused in the doorway as I ventured ahead of her into the room.

"Thank you," I said, wondering where I'd put all the clothes I'd brought with me. There before me, in a moderate-sized room, were three single beds, their heads resting against a wall in dormitory style. There was barely enough room to squeeze between them. At the foot of the beds were two beige-colored chests with seven drawers each. I wondered how it would be to sleep with other people, especially other white people. I had always had a room of my own. I also wondered how Judy and Joan would feel about my being squeezed into their bedroom and into their lives.

Suddenly, I felt as though someone other than Kay was watching me. I turned to the bay window and saw a pair of large, brown eyes looking back at me. "A cow. Eeeeeeek!" I heard myself screech as I backed away.

Almost immediately, the cow answered, "Moooooo." Just beyond that cow was a whole row of the large brown-and-white creatures, standing like a welcoming committee. "Moooooo," she repeated.

"Cows," I heard myself say again. "There are cows practically right here in the bedroom."

"I'd think an Arkansas girl would have seen cows," Kay laughed.

"Not this close up," I answered. Little Rock was a city. I'd only seen cows two or three times in my life at the rodeo or from a car window. I felt a moment of homesickness, realizing how far I really was from everything familiar.

"They come down from the hills to listen to our classical music every day. They have good taste," Kay said, as I tried not to show how dismayed I was. She laughed again and then added, "Not much closet space, I'm afraid. You'll have to make do until we can find you a wardrobe of some kind." She handed me a bunch of various shapes and types of hangers she'd obviously collected for me. "You can hang clothes up later. George will be home soon so we'd better get started fixing dinner." She beckoned me to follow her to the kitchen.

Aha, I thought to myself, *she's already going to try and make me into a servant.*

Chapter 7

"I'M HOME," A DEEP VOICE SAID as the door opened and Rags barked with excitement. I shuddered to think that maybe this George was a white man just like most of those I had already met. Would he object to my being here? Would he hate me? What would he do to show his displeasure?

I had to face up to these two things: I had to tell Kay I wasn't going to be a maid and I had to meet the man of the house.

I felt myself growing anxious as I moved toward the kitchen. What words should I use to tell her I wouldn't be their servant? What if she insisted? How would I defend myself? Would I have to leave right away? Where would I go?

"Here, honey, have a seat there. Do you want more tea?" Kay asked, smiling and pointing me to one of the straight-backed chairs. Here she was, serving me tea. I realized I was wrong, at least for the moment. "George, this is Melba, our guest from Little Rock." Kay smiled at me as she rushed over to embrace a tall man with strawberry-blond hair.

I guessed Mr. McCabe to be just a bit shorter than my father— about six feet two inches. Unlike Papa Will, he was built lean and lanky, and he dressed very differently than Papa ever had. He wore a white shirt, suspenders to hold up his brown tweed trousers and a brown plaid bow tie. His hair was cut into a flattop like those I had seen on television. I was glad to see that Mr. McCabe's smile was warm, which hopefully meant that he was in favor of my being with his family. I could see character lines around his sparkling blue eyes, lines that Grandma said spoke well of a body, showing that they laughed a lot.

"So, you're the new kid?" he said, looking directly into my eyes and placing his hand on my shoulder. "How's it going? I'm George."

"Uh, good. Very well, I mean," I stuttered as I moved backward.

George didn't seem to notice my shyness. He moved away and pulled out a chair and sat down at the table. Kay planted a quick kiss on his cheek and rushed to start preparing dinner. I had never seen such open and joyful affection between husband and wife. It wasn't at all the way my mother and father had behaved toward each other, or toward us children.

"The NAACP called me. Since it's so late in the school year, they wanted me to get going and place you in a school," said George, looking directly at me again.

"Thank you," I said, placing my hands on the table, trying to decide if I should look him in the eye. In Arkansas, for a Negro person to eyeball a white man, woman or child would be a show of disrespect. I didn't know the man's heart or feelings on race, so I could take no chances. I lowered my eyes.

"I talked to the people at the junior college," he continued. "Their rules say you can register only if you're an adult or you have a high-school diploma. You meet neither of these criteria. The NAACP people thought they'd make an exception for you, but the college administration says they can't do that."

"College?"

"Well, I thought you might be more comfortable there because of your age and your experiences. Besides, you'd have a lot more freedom."

"I studied correspondence courses at home with my mother, but I haven't done nearly enough to have completed my senior year."

"Well, we'll have to decide what's best."

I was surprised that he was giving me so much attention. It seemed as though he had done real investigation, which indicated that he didn't mind my being in his home. In fact, his effort to look into schools for me was a sign that he welcomed me. My spirits lifted as I listened to him, and I felt a little more at ease.

"Oh," I said, "I had just thought I'd return to high school."

"Well, maybe you've got a point. You can be a senior and have some fun for a few months." He took a cigarette from his pocket and lit it, drawing in a deep breath.

I wondered what it would be like to attend an already integrated high school. "But won't that hurt the NAACP's court case if I'm registered in high school here?"

"I've checked on that. It'll be okay as long as you don't actually collect the diploma until after the court case is settled." If I received a diploma my name would be withdrawn from the documents in court petitioning for the right to get me back into Central High. We had been told that we might have to double back to Central, even take courses we had completed if suddenly we won our case.

"Sure, why not?" I listened to myself agree again. How could he have gotten all that information so quickly? I guessed it was because he was head of a local college and could get through to people fast. I was also surprised at how comfortable I was talking to him.

I listened as Kay and George thrashed out all the reasons why I should or should not go to high school. As the discussion continued, the two girls arrived. Joanie was the taller of the two, with a round face, happy brown eyes and auburn hair. She was instantly friendly. Judy, a blond, appeared to be a bit distant and quiet, maybe even shy, although she welcomed me with a smile and a sincere manner.

"Whose turn is it to set the table? Somebody's not on the job," George joked. "You girls are probably pleased to add another victim to the work schedule. Did you explain the duty roster to Melba yet?" He laughed as he lowered his cigarette to the ashtray and stubbed it out.

As George continued his teasing chatter, Kay added celery to the beef stew that was beginning to fill the house with an inviting aroma. As I watched the others lend a hand, I realized I was being asked to help with dinner as part of the family, not as a servant, and I happily grabbed for a knife to chop the carrots and afterward helped arrange the plates and silverware on the table. Allowing myself to take part in the laughter that filled the room, I could feel all the muscles in my body relax. I felt suddenly carefree, as though the only thing that mattered was the joy surrounding me. For the first time in two years, I felt a little bit safe. Maybe the McCabes weren't going to harm me after all. Maybe just for this one night nobody was going to harm me.

"Hey, listen everybody." George banged on the table with a spoon to get our attention. Then he began telling a joke. "Oh, no, not again." Joanie voiced the attitude written on the faces of the other family members. "Boooooo," everybody hissed. But he persisted. It was apparent that his attempts at humor, rather than the jokes themselves, were the real source of family fun. What I noticed most was that the children in the McCabe family enjoyed a kind of equal footing with their parents. It was something I had never experienced.

The spirited way the McCabe family gathered in the big kitchen fascinated me. They all seemed so carefree and happy. They acted as if they held the world in their hands. Things were so casual, unlike the ways I was accustomed to. Maybe I was only remembering the hard times since Central High. Once I had gone to that school there didn't seem to be much to laugh about.

Soon, three-year-old Ricky came in from his nap, dragging a wooden truck. Dori had come down from her room, carrying her favorite doll.

"Okay, it's almost time to eat," Kay said. "Ricky, go wash your face and hands."

"I don't have to. Her face and hands are dirty," Ricky said, pointing at me.

"No, sweetie. They're not—she already washed."

There was an awkward silence as I tried to hide my hands behind me without looking as though that was what I was doing.

"Honey, he doesn't mean any harm," Kay said, quick to sense my discomfort. "He doesn't see anyone up here but white people. He doesn't know any better." I could see she was monitoring my reaction.

My heart skipped a beat. Did this mean they didn't have any friends of color? But how could that be? Weren't they in the NAACP? Were they prejudiced after all? Then I remembered many years before, when Conrad was two years old and I was barely five, and both of us hid under the bed when my red-headed, white-skinned cousin was sent to baby-sit us. She looked like a horrible monster, because her coloring and hair were so much different than ours.

This was the same kind of thing, I reasoned. Ricky had expressed the innocent thoughts of a three-year-old. To him I was simply brown. He hadn't said it was wrong or right, just that I was brown. So the knot eased in my stomach and I actually held my hands out in front of me and looked at them. Suddenly the whole thing made me giggle aloud. One by one the others joined.

With the strained expression fading from his face, George pulled Ricky onto his lap for a heart-to-heart. "Well, son, this is something we ought to talk about," he began. "Melba's face and hands are always going to be that way. That's the package she came in." And off he launched into a long explanation. At the end of it all, Ricky looked up into my eyes with the most sincere expression and pointed to me with a very emphatic statement. "She didn't wash hers. They're still dirty."

"I'll take him into the bathroom and show him it doesn't rub off so he understands," I volunteered. The boy reached up for my hand and we were off. But even after our visit to the bathroom, he still wasn't convinced that I wasn't being allowed to violate family rules.

"It'll take time." Kay smiled as she added some finishing touches to the stew. "Oh," she said, "it'll be a few minutes before we eat. Maybe while you're waiting this is a good time to call your mother and let her know you've moved."

"Uh—sure," I stuttered, dreading the call but realizing I had to do it.

"Hurry back, we'll wait for you!"

I walked down the dark hall to the front of the house, grinding my teeth and tightening my jaw as I raked my mind for the best way to gently tell Mother Lois about my "host family."

"McCabe?" she said. "That's a rather odd name for a Negro family. Oh well, times are changing. Who knows where a body comes from."

"Well, Mama, they're not exactly Negro. You see, uh, the family is—well, he's a college professor and she's a housewife. They're real education-conscious; they've already checked on college for me and they seem nice enough and really interested in my welfare."

"Melba, Melba, slow down, honey. Who are these people? Do they know anyone here in Little Rock? Anyone at our church, maybe?"

"No ma'am, uh, they're white folks, Mama. They're not Negroes."

"Precious Lord, Melba, have you taken leave of your senses? You go to California and live with white strangers?"

"Well, not exactly . . ."

She cut me off. Mother Lois's voice was shrill. She didn't have much experience being around nice white people whom she could get to know. I was tense, crossing my fingers that she wouldn't demand I go home to Little Rock right away.

"I'll call the airport now—right now—and get you a ticket. How far are you from the airport?" Her words echoed in my ear. How could I tell her I wanted to stay?

"No, Mama. They were picked by the NAACP. They're members, I think. Besides, Mama, there are some Negro NAACP members and they agree these are okay people."

"What church do they belong to?"

"Mama, I didn't ask yet. I need more time. I'll be okay, all right? The man is a college professor. He teaches." I knew that would help persuade her that I was safe and quiet her fears.

"All right. You call me tomorrow. But Melba, if they call you 'nigger,' make you eat at a separate table or sleep out of doors—you come right home. You hear me, girl?"

"Yes, ma'am. Don't worry, Mama. They gave me a bed with their daughters."

"You mind your Ps and Qs and look after yourself. You don't even know if these are God-fearing white people."

"Yes, ma'am."

"Call me tomorrow night."

"I promise."

I crept back to the table and took my seat. I picked up the napkin to wipe my brow. "Thank you, God," I whispered a small prayer. Kay was pulling rolls out of the oven and savory steam wafted from the stew in its large serving dish on the table.

I was astonished when nobody insisted we say a blessing. I decided I shouldn't make a fuss. I whispered one under my breath. Over dinner I witnessed the most jubilant noises I had ever heard. At first the four McCabe kids spoke at once. Everyone unraveled details of their day. Only after doing that did they ask me a few questions. And those weren't the invading, serious, "Justify why you went to Central and why you want equality" type of questions. Instead, they seemed genuinely curious about my life in Little Rock, wanting to know what the houses were like and whether there were movie theaters. I felt like an equal, just one of them, revealing a bit about myself.

Later that night I felt too embarrassed to undress for bed in front of Joanie and Judy, so I excused myself and went into the bathroom. Fifteen minutes later, I returned in my pajamas. Joanie teased me about being shy. I decided I wasn't only uneasy just because they were white, but also because they were strangers. I'd never undressed in front of anyone before. In my family that was considered unladylike.

Afterward, Judy, Joanie and I lay in the dark chatting and giggling while they told me what Montgomery High School was like. Long after they were snoring, I lay awake trying to accustom myself to their presence. I'd never shared a bedroom with anyone, much less with white girls. I lay in the dark remembering all the times I had watched television families and wished for a much larger, ordinary family of my own with a happy dad who came home to read the newspaper and chat, and a happy mom who didn't have to work and prepared the evening meal as we all gathered in the kitchen. It dawned on me that since there were none of my people on television, I forgot to specify to God that the one he sent me should be Negroes. Grandma India had always said, God gives you exactly what you ask for. And, once again, Grandma was right. I wrote in my diary:

Dear God,
Is this the family you want me to have? Can't you find me one that is made up of my own people? The McCabes are very sweet but how

*will I ever, ever fit in? And will they stay as sweet as they are today?
I'm not lost but it seems I am in the wrong place. Please let me
know what your will is for me.*

The next day, George and Kay took me to register at Montgomery High School. The school was a cream-colored, one-story
building a block long. One side was a series of classrooms and the
other side fronted an open field. I frantically looked around for more
people like me, but at first there were none.

"Where are they?" I questioned George as we stood in the reg-
istrar's office. He was a teacher, he should know, I thought.

"Where are who?" A puzzled look crossed his face.

"You know—Negroes—like me?"

"Oh, honey, that's right. Well," Kay had a strained expression
on her face. "The truth is . . ." Her words came very slowly. "There
really aren't very many nonwhite students."

"How many are there?"

"As I remember there are ten," George said, winking, not really
understanding my distress.

"Ten?" I gasped.

"Well, give or take one or two. But there are about eight hundred other students, so you won't be lonely."

Ten. The word rang in my ears over and over again cutting me
off from the others, as though they were speaking to me from the
other end of a long hollow tunnel.

George continued, "I think some of them are Mexican or
Asian."

"Honey, it'll be all right." Kay must have seen the fear in my
face. She took my hand in hers.

"Does the NAACP want me to help integrate here too? I
wouldn't have come if I'd known. I want to go home." My words
came out all in a loud rush before I had time to think about them or
hold them back.

"No. No. I promise you, it'll be all right." Suddenly understanding my predicament, George tried to console me. "This school is already integrated. It's just that there aren't very many Negroes living
in Santa Rosa. They haven't moved up here yet. You're gonna be just
fine, Melba." Kay gave me a parting hug. I stood motionless watching

as the two of them moved down the hall, leaving me there all alone. I felt panic rise in my chest.

With a class assignment card and books in my hand, I stepped outside into an open walkway covered by a roof. Beyond that was the vast dusty open field that stretched to the horizon. The bell rang for the change of classes and that's when I saw them, hundreds of strangers, strangers who had the same white faces as the hostile students I thought I had left behind at Central High.

I took a deep breath and braced myself. But suddenly I couldn't catch my breath. I looked at the faces, at their eyes all coming toward me. I turned and behind me there were more of them and I was alone . . . with no one to protect me. My heart was pounding in my chest and all I could hear were the voices in my head—the chant I had heard every day at Central, "Two, four, six, eight, we ain't gonna integrate!"

Chapter 8

THE CLOSER THOSE WHITE STUDENTS came to me, the more I felt my throat tighten. My body was on fire. My vision began to blur.

Frantic, I began to burrow through the crowd. A queasy sensation in my stomach was like a geyser, foaming up into my chest. My legs felt like elongated sponges trying desperately to hold up the trunk of my body. Nevertheless, I was moving fast. I had to get out of there.

Finally I was in the open field—beyond the faces—but I couldn't stop running. My legs were carrying me faster than I had realized I could go. My feet were churning up the dust of the desolate field where I sought refuge. Maybe, just maybe, I would keep running forever.

Soon the muscles in my legs ached. My breath came in jolting gasps. Suddenly I felt my right foot sink into a pothole; my ankle twisted in pain. I stretched my hands out in front of me to brace my fall forward into the dirt. When I could get past the throbbing pain of my ankle, I sat up and buried my face in my hands. Cascades of tears flowed from me. My throat was hurting and my body was sore. Lost within the nightmare that engulfed me, I wasn't aware of anyone coming after me. Through the fog of pain, a voice called out to me.

"Melba? Uh, Miss Pattillo? You are Melba, aren't you?" The white face was so close to mine I could see the tiny lines around the soft mouth that was speaking words to me. What was she saying? Huge, sympathetic green eyes commanded my attention. She was small-boned and delicate, but very tall. She was bending over me. I turned my eyes away from her to look down into the dust.

"Yes, ma'am, I'm Melba."

"Are you all right?"

"I think so."

"Was someone chasing you?" Her long, slender hand touched my shoulder. I looked at it. White people—strangers—didn't often touch and speak in soft voices.

"No, ma'am."

"Well it certainly appeared that way to us. You were running like a wild woman—like you were being chased. It took me a while to find you."

"Uh . . . ma'am," I didn't know what to say. I stole a glance at her and saw that she had a pleasant expression, almost a smile, as she waited for me to speak.

"I'm Mrs. Jefferds, one of the assistants in the office, and I'm here to see that you are all right and that you get back to class."

Try as I might to convince her that I didn't need her help, she insisted that I did. As I stood to brush myself off, she picked up my purse and notebook and began brushing off the back of my skirt. Looking down at myself completely took away any hope that my clothes had remained starched and ladylike. I had made an awful mess of the new dress Mother Lois had sewn for my first day. The dust had stained my yellow skirt and the matching blouse was rumpled. Besides, I was hobbling on my hurt ankle.

"Do you think you can make it back?" Her large, kind eyes invited me to speak.

"Uh, yes, uh, I mean no, no, I don't want to go."

"Why?"

"It's just that . . ." I stopped myself. Who was this woman? Why should I trust her with my truth? Despite her kind tone, she was one of them and I shouldn't . . .

"It's just what?" she pressed me.

"I want to go home."

"Well, the McCabes have left. You can't very well go back to the McCabe house by yourself. I think that they would really prefer it if I got you settled in your classroom so you can get on with your school day."

"Yes, ma'am."

"Perhaps it's just your fear of being in a new school. But you'll get over that," she smiled and reached out to take my hand. At Mrs. Jefferds's insistence, I was ambling as slowly as I could manage, back across that dusty field to the school that frightened me out of my wits. After several steps, the pain in my ankle lessened. Mrs. Jefferds coaxed me back into the hallway where she pointed the way to her office so I could sit and rest until the bell rang for the next class.

I realized I desperately needed to go to the restroom so that I could spruce myself up. When I returned to her office, Mrs. Jefferds stood and offered to go with me to class. It wasn't easy convincing her that I could go on my own. "I promise I won't run away," I said with a fake smile and looked directly at her for just an instant.

Drawing a deep anguished breath, once more I found myself standing in the hallway, awaiting the next bell that would signal the start of a new period. I certainly didn't want to walk into any ongoing class and stick out like a sore thumb.

The bell rang, but I remained frozen, unsure what to do. Students began filling the hall.

"Melba, don't just stand there. Let's go!" With an anxious voice and manner, Judy McCabe rushed up to me and explained that she had come from her class to introduce me and show me around. "Hurry, we're gonna be late." She clutched at my arm, a red flush of enthusiasm painted across her face.

"Where were you? I looked all over for you last period so I could take you to class," she said, sticking her arm through mine and urging me to go with her through the now crowded corridor to my next class. But I still couldn't make myself move. My body stiffened.

"Judy, please, wait a moment!" I just wasn't ready to face the task before me. "Uh, promise me you won't tell anyone I'm from Little Rock, or about Central High and all."

"Why not?" she asked, with a puzzled expression on her face.

"Because somebody might think I came here to integrate."

"Okay, sure, let's just go." She tugged at me, insisting that I come with her despite my hesitation. I was sure Montgomery High students would be just as cruel to me as the ones at Central High had been. Who would be the first to call me "nigger," or to trip me or spill ink on my clothes?

"Judy . . . Judy, we're over here." Voices were calling out over the noise from the opposite side of the corridor.

"Hey, Melba, come and meet my friends." Judy clutched my arm and off we went to meet a group of girls. My heart thumped in my ears. Why would they want to meet me? Suddenly a rush of words whirled about my head. Their hands fluttered in the air like a flock of birds, their strawberry faces and sparkling eyes only added to the colorful palette of their dresses. They were all speaking at once, breathlessly describing their weekend experiences and at the same time complaining about teachers they disliked. For the moment they weren't paying any special attention to me, but I held my breath, waiting to see what rude things they were going to say.

"This is Melba," Judy said in her matter-of-fact way. "She's going to live with us and go to school here." Each one hesitated for only a moment to look at me with glances of acknowledgment and then, once more, words began flying out of their mouths.

"Great," said a blond girl with a shoulder-length pageboy and bangs. Her wide full lavender skirt and blouse made her resemble a picture from *Seventeen* magazine.

"How long are you gonna be here?"

"I'm gonna . . ." But without stopping to wait for my answer, she raced over my words, talking with the others in their rapid-fire fashion.

"What classes are you taking?" a wide-eyed redhead asked me.

"Where did you come from?" yet another girl asked.

Each of the girls asked questions, but none of them waited for an answer. Instead, they launched back into their breathless ex-

changes, including me with pointed fingers and eye contact, and behaving as though they had nothing against my being there.

When the bell rang, once more I took a deep breath and said
goodbye to them. I didn't want to take Judy away from her friends,
so I didn't wait for her to escort me to class. They called out, "See you
later," in unison like a choir as they smiled at me. Nevertheless, I told
myself, I could not let my guard down. The muscles in my jaw, shoulders and tummy tightened as if to shield me from what was surely
coming any moment.

At my first class, I was greeted by a smiling teacher. "You must
be the late registrant," the social studies teacher said, as he approached me with an extended handshake and a warm smile. Well, so
what—lots of white people are pleasant on the first go-round, I told
myself as I shook his hand with reluctance. Three or four of the
teachers at Central High were polite at first, but that didn't change
the fact that they later treated me as though I were a plague upon
their house.

"Yes, I'm Melba." Sunlight shone through the bank of windows
into the room filled with about twenty students whose giggling and
chatter didn't subside as I walked further in.

"We're expecting you. Let's see, looks like there's an empty seat
over here." The slender brown-haired man smiled and spoke with a
kind voice as he pointed to a desk near the front of the row closest to
the door. Ignoring his direction, I headed for the desk in the rear
where I knew, with my back against the wall, I would be safe. To my
amazement only a few people looked up at me. They smiled and said,
"Hi."

"This class is murder," whispered a boy with slicked-back, car-
rot-red hair and freckles as I walked past him. I noticed that he wore
brown-and-white saddle shoes just like my own. I hesitated, waiting
for a harsh word, but he and the other students smiled and then
turned their attention back to their desks or to the front of the room
where the teacher was preparing to begin his lecture.

As I made my way to my seat I noticed a pile of books blocking
the aisle in front of me. *Aha, here we go,* I said to myself. *It's happening
now! Of course, they'd been purposely put there to trip me up. Okay, fine, I can
deal with that,* I reassured myself. *I'll quietly step over—no, I'll turn and
find another seat.*

"Wait. Sorry. Oh here, let me move these." The girl smiled through her blue-rimmed glasses with rhinestones on the outer edges of the frames as she moved her books further under her desk. Squeezing out a "thank you," I walked past and sank down into my seat, breathing a sign of relief. The teacher's voice filtered through the competing voices. All my classmates were beginning to quiet and focus on him. I took a deep breath. Maybe everything would be okay for the next few minutes. Maybe I could focus on learning something.

The social studies teacher cleared his throat as he leafed through the large white sheaf of pages connected to his huge easel board. After a few minutes had passed, my head was reeling as he lectured, analyzing a long chain of world events. He might as well have been speaking Greek. Finally, he paused to write the names of several countries on the blackboard. Korea. Japan. The Soviet Union. China. Cuba.

"Gregory, explain to us the American point of view on the Korean conflict." I held my breath as the boy next to me began to speak. Did that mean I'd be next? I could hardly understand the question let alone give an intelligent answer. A stupid answer would let them know how little I really knew. As Grandma India had said many times, "First impressions can be everything. A person ought always to put forth personal best, but most especially the first time out."

I had taken two years of social studies classes but our questions and discussions were not nearly as sophisticated as what I was hearing. It was true, I liked to read the newspapers and I paid attention to international events, but I hadn't ever been exposed to this kind of wide-ranging analysis. Besides, my year without school when I faithfully watched soaps must have dulled my academic skills. I had also been obsessed with Little Rock integration, closed schools, legal suits and the like. Now, as I heard about things far removed from Little Rock, my pencil raced and my hand cramped from taking notes. As the period continued, I discovered just how little I really knew about world affairs.

How would I ever catch up? Before I could worry about it too much, the bell rang and I braced myself to go back into that crowded, noisy hallway. I took a deep breath and let it out slowly as I squeezed through the mingling students.

"Let's go. I'll give you the tour." Judy was outside waiting for me. "I'll skip study period, so we'll have almost a whole hour."

"Tour? What tour?"

"Of everything. You know, you've gotta learn where we assemble for rallies, where we eat and goof off."

And she certainly kept her word as she dragged me, racing, through the entire school. I was preoccupied with keeping my guard up and trying to spot the other minority students George had told me about. I figured they would explain what kind of treatment I should prepare to endure at Montgomery High.

"There," I said excitedly to Judy. "Wait a minute."

"What?"

"I wanna meet that girl. Who is she?"

"Oh, that's Ginny. She's not going anywhere, we can do that later." It was apparent that Judy didn't understand my urgent need to talk to one of my own people.

Ginny, I thought, making a mental note to myself. I really wanted to talk to her now, but Judy was pulling at my arm again. I felt it was bad manners to complain, as Judy walked me to my next class, pointing to other people and places she thought I needed to know about.

My worst fears were realized as I emerged from the classroom. Judy was nowhere in sight. I had to get to my next class on my own. I ventured into the waves of noisy people and made my way down the hall, assuming the direction I had chosen was correct. I dared not ask anybody for help for fear of picking the wrong person.

As I walked alone for the first time, I hoped I would see the boy Judy described as really important—some sort of school officer—and not a white boy. I had assumed she meant he was one of my people. There he was—a real live Negro boy walking down the adjoining corridor. I could hardly contain my excitement as I forded the streams of students and made my way toward him. He had paused just in front of the glass case that held trophies.

"Hi, hi . . . I'm Melba." I felt my right arm flutter in the air as though I were flagging down a longtime friend I hadn't seen for a year. I didn't want to let him know how anxious I was, so I tried to calm down before calling out again. I was certain he saw me and yet he wasn't making any effort to push through the crowd toward me. Perhaps he was preoccupied. I called out to him once more as I moved his way.

"Oh, uh, hi," he said, his nose in the air, looking at me as if I was an intruder. He wore a flattop haircut and dark sunglasses. With his bow tie and a varsity vest over a white long-sleeved shirt, he, too, resembled a picture out of a teen magazine. I'd never seen a black boy dress like that or look so totally in charge.

"This is my first day. I'm lost, can you help me find my next class?" I figured asking directions wouldn't reveal my real motive for contacting, wouldn't make me seem too eager.

"Why are you asking me?" His eyes were cold as he pulled his dark glasses down on his nose and glared at me as though I was an insect. Pausing for only a moment, he moved his shades back into place and with that, he walked off.

His words wounded me. My hurt feelings welled up in my throat. He was making me feel small and unequal—as though I wasn't good enough to rate his friendship or even a moment of his attention. He was a real snob, really no different than some of the Central High whites. I had little time to think about it, though, because suddenly the bell rang and I was being pushed along by the momentum of the late crowd scurrying to class. I had to concentrate. Maybe I was going the wrong way. Where was my next class? I decided I'd deal with what's-his-name later.

Suddenly, I was surrounded by silence. The halls had emptied. I panicked and started hurrying toward one corner of the U-shaped corridor. Just as I reached the corner I heard voices—boys' voices. There they were, blocking my path, a group of James Dean look-alikes, boys wearing white t-shirts and straight-legged jeans. Some of them had their hair slicked back into ducktails and their shirt sleeves rolled up. One boy's rolled-up sleeve revealed a tattoo. From my experience at Central High I had learned that boys wearing the ducktails were the ones to avoid. But how could I avoid them when they were in front of me? Frantically, I looked around. There was no way to escape. They had seen me.

I braced myself for what would inevitably come from these "sideburners." Would they lash out at me by using the "N" word, surround and trap me, punch and kick, throw raw eggs and maybe something worse?

Taking a deep breath, I tried to appear nonchalant. I lowered my eyes, stared at my feet and quietly slipped past the boys. My jaw clenched tight to allay my fear. I didn't dare look up, but I anticipated the slap to my head, waited for the vicious words to assault my ears. But before I knew it, I was down the hall and well past the boys. Slowly, I lifted my head and looked over my shoulder. The boys were still there, talking and laughing, but it was as if they didn't I know I was there. They plumb ignored me without even so much as a glance.

"Thank you, God," I whispered, breathing deeply and relaxing my muscles. I walked a bit further and once again looked back. I could hear Grandmother's words in my ears, "Sometimes it's the expectation of evil rather than the real thing that does us in."

My nerves were jangled. I was weary. As I continued to look for my next class, I started to repeat the Lord's Prayer. Looking over my shoulder one more time to make sure the boys didn't change their minds, I walked close to the walls to protect my right side.

"Hey," said a boy who was at least six inches taller than my five feet eight inches. He blocked my path and towered over me. His shiny black hair and horn-rimmed glasses made him appear sinister at first glance. He came so close to me that his book satchel touched my skirt made wider by my crinoline slip. I adopted a go-away attitude and brushed past him.

"Hey, did you hear me?" He persisted in talking to me. I felt my cheeks go hot and my temples pound like a kettle drum. What was he going to do to me? He moved closer, but he didn't appear to be making a fist to hit me.

"What do you want?" I asked, as I backed up slowly, stiffening my body in preparation for a quick getaway. So he was to be my first attacker. At Central, they hadn't stopped to talk before striking. Was he alone?

"Hi, I'm a hall monitor. You look lost."

"I'll be fine." I moved away but he followed closely, continuing to talk. What kind of ruse was this?

"Where are you going?"

"To class." I spoke emphatically and turned to walk away.

"Where's your next class?" He walked after me and flashed a broad grin as his eyes danced back and forth searching mine for the answer to his question. I slowed to take a closer look, intrigued because his pupils were outlined by a golden halo and they appeared huge behind the thick lenses of his glasses. That's it—he resembled a young Clark Kent.

"I don't know," I mumbled.

"Well, didn't they give you some sort of schedule? Didn't you write down your classes?" Geez, if this was a trick, why would he take so long to get it going and why was he so very cordial?

"Uh, English, I guess." I stuttered as I glanced at the card I held in my trembling hand. At the same time, I was trying not to take my eyes off him. What did he really want?

"Here, I'll show you the way," he said.

"But I . . ." My words wouldn't come. I pulled back. Perhaps he was leading me into a trap. Falling for a nice greeting and hoping for friendship had led to lots of painful traps at Central High. *Don't be silly, Melba,* said a voice in my head. *This building is so much smaller than the seven-story castle of torture that was Central High. There are no places to be trapped here.*

"Well, come on, you don't want to be any later," he began to move, beckoning me with his eyes to follow. My heartbeat raced so fast I wondered how I would ever be able to slow it down. Reluctantly I began to follow him.

"Where are you from?"

"Uh, the South," I stuttered. Suppose he had read about me and been sent by the Klan to do me in.

"Southern California, Los Angeles?" He was pressing me. Why?

"No, uh, you know, the deep south like Georgia or Alabama."

He continued chatting but I couldn't focus on what he was saying. We were moving quickly through the hallways and unfamiliar things seemed to be whizzing by like a film projector set on fast forward.

"Oh, by the way, what's your name?" he said as he pointed me toward a door.

"Why do you need my name?"

"Just wondered. My name is Evvie," he said as he hustled me to the classroom, pulled open the door and nudged me inside. "See you later," and he was off before I could muster a thank you. I stood there a moment. That's when I saw that Judy was seated inside the room. We would be taking a class together. How would she treat me in front a whole class full of people who knew her but weren't necessarily special friends of hers? I stood there holding the doorknob, sorry that I was too late to sneak into the room and find a seat without drawing attention to myself.

Chapter 9

"Hey, guys, this is Melba." Judy's announcement was loud enough to wake the dead, and for certain it attracted almost everyone's attention. I wanted to fold into myself like a turtle into its shell. All those eyes in white faces looking at me meant I would surely be a target of their wrath—the only question was, would it be verbal or physical? Would they say things so ugly it would make Judy turn on me too?

"Hi." I spoke softly.

"Welcome." The teacher walked over to extend her hand to me. Tight, almost kinky, brown curls framed her round, tanned face. Her thin lips held a genuine smile, and her blue eyes were like clear pools. As she looked me over, I felt no twinges of disapproval or disgust. Her manner was welcoming.

"Have a seat, and when you get a chance, you should review Judy's notes on James Joyce. I'm certain you're already familiar with his work, but it's a good idea to get used to our approach."

James Joyce. The name rang a bell. What did he write? I had heard Mother Lois mention his name but I had never formally studied him. The teacher continued talking, explaining how we would be dissecting *Ulysses,* and I knew for certain I would be spending some time in the library.

"We'll also be reviewing the works of Shakespeare."

Shakespeare! Great—a name I recognized. *Macbeth*, I remembered *Macbeth*. My heart skipped a beat. She was walking toward me.

"Melba, this reading list includes most of the works we will brush through this semester." She handed me three typewritten pages, single-spaced. I glanced at the list of authors' names: Molière, Ibsen, O'Neill and Faulkner . . . God bless Faulkner, the only writer I recognized on the first page. I was still staring at the list, somewhat oblivious to her lecture, pondering how I would get through the class when the bell rang.

"Enough to scare you to death," Judy said as if she knew exactly what I was thinking. "If I have to review all these books it could ruin my whole life."

"Yeah, you're right." How could I admit to her that I had to start from the very beginning? I could not review what I had never read.

"Choir class is that way." Judy pointed me down the hall. "I'll meet you just outside this door afterward and we can eat." She waved goodbye and scampered down the hall.

Did that mean we would go to the cafeteria? That word unearthed miserable memories. I knew I would fret about it all through choir. I couldn't bear to think of being in a large room full of unruly white teenagers.

"So you're joining our stars this semester," the music teacher teased me gently as I entered the room. He was about my height with flaming red hair that framed an expressive and kind face. His manner was as playful as his smile. As each person entered the room he had something positive and funny to say. He had such a welcoming way about him.

The sight and sounds of the piano made me comfortable right away. I climbed up the steps to seats mounted on risers which stretched almost to the ceiling as if the room were a miniature Greek theater. The teacher's desk and piano were directly below on a hardwood floor.

He didn't vie with the chatter for attention. Instead he sat down at the piano and began playing one of my favorite spirituals, "Old Rugged Cross." It was a familiar touchstone in an unfamiliar world and my heart leapt for joy. The music brought back to me the life I had left behind: our Sundays at Bethel AME Church and the sweet voice of Mrs. Marlene Smith singing that solo at least once a month as I grew up. Suddenly I was homesick for those church services, sitting between Mother and young Conrad wiggling and squiggling and making a fuss.

"Negro spirituals are a rich part of our culture, and provide a backdrop for much of today's music from gospel to show tunes and rock and roll." Rich part of our culture? I couldn't imagine that white high-school students would be studying my folks' music.

"Listen to the words and hear the honest message they contain," the teacher instructed. "Usually they are about gratitude or about asking for mercy or about pain being healed by words of praise. These songs express feelings we all have from time to time.

"Melba, do you know this song? It's called 'I Have a Mother in the Heavens.'"

"Ah . . . yes." I stammered.

"Why don't you sing it for us?"

What? Sing by myself? In a room full of white students? I couldn't.

My knees shook so hard I thought they must have sounded like castanets. It was only the second time in my life I had ever sung before an audience of white people. When he invited me to come down front I begged off, I was too embarrassed. I wanted to stay in my seat; I was also afraid my voice would croak like a frog's evening song if I stood up in front of the class. And yet, when he started to play the notes I had heard so many times, the words flowed out of me. I surprised myself when my own voice rang in my ears. Soon I was lost in the verses that Grandmother India had sung to me so many times. It made me miss her. Then I imagined her smiling down on me and the tears that had come to my eyes when I began singing started to dry.

The class listened intently and I smiled as I sang. I felt appreciated and that made me proud of myself for the first time in a very long while. The class applauded when I came to the end. Their praise embarrassed me.

"You were great," the girl next to me whispered.

"Nice voice," the girl on the other side said.

I didn't know quite how to respond to the praise of all these white students. They looked no different from the students in Central, yet they were applauding and smiling. I felt such joy surge up inside of me that the rest of the hour sped by quickly. All of a sudden my rapture was interrupted by the bell and I was gathering my books once more to trudge through that hallway.

"See you Friday," the teacher called after me. "We're doing show tunes."

I was floating as I left the room. I would count the hours until the next music class. It made me proud to watch white students sing and listen to the hymns of my people with respect and admiration.

But pride quickly turned to fear as I realized it was time to go to have lunch. The cafeteria had always been such a nightmare at Central High. Judy was waiting for me as promised, and as we entered, I could see it wasn't really a cafeteria like the one at Central, which had been the size of a football field. It was a regular-sized room, and students sat around talking, laughing and eating bag lunches. Even though the room was much smaller, the chattering voices brought back frightening memories. Lunchtime at Central High had been an hour of terror each day. I would huddle in the corner with four other integrating students, waiting for someone to strike me, pelt me with something, or, for certain, call me "nigger." But with fewer people, I did feel a bit less threatened.

"What's the matter with you now?" Judy sensed I was nervous.

"Nothing. I mean, I'm worried about homework," I lied. How could a white girl in California even begin to imagine the torture a cafeteria could be?

We seated ourselves at a table occupied by several of Judy's friends and opened our brown bags. But I couldn't relax enough to eat. I set my tuna sandwich aside and looked around for some of my own people. Though I would be cautious about approaching them now, I felt a real compulsion to at least try to make friends.

Across the room, about twenty feet away, I saw a very pretty Negro girl calmly eating her lunch. I watched her as she laughed and chatted with white students, just as if they were her friends. Mustering my courage, I headed over to introduce myself.

"Hi, I'm Melba," I said, smiling at the girl with a neatly cropped haircut who was just finishing the last drop of her juice. She wore a beautiful forest-green gabardine jumper.

"When did you get here?" She was friendly, not like that snobby Negro boy.

"May I sit down?" I gingerly reached for the straight-backed chair, pausing for her permission to join her.

"Sure, but I've only got a moment."

"I just wanted to ask how things are here." Should I come right out and ask, How do the white people treat you? *No*, the voice in my head said. *Melba, you don't want to appear to be the country hick.*

"Things are fine. I didn't get the gym class I wanted and tryouts for cheerleading are coming up sooner than I thought, but, oh well."

"You mean you're allowed to try out? I asked, trying not to sound flabbergasted.

"Oh, sure." Sure. She said "sure" as though a Negro trying out for cheerleading was the most ordinary thing in the world.

"You mean they don't object, uh . . . even if the person is Negro? You mean, even I could try out?" I almost couldn't believe it. I was so excited.

"If you think you might make the cut, give it a try," she said cheerfully. She stood and gathered up her things. "See you later." She waved to her friends and sauntered out of the room, as though she weren't at all afraid. She behaved like an ordinary student. Was it possible that I could be ordinary here, as well?

Maybe things wouldn't be so bad here. After all, everyone had been really nice to me so far. I went back to my table feeling a little more comfortable. But no matter what my head told my stomach, it wouldn't calm down enough to let me eat. I put my sandwich back in the bag. I couldn't take an easy breath until Judy and I were out the door of that eating room and on our way to afternoon classes.

Nobody had behaved in a threatening way during that entire day. I was surprised, and in some ways, it frightened me more . . . were they waiting for something? The expectation of evil had tuckered me out. By the time I made it onto the school bus to go home, I was exhausted.

"Well, how'd your first day go?" Kay smiled at me when she arrived home from her League of Women Voters meeting. Now she was standing at the kitchen sink washing lettuce for a dinner salad.

"Nobody bothered me." I caught myself before I revealed to her all the fear that haunted me that day. I didn't want to worry her because I knew she wouldn't understand.

"What, honey?"

"Oh, it went fine." I didn't trust her enough to confess I expected trouble.

"We'll have an early dinner. I'll bet you've got lots of homework."

"Loads of it."

"Oh, you'll do just fine. I'm just so pleased you had a good day. George and I were kind of worried when we left you. We didn't think about how few Negroes there are in that school, and we could see that you were genuinely frightened."

"Where are they? Is there segregation here—in Santa Rosa—in Montgomery Village?" I knew what George had said, but I wanted to hear what Kay thought, too.

"No. It's not an issue here because there aren't a lot of minority people. The standard of living is so high that only the financially well-off can afford to live here, that is, unless you live out here in the countryside like we do. Basically, this is a retirement center for those who can afford it, or a bedroom community for commuters." I didn't understand what she meant because I'd never heard the term "bedroom community" and I didn't know anything about retirement communities. The older people in our community lived with their families.

"Well, nobody's bothered me so far," I said.

"Well, honey, did you think they would?"

"I didn't know. Yeah, I guess I did." I felt myself loosen up a little bit, but I still couldn't tell the whole truth—that I was terrified that my experience at Central would be repeated here.

"We wouldn't have allowed you to go if we'd thought there was any danger. This is definitely a conservative community, though. Look at all those signs on the back of cars saying 'Goldwater for President.' So they might not invite you to dinner or want their children to date you, but they're sure not gonna hit you or call you names." She placed her brown knit shawl-like jacket on the back of a chair, pulled an apron around the front of the matching skirt to protect it, and began stuffing a huge fish with onions and herbs to be baked for dinner.

Meanwhile, I went onto the front porch to sit alone and think about her words. I suppose that I had some vision that all of California was integrated. I was so homesick for Negro people. I yearned for a place where no one asked questions about my color, but instead welcomed me and automatically included me.

At dinner, once again, the jokes and wonderful stories about the day made me forget my woes. I actually laughed and enjoyed myself. George had a kind, deep voice and his funny stories and stream of comments filled me with wonder. Sometimes he behaved as though he was a performing star, as if he was on stage.

When he leaned across the table and asked me about my first day at Montgomery, I found myself daring to look him in the eye. His question stunned me because he was treating me as an equal. I felt comfortable talking to him because he seemed so playful and accepting of me. When dinner was over, George said just this one night he would let the three of us off from dishwashing duty so we could get a head start on our studies, but we had to listen to his one last joke and laugh at the punch line, whether we understood it or not. Giggling, Joan, Judy and I reluctantly retired to our study room.

Oh, how I wished for a cup of Grandma India's warm chocolate and for Mama's tips on James Joyce. Although George and Kay were wonderful, I noticed that home life was different when there was a mother and a father. They paid attention to each other. That didn't leave as much time to tend to the kids. I realized I had been spoiled by all the attention lavished on me especially during my study periods by my mother and grandmother, who had spent almost every waking moment tending to Conrad's and my needs.

"Lights out, girls. Time to go to sleep if you're going to be ready for a fresh start," Kay called from upstairs to interrupt Judy and Joanie's gossip and my giggles just after 9:00 P.M.

A few minutes later, I lay in bed reciting my prayers to myself, too self-conscious to get on my knees as I had done each night at home. I had to ask God's forgiveness because I hadn't been thinking about the Lord's will or reading my Bible very much. Now, what with being in a room with two other people and so much catch up in my studies ahead of me, I knew I'd have little time to myself. I was beginning to worry about being hell-bound because I wasn't doing all the things Mama and Grandma said a body had to do to get to heaven. The McCabes were Quakers, I knew, but I didn't know what that meant. I noticed they didn't seem to read the Bible or bless the dinner table. But I knew that Quakers were very peaceful, loving people, because they had come to Little Rock to try to negotiate peace between the segregationists and integrationists. They would always reach out to me with respect, and they were fearless in their efforts to protect us against harm.

In the morning I awoke at dawn to a deep gray overcast sky with only small streams of light filtering through the clouds. It was still and I felt alone as I peered out the window, waiting for the cows to go to the barn for milking. Judy and Joan were in the room with me, but I could not tell them how ill at ease I felt. As I thought about the day ahead and tried to imagine what school would be like, a wave of panic thrust upward in my throat.

Stop it, Melba. If you spend all your energy worrying, you'll have nothing left for living. I decided I had to trust God for my protection. If He got me through Central, I had to trust Him to get me through Montgomery High. I could no longer afford to spend all my time trying to figure out who would harm me. I had to get busy learning new things.

Beginning with my first class that morning, I allotted myself recesses from worry. In all the places I had gone during the first two days where nobody harmed me, I let myself feel kind of safe. I even began to imagine what it would be like to attend school for a whole week without expecting awful things to happen. I also stopped frantically searching for my own people. After English, when Evvie, the hall monitor who looked like Clark Kent, spoke to me, I spoke back without a scowl on my face. By noon, my heart wasn't pounding one bit and my stomach didn't hurt. I felt just fine.

I was able to string together three more days of feeling okay about myself and my surroundings. Judy and Joanie were a real help to me because their attitude toward me wasn't affected by the difference of my color. I was always and at every turn treated like their friend and a welcome new family member. Several days later I wrote in my diary:

Except for my stay with Sarah, this is the first time I've ever lived in a white home. It's one week and nothing bad has happened to me. In fact, here at home with the McCabes only good things have happened to me. Sometimes I actually forget to wait for the other shoe to drop —for something awful to happen. No has called me "nigger," no one has hit me or said bad things to me. Only good has happened.

One afternoon during the second week of classes, just before noon, Judy rushed up to me in the hall, obviously with a plan in mind. Fresh-faced and apple-cheeked, her blunt-cut blond hair danced across her forehead as wisps of hair cupped her cheeks. She reminded me of the pictures I'd seen of Dutch girls standing in tulip fields. While Joanie was effervescent, Judy was even-tempered and always calm. Even when she was in a hurry she had a calm manner, which was one of the reasons she was so good with the cows and other animals that she loved to care for.

"Hi, Melba, come with me. We're going to the Pick-up to eat lunch." I could tell Judy was in a hurry and she wouldn't take no for an answer. I was apprehensive, wondering how her friends would feel about me joining them in a different setting, a social setting away from school.

Outside in the parking lot, Cindy, a girl in my choir class, sat behind the steering wheel of her '57 Chevy convertible.

"Well," said Cindy, "what's the hold-up?" Girls were all piling into the car. I was holding back. First off, I didn't think we'd all fit, and secondly I wasn't certain I should go.

"Come on, Melba!" Judy was becoming annoyed with me. "Now get in!" She had a firm, commanding style and I noticed that people tended to go along with her plans when she'd set her heart on something.

There we were, in the parking lot behind the school, with car engines revving all around us. At my old Negro high school in Little Rock, none of my friends owned cars. And at Central, where I noticed lots of kids did have their own cars, I wasn't a part of their social life, so I was never asked, nor would I dream of getting into one. This felt strange to me. If I went off with them there would be no adults there to rescue me if someone decided to turn on me. *It's all right, Melba, it's all right,* a voice whispered in my head. *This is Santa Rosa and they won't hurt you.*

"Well, get on in. We haven't got all day," Cindy motioned for me to get into the back seat. Once more I balked. I'd be trapped in that car. Where were they going to take me? I didn't know how to find my way around that countryside. Suppose they were going someplace I wasn't welcome? How would I get back? And what if it was a trick to get me away from school and they were going to be mean or even cruel to me?

"You're holding up the parade. We've gotta get started or we won't have enough time." Judy pushed me from behind and I landed in the back seat. There was no turning back now.

"Ever been to the Pick-up before?" Candy, sitting beside me in the back seat, asked.

"Uh, no . . . no, I haven't." I scooted over to the right, resting my right arm on the metal exterior of the car so Judy could slide over and let yet one more girl, Marty, a giggly blond, slide in.

"Hey, guys, this is Melba . . . she's gonna live with us for a while."

I waited for a response, but Marty slammed the door as Cindy shifted into first and we zoomed off. No one said anything except Cindy, who looked in the rear mirror at me and said, "You'll love the Pick-up. It's a blast."

"What's the Pick-up?" I couldn't pretend any longer that I knew what it was. I wanted to know where I was going and how I should behave.

"It's the local hangout," another girl said.

Hangout, I thought. My Negro friends and I didn't have "hangouts" in Little Rock. There had been no place for us to go after school until the community center was built. It was becoming a meeting place, but nobody talked about it like these girls talked about this "Pick-up" place.

"It's a drive-in . . . you know."

No, I didn't know. I had never been to a "drive-in." I felt ignorant and out of it, as though I had come from Mars and was visiting Earth for the first time. As we sped along the countryside, I was dazzled by the picture-book fields with an occasional mansion set at the end of a long drive. The breeze blew my hair and chilled my ears. I sat listening to all the chatter about things that never mattered to me.

So much ado about topics that I had never had time to ponder. I envied their freedom.

From what I could gather, these girls' chief concerns were having fun, finding and keeping the right date, wearing the right clothes, being good at sports like golf, tennis and boating, and meeting after school at this Pick-up place. This was a far cry from what I was accustomed to. Many of my friends back in Little Rock were concerned about survival: paying rent, keeping jobs, eating, and just plain keeping body and soul together. And always, that dark cloud of how to keep the white man off your back. Most of the social energy in my community was spent praying for better times in the church, which was at the center of our lives.

"Melba, there it is." Judy turned to me and got my attention as she pointed.

The Pick-up was a white building with blue trim set in the middle of a dusty parking lot. It was the size of a Little Rock family home with open windows across the front. Hot rods, convertibles, pickup trucks and cars of every description were parked all around the front. The aroma of onions and french fries filled the air, but I didn't see any restaurant. Then I saw the girls in white and blue uniforms carrying trays of food which they clamped onto the open car windows as they giggled and chatted with their customers.

"Hamburger, chocolate shake and french fries. What about you, Melba?"

"Uh, a Grapette," I sputtered.

"What's a 'Grapette'?" Cindy asked.

"That must be something they only have down South," Marty guessed.

"Melba, how about a cherry Coke? Sure you don't want a hamburger?" Judy asked.

"I'm sure." How could I possibly eat when there were so many new things going on around me? Everyone was smiling as though they didn't have a care in the world. Some were giggling and telling jokes and playing tag from car to car. It was like a huge party—bigger and more jovial than any I'd ever seen. I sat staring in awe. Kids were yelling to each other over the roar of engines, and jukebox tunes like "Tequila," "Bird Dog" and "Mack the Knife" blasted from the car radios at high volume.

While Judy visited from car to car with her friends, I just sat alone in the back of the convertible and tried to take in as much of the scene as I could. I wanted to bathe myself in the joy of it, because it was like nothing else I'd ever seen. I had never seen a restaurant where food was served outside. In my hometown I had never even seen the inside of a restaurant. In Little Rock, Negroes couldn't ever go to restaurants, had to sit in the balcony in the one movie theater open to us and were barred from the local amusement parks. Only my Sunday school friend, Vince, had a car. Everybody else rode buses or walked or hitched a ride with parents. There was no place like this in Little Rock to gather and just be happy.

I never wanted to forget how these people enjoyed all-out fun with absolutely no thought for their safety or welfare or what observers might think of them. They weren't looking over their shoulder, afraid of standing out. They weren't fearful of being criticized or humiliated. They were focused on serious pleasure taking, just enjoying themselves.

I realized I had spent a year figuring out how to respond to mean white people, arming myself to be the warrior, but I hadn't developed the social skills an ordinary teenager needs to get along. And I certainly hadn't developed the ones needed to be among these white California teenagers.

I had no idea how I should behave, so I did nothing. I stretched my neck, trying to see all the sights, then stretched my brain to fit them into categories to store them so I could figure out later why everybody couldn't live this way, at least some of the time. I knew this trip to the Pick-up would take up at least five pages in my diary. That night I wrote:

> *Dear Diary,*
> *There is this whole world I didn't know about, a world where people are totally free to just have fun. I wish Mama and Conrad could be here. I wonder if Grandma India knows about this kind of world. I hope there is one wherever she is. She deserves a good kind of life.*
>
> *Until now I never realized that prejudice is not just about not being able to drink from a water fountain or ride in the front of the bus . . .*

Segregation takes away so many other parts of our people's lives. It's a much bigger monster than I'd ever imagined. I wish all my Little Rock friends could see this new world.

So much has been withheld from me. How will I make it up? How will I ever be able to catch up to California white people and is that really what You would have me do, dear Lord?

Chapter 10

THAT DAY AT THE PICK-UP was the first of a series of giant volcanic eruptions inside my head that expanded my mind and compelled me to see the world in a new way that I never could have imagined. In my Little Rock world, the primary focus for me and all my Negro friends had been on survival. In this Santa Rosa world the focus seemed to be on having fun. They must have already learned how to survive. No one spoke of not having enough food, or not having heat or electricity because the bills weren't paid.

Much of my time at home had been spent listening to Grandma India and Mother Lois worry out loud about two things: how to squeeze money out of turnips and make those dollars and cents go far enough to keep us housed and fed; and second, how to keep the white folks' feet off our necks—how to live day to day without breaking the rules of segregation and getting trounced or hanged.

I had fretted most of my life about Mother Lois's money shortage, watching her struggle to pay back the loans she had to borrow each spring to make it through the summer, and taking in sewing and such to keep Conrad and me fed. When I wasn't worrying about that, I worried about constantly trying to comply with the strict rules of the white world: riding the seats in the back of the bus, keeping my eyes downcast around white people, drinking from a water fountain marked "Colored." Even at age five I could remember worrying about these things. Now, I had a brand-new set of worries, some of which I couldn't clearly describe. I wondered about the carefree mindset of the students. What would it take for me to feel this way, and what would they have to see and feel and know about me to accept and include me? But the biggest question was, Did I wish to be a part of their group? Would it make me content?

Now, in Santa Rosa, not only was I struggling to understand these teenagers and such fun-filled lives, I felt like an outsider here in every way, struggling to fit into a strange new place where I wasn't certain people wanted me. And even though Kay assured me Santa Rosa was not like Little Rock, I felt as though I was integrating the school and the town because I saw so few Negroes. I couldn't figure out what was expected of me. I wondered how these strange white people saw me, and what they thought of me. No one was officially asking me to integrate, in fact, they were totally ignoring me. My continual discomfort was growing into a hard knot deep inside me. I felt weak and unable to face things; tears were always just beneath the surface and I would spend all day fighting to keep them back.

At home, I still didn't trust the McCabes completely. I was on guard—watchful and expecting them to turn on me. They didn't behave like any other white people I'd met. Not only were they nice white people, but they were Quakers and committed to nonviolence. Kay was so sweet. She always spoke with kind words, which made me suspicious. It was the waiting for her to behave differently, to say something unkind to me, that was unnerving. The more wary I became, the more they all behaved as though I were one of them. After a while it became apparent that they weren't predators lying in wait to trap me. Their attitude didn't hide an agenda. They seemed to be drawing me closer into their family circle without reservation and with unconditional love.

Still, I felt ill at ease because I did not understand their carefree attitude. I had not accustomed myself to sharing a room. Judy and

Joan seemed so free and unashamed of their bodies. I was caught up in all Mother's lectures about never displaying one's private parts. I rushed off to undress in the bathroom both morning and evening. Late at night I was awakened by their snoring, even their breathing. Sometimes I hid a small radio beneath my pillow and played KSFO so I could hear that choir, the clang of the cable car bells and Mr. Johnstone's voice. I had never seen a cable car but the sounds somehow made me feel the nearness of home. The sound was like the clang of the church bells on Sunday morning.

Lack of familiarity with the family routine also contributed to my daily discomfort. I strained to remember the McCabe rules, to try and measure up to their expectations. They insisted that I call adults by their first names, and encouraged me to speak my mind. I had to admit that I was finally able to look both George and Kay in the eye and feel comfortable, which was a big step for me. But they ate strange foods — baked or boiled cow tongue was the worst. They listened to classical music. And they turned the heat on only in the frigid cold of morning.

I complained constantly about being cold. I was accustomed to a very warm, cozy home. Grandmother India and Mother Lois believed the one item a body spends money on is gas heat. I had whooping cough since I was two years old so they'd taken special care to have the house warm. In the damp cold of a Santa Rosa autumn, I was shivering all the time. Kay and George had taken me to the doctor who came up with a bizarre solution. When the doctor warned that my body temperature needed to be elevated, he suggested that I sip wine to ward off the constant chill I was having. "Oh, no, I can't do that," I blurted out. I was stunned because I knew drinking wine would be committing my soul to hell. I would just have to wear woolens because I couldn't risk hell.

Many of the traditions that stood at the foundation of my life were being pulled from beneath me. The core and foundation of all my choices, my behavior, and many of my feelings had been dictated by the Church. God's expectation of me was the lens through which I viewed all of life. It had always been my strength and hope.

I wondered how it would feel to be like the McCabes, to belong to a religion that did not require the ritual mine did. The McCabes were Quakers and, unlike our church, regular attendance was not preached as a requirement to save one's soul. Their service was not like ours; it was what they called a "meeting," in which they all sat in silence. There was no singing gospel choir or preacher shouting instructions for getting into heaven. If I didn't pray three times a day on my knees, read the Bible every morning and evening, keep my mind on the Lord and treat everyone as though they were the Christ child, I would be hell-bound. And yet, I was noticing that the McCabes, as Quakers, treated me and the people I had seen them with as though we were the "Christ child." But they did so without ritual. There must be more ways of being a good Christian than I knew about.

Even if I found a church, I knew there was no bus transportation on Sunday, so I would have had to get George out of bed to drive me. I speculated he would probably be willing, but it would be unfair to ask him on his only free day. Saturday was mandatory chores and family day, so Sunday morning was the only day he had left to find peace in his own way.

I also had to admit that I was frightened to attend a new church alone. Since I rarely saw any of my own people in Santa Rosa or Montgomery Village, I was certain there were no Negro churches in the area. And although I had asked several times about churchgoing for Baptists or Methodists, I never managed to explain to George and Kay how important it was to me. It had been not only a source of strength, but the very center of my social life.

"Prayer meeting," I heard myself whisper one day. I would have given anything to attend an old-fashioned prayer meeting. Then I thought about how Mother Lois, Grandma, Conrad and I used to go to prayer meetings. There would be lots of singing and pretty organ music, and sometimes afterwards we would gather and play parlor games in the basement of the church and eat delicious baked chicken and rolls and lemon pie.

I had been with the McCabes for a month and a half, and I hadn't been to church once. I had never in my life missed church for even two Sundays in a row. Although Kay promised I wouldn't go to hell for not attending church, I knew Mama Lois would say just the opposite. "If you don't have time to serve the Lord, then he won't have time for you," she would always say. And if she thought I was not giving the Lord my time, she'd have me on a plane home faster than I could say "Amen."

At the same time, I was also feeling like a square, a social misfit at school. I wasn't making very many friends on my own and I certainly didn't fit into Judy's circle of friends, regardless of how hard we both worked to make me fit in. I decided one reason was my clothes. They were like neon billboards advertising that I was different.

"Why don't I take you shopping? That'll make you feel better, honey." Kay had been a patient listener, tactfully agreeing as I explained to her how my clothing was making me feel self-conscious, like a real hick.

My clothes were the ones Grandma India and Mama Lois had made for me out of fabric they found on sale. I knew they had done their best, and at times before I had come to California, I had been proud of the way I looked. I'd worn those same clothes to Central High. These were the outfits I wore on national television. But when I compared the way I looked to the way Judy and the Santa Rosa girls dressed, I was ashamed of my homemade appearance.

While I wore quilted flowered skirts and cotton blouses, lace-up brown-and-white saddle shoes, and a rubber band to hold up my ponytail, they wore gabardine jumpers over white ruffled blouses with thread-thin black ties at the neck, cashmere sweaters, silver chain belts, leather loafers and fancy clips to hold their ponytails.

"Oh please, can we do it today—right now? I've saved up my allowance, and Mother Lois sent money for a winter sweater, so I think I have enough."

"Sure, why not," Kay said, to my delight. Just for an instant I felt a twinge of fear, wondering how white store clerks would treat me, but I was more concerned with fitting into my Santa Rosa world. As we drove along asphalt roads lined with trees turning to autumn's orange and gold, I was certain my new clothes would be one key to help me feel as though I belonged.

"Shop for things you can mix and match with what you already have," Kay advised as she looked through the racks. It was the first time I'd been shopping in more than a year. I was excited as we stood there in The White House department store. I bought a green tweed

A-line skirt with a kick pleat at the bottom, a white blouse with ruffles on the front, a tiny black tie and a green sweater.

"You'll dazzle 'em, girl," Kay said when I modeled for her. As I paid the clerk for my purchases, I found myself growing sad. I wanted more pretty skirts and blouses, more sweaters. All the way home I was thinking to myself that I'd have to wear that same new outfit every day. None of my own things made me feel proud any more. If I could have a nice wardrobe I would become popular and have a good social life and some Negro boy would ask me out on a date. That night I wrote:

> *Dear Diary,*
> *Oh dear God, please help me to remember that I really have plenty. Thank you for my new clothing. Please help me to afford more new things so I can fit in here.*
>
> *But also, please help me remember that money is not really so important. I want to keep gratitude on my mind and think of what Grandma India always said . . . "Money is only green-colored paper. Invest your time in accumulating spiritual wealth, 'cause it travels with you. No one has ever seen a U-Haul trailer hitched behind a hearse."*

The next morning when I walked into school I was prancing, strutting my stuff, smiling at strangers and holding my head up high.

"Hi, Evvie." There, I said it first, I thought to myself as I passed his monitor's post. Totally immersed in a stack of papers and surrounded by two girls, he barely mumbled hello. That's how it went all day. I made a special point of walking places I usually didn't walk and smiling at everyone. But it wasn't as though hordes of people came up and offered to be my friend. By the end of the day I was disappointed that this first effort hadn't yielded more dramatic results.

I had to admit to myself that maybe I was expecting too much from one day and, despite the day's failure, I did feel better about myself. I vowed to get more new clothes no matter what I had to do. I also promised myself that I would buy a record or two so that I could listen to the music my new acquaintances enjoyed, like Bobby Darin,

Paul Anka and Frankie Avalon. I was already familiar with this music because in Little Rock, we always watched the Hit Parade.

I was fascinated by the way the high-school students around me discussed their lives away from school. They talked about fun endlessly and they invested lots of energy in making plans for fun. They were very serious about making sure their lives were entertaining. It was the first time I had been close enough to observe people who had both the opportunity and the means to take tennis, golf or horseback-riding lessons. These people reserved seats at plays and competitive golf tournaments. They did all sorts of new things I had never heard of like river rafting and kayaking, mountain climbing or rock collecting. So, I thought to myself, fun just doesn't happen. God doesn't decree it. A body plans and anticipates. I had never observed my group of relatives planning fun. This was an exciting new possibility.

One day in November, as I trudged to the library after school for what seemed like the hundredth day in a row, I pondered just how I could completely make myself over in order to become accepted. I folded my arms across my chest to fend off the early winter wind, thinking about the clothes I should wear, the way I should talk, and the friends I might have. But as I reached out to open the heavy library doors, I decided that if I changed all the things about me that made me Melba, I'd then be somebody else. Maybe what I sought was some combination of who I had been in Little Rock and who I would like to become in Santa Rosa.

LATER THAT WEEK, everybody in school got totally caught up in an upcoming big football game. We were playing our biggest competitor over in Healdsburg. As the football frenzy took over the entire school I got frightened. It reminded me of the Homecoming Week frenzy at Central High, which often, for some reason, resulted in even more abuse to the Negro students.

Meanwhile, Judy told me everybody had to dress up like Vikings because our team was called "The Vikings." She brought home horned helmets and yellow yarn so we could make braids to hang beneath our helmets. The yellow braids made me feel so self-conscious—so different—so out of place. There was no denying that I stuck out like a sore thumb.

When I complained to Kay about how embarrassed I would be in yellow braids, as though my hair could ever be blond, she volunteered to drive me into downtown Santa Rosa where we found a shop that sold black yarn. On our return trip home, I stared at her profile and wondered why she was so kind to me every single moment of every day. Could I begin trusting her now?

At school, I had begun to feel that unless I suddenly turned into a white, native Santa Rosan, from the right family, I wasn't going to become a full-fledged member of any popular clique. I continued to feel ill at ease in social situations. It wasn't anyone's fault. It was just that I had brought so many memories with me, so many sad and painful scenes, that they formed a kind of a glass wall that stood between me and acceptance. I was seldom willing to risk breaking through that wall for fear of being rebuffed and hurt again.

The truth was that most of the students ignored me. Even though Kay and George tried to soften things time and again by explaining that what I was experiencing would be true for any new kid in school, it didn't make me feel any better. The fact was, I was isolated, just as isolated as I had been at Central High, only this time it was without the deliberate physical and mental torture. I found myself refusing even those occasional after-school invites from Judy and her friends to go to the Pick-up. With Judy and her friends I was always on edge—always stretching to fit in.

As I tried to soothe my hurt feelings, I turned my attention to an area where I was pretty certain I could earn acceptance and perhaps even admiration. I devoted even more time to my studies, rushing to the library after classes. This made me confident about reciting in class and as time passed I even raised my hand to volunteer. And, always, music class remained a haven of safety and pleasure. I felt the warmth generated by the teacher's smile and genuine caring. That was the place where each day I felt normal.

I anxiously awaited the day when grade reports would be issued. When it finally came, I felt my whole self smile. Yes, I had done it; I caught up to my classmates. "Oh honey, let's make certain George gets a look at this as soon as he comes home," Kay said as she examined my report card and squeezed my hand. "He'll be so proud of you. My goodness, two A's even though you arrived late."

Kay dazzled me with more accolades as she crushed potato chips for the tuna fish casserole. Over dinner, George joined her in applauding my good grades, grinning with pride. The McCabes continued to encourage and compliment me in the days that followed. Their response made me feel extra special and I vowed to work even harder.

I allowed myself to wallow in their compliments, knowing all the while that when Saturday's phone call came, Mother Lois's response was going to be much different.

"Send the report card home so I can get a close look at the problem," she said. "Only two A's? That's just not like you. Perhaps it's the adjustment period that's taking its toll. You'll do better during the next grading period."

"Yes, ma'am," I said.

Mother Lois insisted on asking all sorts of unpleasant questions about my classes and how I stood in each one. She was no longer focused on finding a Negro family with whom I could live, finally accepting George and Kay as being gentle, loving human beings who had my best interest at heart. If anything, she was curious and a little concerned that I had such a comfortable relationship with these white people. I could tell it made her suspicious of me and I knew she worried that I might be losing my moral standards.

As was the case after all of her phone calls, I felt trapped between her stringent rules and expectations and the freedom of the relaxed value system the McCabes imposed. I had only begun to question Mother's rules since my arrival at the McCabes', where teenagers' relationships with their parents were so different.

"Melba," Mother Lois chided, "we're not white, so we have to go a step further than other people to prove our worth. You know how important grades are in this family. Don't get caught up in that casual, white folks' pleasure-seeking lifestyle and forget who you are."

There was a long pause in our conversation, as I shifted from being Melba of Santa Rosa to being Melba of Little Rock so that I could earn and keep my mother's approval. Talking to her made me feel guilty for the freedom I felt in Santa Rosa; guilty for not suffering the abuse at the hands of Little Rock's segregationists that she and Conrad still had to endure.

"Discipline is the key to a productive and successful life," she would remind me time and time again.

"Yes, ma'am." I had to remember to say "ma'am."

"Tell me about your new church family. Have you volunteered yet to be an usher or sing in the choir? You do go every Sunday, don't you?"

"Of course, Mama," I lied. I hadn't attended church in eight Sundays. But I knew if I told Mama the truth, she might insist that I come home right away, or worse yet, she might get on a plane and come to Santa Rosa to correct my sinful ways. I quickly changed the subject so she wouldn't ask for more details about church.

"So, how are the NAACP folks getting along?" I asked.

"Many of our folks are still out of work, even those who lost their jobs back last year when the segregationists were punishing us. And we're losing our only newspaper."

"You don't think Mrs. Bates will have to shut down, do you?" I asked. *The State Press* had been the only Negro newspaper in the whole Little Rock area; it was the only place where we could list our events and read stories about our community and our people. It printed notices of our dead with respect and gave us dignity. It was the only newspaper in which we could see pictures of our weddings and our ministers. But since Mrs. Bates, as NAACP president, had been sympathetic to our cause of integrating Central, segregationists threatened to put her out of business.

"I don't know for sure. We've paid a dear price . . ." Mama's voice trailed off.

"Well, it makes me sad to think we might not have any newspaper."

"Our fair share of the pie . . ." she mused. "Lord, they seem so reluctant to share."

There was silence for a moment. I could feel the guilt seeping through my pores. I was enjoying breathing the free air in Santa Rosa.

Then I said, "Well, Mama, gotta go, I love you."

I lingered in the twilight, sitting alone, wondering what would become of me. I also wondered about the other eight. Mother Lois had told me that Ernie was in his second year of college at Michigan State and Thelma and Elizabeth were with families in Illinois. Gloria was also off in college, while Terrence was doing well with a family in southern California. I wasn't sure about the rest. The names of the eight people who had attended Central with me rang in my heart like those of beloved relatives whom I missed terribly, but didn't really want to see. Even being in touch by phone would bring back too many painful memories.

Jolted out of my daydream by the sound of Kay in the other room, I realized I was becoming comfortable with the McCabes. I sank down onto the lush old wine-colored couch and touched the mahogany end table. I dug my toe into the pink and wine carpet. Despite everything that had gone wrong, there was lots I adored about being here and not being identified as one of the Little Rock Nine every moment of every day. This was home now, and it was beginning to feel good.

"Melba—" Kay was calling from the other room, jolting me from my reverie. "Honey, what are you doing in here sitting in the dark?"

"Just thinking about things."

"The NAACP phoned earlier today. They want you to speak at one of their events about your Central High experiences and be interviewed by the television and the newspapers. Why don't you sleep on it, we'll make the decision together, tomorrow."

Chapter 11

"SOMEBODY WANTS TO LET THE CAT out of the bag," George said as we finished Saturday morning breakfast mulling over the issue of why the NAACP wanted me to go public and what it would be like to have the press reveal my whereabouts. He and Kay had purposefully avoided exposing me to any news reporters. "What would really be gained by your doing this?" His words trailed after him, even after he and Kay excused themselves and withdrew to the living room to discuss my fate, closing the door behind them.

The phone call the day before from the NAACP requesting I give a speech and do interviews had me tossing and turning all night long. My mind was cluttered with "Yes, I should" and "No, I can't," as well as apprehension and excitement about being the focus of attention again.

From my station at the kitchen sink where the girls and I were cleaning up the dishes, I could hear George and Kay in a heated discussion about whether or not I should be allowed to comply with the requests.

During my marathon worry session, I had decided that some part of me really wanted to do the interview and make the personal appearance. Speaking on stage or before rolling television cameras were the times I had felt most confident about myself. That was in contrast to my feelings of inadequacy in relation to Montgomery High School students in their classes and social circles. I wanted and needed so much to feel important again.

But at the same time, I wanted to please George and Kay and to not be considered so much an outsider by either the school or the community. I wondered whether appearing on television and speaking about Little Rock would make me feel more included or less.

Thirty minutes later, George came into the kitchen, walking over to the table where Dori and I were sitting, kneading bread for her 4-H project. Judy and Joan were outside tending Vodka, the calf Judy was growing for 4-H. George took a seat across the table from us, pausing for a long moment to light his cigarette. At first his eyes met mine and then he looked down at his ashtray. Kay trailed in to the room behind him and wore a slight smile as she sat down.

"Dori, would you excuse us?" Kay said.

During the long silence as Dori walked from the room, I heard breathing—maybe my own—uneven and shallow in anticipation of what they were going to say or do.

"We don't think you should give the speech or talk to the press." I could see by the expressions on their faces that their decision had not been an easy one. I knew they risked alienating members of the NAACP by telling them no. I feared angering both the NAACP and the press. Besides I was so uncertain myself—I was torn between what I thought I should do and what I really wanted to do.

"Why?" I blurted out. "The NAACP has done a lot of work on the Little Rock case. I owe them." My hands were shaking as I squared my shoulders and picked at my fingernails. I was anxious because I didn't know whether they might think I was "talking back" as Mother Lois would have thought. "Children are to be seen but not heard," Grandma would always say.

"We're certainly willing to discuss this with you and to hear your point of view." *Whew,* I thought, as my muscles relaxed. *I'm not talking back. I'm presenting my point of view.*

"I know the NAACP is important to you but as your guardians for now, your welfare is what's most important to us. We believe it's best for you to stay out of the spotlight, and focus on your studies and just being you."

"Chrissake, give yourself time to breathe," George said. "You've done your fair share already."

"Inevitably, there would be more speeches, taking time away from your homework — more controversial articles, causing people to have to take sides," Kay said as her brow furrowed and she reached up to brush her hair from her face. "You wouldn't have any time to be a real member of our family. You'd become a visiting celebrity we saw every now and then."

A visiting celebrity, I thought to myself. *That might not be so bad.* Sometimes I was bored with ordinary life. I missed the glamour that went along with being a celebrity — limousines, applause, excitement. I remained silent, as I placed a towel over the bread pan in order to allow the dough to rise. Carefully I chose my words and cloaked my comment in a calm tone so they could not think I was being sassy. "Maybe I should do it just this once and make everybody happy — you know, the NAACP and all."

"And risk losing your anonymity?"

"Maybe because I'll be speaking in San Francisco and talking to the San Francisco news, nobody up here will know about it."

"Honey, you know we get San Francisco stations and newspapers. Everybody will see."

"Melba, you can't live your whole life as a part of the Little Rock Nine — or as a lifetime member of the NAACP. You have to build a life for yourself, make plans for a career." I watched as George stood, rolling up the sleeves of his rust-colored Pendleton shirt. He took hold of the chair back, and shoved it beneath the table as he began pacing across the linoleum and wood floor. "You've got to focus on getting the right education," he said. "It's the foundation for everything else you'll do in life."

For once, I was beginning to wonder whether or not the McCabes and Mother Lois had the same script writer. They spoke the same words I had heard from Mama so many times about education and success. Listening to him was like hearing an echo all the way from Little Rock.

"Well? It's your turn. What do you want to do?" They looked at me as though they really valued what I had to say.

"I think maybe I'm obligated to do the interview," I said as George turned his back to me, circling around near the back door and staring out into the bright sunlight. Kay stood still, looking into my eyes, taking a deep breath, slipping her hands into the pockets of her jeans, waiting patiently for my words. I mumbled some other reasons why I might want to give speeches, but I couldn't tell them that I hoped getting my picture in the paper would result in my being asked on a date by some fabulously handsome black boy—perhaps one from San Francisco.

George moved closer, looking me in the eye. "This is a conservative community, doggone it. The press is going to want the real Melba of Little Rock. Ask yourself: Are you ready to perform in that way—to bring up issues that might anger people, to expose yourself to the criticism that might bring?"

His words struck me like a hot poker. "No, no, I'm not," I said in an artificially loud voice. A lump was growing in my stomach. A band tightened around my temples.

"So you agree, the answer is 'No,'" Kay pressed.

I nodded my head in agreement with a decision I felt was largely George and Kay's. His questions had frightened me, compelling me to answer quickly and perhaps more honestly than I had intended. But I didn't feel they were totally wrong. On some level I relished being unknown, loved being an ordinary student and dreaded the thought of dragging my Little Rock ghosts out of the closet. But in saying no to the interview and speech, I felt as though I were killing off Melba. Was I ashamed of what I had done in Little Rock? In refusing that NAACP request, I felt I was betraying them.

However, having finally acquiesced to George and Kay's decision, I discovered I could breathe deeply once more and the band around my head loosened. My chance for press stardom in California had been vetoed, but at least my body agreed with George and Kay.

I withdrew into the living room and sat in my favorite brown leather chair, feeling my stomach muscles relaxing. Sitting in that room alone, I felt peaceful and contented once more. I realized being a member of the McCabe household provided at least a temporary haven for me. Occasionally, I heard myself giggle and behave like a carefree teenager. I enjoyed a kind of security I had never experienced before.

What I loved most about my new home was the fact that there was no major racial conflict in Santa Rosa. Of course, this was because, with few exceptions, there was only one race. There were no reports of Negroes being refused service at various downtown businesses and being attacked or abused. For the first time in my life there were no dinner-table discussions about what awful things the Ku Klux Klan might do on their late-night rides or how white people preferred us to behave. The McCabes were the white people! They were in control. I was sitting in the winner's circle for once in my life.

From my place in the living room, I could see George on the phone. I watched as he took charge without fear of the consequences, explaining to the NAACP people that I wouldn't speak or give interviews. I could tell the person on the other end of the line was threatening him.

He was unyielding in his position, but by the time he replaced the received on the hook he seemed to have brought the conversation around to an amiable agreement. "Yes, she will consider doing interviews when she leaves here to attend college," he promised.

I thought about how passionately he had argued his side of the issue and what was best for me. I took a deep breath. That crisis was settled. Only two reasons for worry remained. One was that I was still certain I would eventually be carted off to hell by God for not attending church. But there was a more immediate crisis: 4-H.

There existed the possibility that I might actually have to feed, walk, milk and shear a real live, hairy, smelly animal. Even the thought made me queasy. Even though I was from Little Rock, I was a city girl with no interest in changing.

"Melba, everybody has to have a 4-H project," Kay explained last week at the dinner table.

"What does 4-H stand for?" I asked Kay, hoping to distract her as she sat at her desk organizing papers for her work as chair of the International Committee of the League of Women Voters. She appeared to be deeply engrossed in what she was doing, with her glasses perched on the end of her nose. But as usual she was willing to take the time to explain.

"Well, dear, let's see now. I think it's heart, home, head and health, as I remember, but not necessarily in that order. It was started by the Farm Bureau. It's farmers helping young people develop the skills they need to be good farmers and good citizens."

I'd never heard of them, but I'd already done 4-H with Grandma India, I thought to myself. "Fine, I'll take over a household chore. How's that?"

"I should think you'd want an animal to tend and sell at the fair." I had noticed that all the McCabe children—except baby Rick—and all of their friends were raising animals. Judy had Vodka, the calf, and a lamb called Strawberry.

"No, ma'am." Even the thought made me forget myself and say ma'am. My mind was trying to figure out how to get me out of this situation without appearing uncooperative.

"I suppose you could raise chickens."

"Chickens," I whispered. *How disgusting,* I thought to myself. I didn't like to think of chickens as having ever been alive. To me they were those things that came wrapped in butcher paper, preferably quartered and ready for the skillet. I couldn't even bring myself to watch as Grandma India cut them up.

Besides, I remembered visiting my relatives in Carlisle, Arkansas. They had chickens. You could smell them for miles around. I recalled standing by, watching my uncle chase a poor hen and then kill it. Grandma stood over the sink defeathering it. The whole thought made me cringe. There had to be a way out of 4-H, even though 4-H was almost like a religion to the McCabes.

It seemed an insolvable dilemma. I told myself dramatically that I'd rather reenter Central than milk each morning at dawn or remove cow pies from the stalls.

"Fine," Kay said, finally. "It doesn't seem 4-H is your bailiwick. You give moral support to the others. But you realize this means you won't have your own blue ribbons."

"That's okay," I said, hardly able to keep a straight face as I rushed to the pasture to shout with glee.

As a sort of penance for not being a 4-Her myself, I spent most mornings standing in the barn, shivering in the early morning cold, while Judy fed and milked the cows. I shuddered in the early morning chill and felt resentment at being forced to participate. But as the days wore on, I focused on the process of what Judy was doing. Her contentment with her chores impressed me until I felt some peace standing there, and actually looked forward to the milking time. After all, I told myself, now my fretting was merely about not having to milk cows, and not about being chased or hanged by an angry mob.

All in all, daily life at the McCabe house was lively, fun, and always busy. After breakfast and a struggle to get Dori ready we would all race for the school buses, late most of the time. The polite drivers would stand by urging us to hurry.

Evenings often meant rousing discussions of current events and hot political issues. George's forte was political debate. In addition to building a university, George fancied he'd run for political office one day. The ongoing debates around the dinner table on issues like the death penalty, birth control, Cuba, and women's voting rights kept me up on my current events and helped me in class.

Sometimes several of George's university colleagues and Kay's politicking partners would join us for dinner. With classical music playing, they sipped their wine and talked for hours on end about John Kennedy's run against Governor Rockefeller or Richard Nixon, the far-reaching implications of Fidel Castro's overthrow of Batista, and the disparity between the Soviet and the American space programs. They would also ponder how George could speed up his project of building a college in Santa Rosa or how he could maneuver things to help a young black teacher get a job.

Listening to those sessions was an education in itself for me. I learned how white people held the power to make things happen. I had never observed such power while living among my own people. I yearned to know more about their world where human beings could mold their lives like Grandma molded her clay for pottery.

Despite our hectic schedules, Saturdays were special days for all members of the family to be together. We'd pick up walnuts to dry on the screens and sell at the county fair for extra money, or go walking in the hills behind the house to look for cows that had strayed far away from their usual path, or we'd hose down Poncho the donkey.

On some weekends, we would all crowd into the family car and go into Montgomery Village for a shopping spree.

By mid-November, the McCabe family serenity had begun to transform me into a somewhat carefree teenager. And yet, as content with that serene farm life as I had become, there was still a part of me that was homesick for a real social life. I continued to yearn for time with old friends, home cooking, Nat King Cole's songs, and the cadence of southern Negro speech from the mouths of the church elders telling stories across the dinner tables at the church suppers. But most of all, when Friday night rolled around and Judy and Joan made a big fuss over getting dressed for their dates, I longed for my own date with a Negro boy who would hold my hand and tell me I was pretty.

As I sat watching them, I would join in the gay laughter and give advice on their makeup, hair and wardrobe. But when that front door slammed behind them and I could hear the loud chatter over engines revving up in the driveway, I would feel abandoned and left out. They would always invite me to come along, but I knew I wouldn't be comfortable because inevitably I'd be the only person of color. Also, everybody else in the group would be part of a couple. I'd feel like a fifth wheel, a sore thumb and all those cliched things.

On one occasion, Judy looked at me with a saddened expression. "I guess it's hard for you, lonely, I mean."

"Maybe I can fix it." George was pacing again with that devilish look in his eyes that always intensified when he was making a plan. He always paced when he was concocting a scheme.

"Fix it?" I whispered.

"Ooooooohh, no," Judy gasped.

In the days that followed, he called all the football coaches at surrounding schools. I was absolutely mortified as I heard him describe what he was searching for: "An honorable Negro boy who might be interested in dating a very healthy girl with a cheerful disposition and a good mind. She's a very nice Little Rock girl. He must be from a respectable family and be earning high grades."

I was so embarrassed I thought I would die. I wanted to say, "Shh, please, George, stop. You're announcing to everybody that I'm not pretty enough to get my own boyfriend."

During the time I was supposed to be studying, I agonized over how I could tactfully announce that I didn't want to use his dating service. I had to stop him before he scheduled a date; he was close to choosing a candidate for the following Friday evening. I decided to announce that I couldn't date until I was older for religious reasons.

"Funny, you never mentioned this before and your mother never said a word about religious restrictions." Kay had a curious expression on her face as she brought the warm rolls to the dinner table and took her seat.

"I'll wait until college," I said, my eyes cast down on my dinner plate to avoid George's stare as I used my fork to push my string beans and baked cow tongue about as though I were eating them. Not wanting to offend Kay, I had never told her how much I hated both string beans and cow tongue, so I pretended to eat whenever they were served.

Although George seemed to be somewhat hurt that I didn't appreciate his matchmaking, he promised to stop the canvassing. "So, I'll dismiss my candidates," he said with a forlorn expression, "but personally I think you're making a big mistake." I suspected he didn't for one moment believe my religious restrictions story; nevertheless he didn't question it ever again.

Meanwhile, resigned to my fate, I settled down to make myself enjoy weekends alone, with my trusty a cappella choir singing the KSFO call letters, the KSFO music which included some of my favorite show tunes, my movie magazines and my daydreams.

In November, to brighten my dreary social schedule, George and Kay decided to resume and increase their weekly family outings that had been a part of their activities before my arrival. The first venture was to a group swim at a local indoor pool, followed by a movie. It was to be especially exciting for me, since I didn't know how to swim and they would give me lessons. We planned for it a week in advance with Judy and Joan relinquishing their other plans in order to come with the family.

At the pool, we were greeted by a man who stared at me with an expression that revealed exactly what he was thinking. It was the kind of look that immediately tightened the muscles around my heart. It was that beady-eyed look of prejudice I'd seen on white faces in Little Rock.

"Where you going? You don't think you're coming in here, do you?"

"Going swimming," said George.

"Oh no, sir, you're not. Not with her," and he pointed at me, squinting, "not with her, you're not."

"Why can't she swim in there?" George spoke in a very loud voice.

"No, sir," the man replied. "That's, uh, that's just the way it is." And he crossed his arms and stood in front of the gate, staring at us.

George continued to press the man. "Just give me one good reason why she can't swim in this pool like every other red-blooded American citizen."

"Well, uh, sir, uh, she can't." The man began to get flustered, although just as determined in his stance as George was. "We've never had . . . uh, we don't . . . let them swim here and I just don't know how the other swimmers will feel about it."

"Is there a law or a rule against it? If so, let me read it," George demanded.

"Uh . . . well, naw, but, uh, we just don't let them."

"What?" George raised his voice even louder, so loud that it hurt my ears as he shouted at the man. "You're violating her civil rights. I'll have your job for this. I'm a taxpayer and I have every right to bring my family here no matter what color they are." On and on George shouted as Kay ushered us back to the car. I felt waves of fear and sadness washing over me. Ignoring the fact that this might be an isolated incident and I was mostly safe in Santa Rosa, my stomach coiled into a Little Rock fear knot. That feeling of comfort, of belonging, of safety faded away. It was as though someone had picked me up and set me right back into Central High.

"Now, Melba, this is a rare instance of one person's ignorance. Please don't be upset by it. We won't let it ruin our plans." But it did ruin things for me. It took away all the power I thought George and Kay had to protect me because they were white.

Even as Kay tried desperately to console me, I couldn't hold back the tears. The others were pretending everything was all right, pretending to be happy, but George's face remained red and his eyes were squinting.

He hustled us to a fancy, budget-breaking restaurant to try to make us all feel better. "Don't you think for one moment I'm going to let them get away with this," George said, with anger in his voice. Later that night I lay awake in bed sobbing into my pillow, trying not to wake Joan or Judy. I hadn't escaped the Little Rock segregationists after all. They were living right in my California neighborhood.

Chapter 12

ALL THE GREAT FOOD, LAUGHTER AND PROMISES in the world couldn't erase what happened at that swimming pool. Wasn't this Santa Rosa? I was accustomed to being free from that kind of insult. Being rejected so rudely, so publicly, left me once again saturated in Little Rock fears. In the days that followed I held my breath, waiting for the next time a white person would forbid me some place or some activity.

I became obsessed with finding other, similar instances of prejudice. I felt myself magnifying the minutest occasion when anyone was chosen over me for any reason. I relived the rejection at the swimming pool over and over again, feeling once more surrounded by the enemy, whereas only days before I had felt liberated and grateful.

A few days later, I heard George on the telephone angrily threatening various city officials about the swimming pool attendant's refusal to allow me to swim. When he caught me listening, he promised me that no matter what, I would be able to go to that pool and anywhere else I wanted. I was impressed with his persistence and his apparent sincerity. Nevertheless, his good deeds did not alleviate my apprehension. I told myself I had to be on guard, ready to defend myself.

Was there any place on Earth people like me were totally free and never victims of the whims of bigots? I pondered that question over and over again. What Negro person is truly free to make decisions about where they will live and work, where they will socialize, free to take action if they are put upon? The answer was always the same: my idols, Sidney Poitier, Nat King Cole, Johnny Mathis, Lena Horne, Dorothy Dandridge. They were Negroes but they seemed able to totally carve their own fate—to shape their lives as they wanted.

I wanted to have the freedom that seemed reserved for Negro celebrities. I decided to take up the dream I had long before the Central High integration had consumed every part of me. I was going to become a singer and hence, a star!

I started planning my strategy, daydreaming for hours. I would begin by calling the NAACP and offering to speak about my Little Rock experiences; a television interview would inevitably follow. Maybe I would even be filmed by several television stations.

I would repeat that process until demand for my services grew to the point that I was compelled to quit school to devote all my time to speaking and being interviewed. When I became popular I would offer to sing or dance. Someone important in show business would discover me and sign me to a recording contract and pay for the extra training I needed.

When I wasn't making plans for my stardom, or feeling exhilarated about the prospect of being a star, I sank into self-pity. I would relive the pain of Central High, and bemoan the fact that I wasn't in a racially balanced school where I could be a popular member of a respected social group and have lots of dates and lots of fun.

Despite the awful storm brewing inside me, my daily life seemed to move along in an ordinary, even banal, fashion. I got up; I got dressed; I made my bed; I went to school and behaved like an ordinary student. During class I struggled to focus, but I would find myself drifting off. I felt as though the teacher and other students or whoever spoke to me were talking from the opposite end of a long tunnel. I was at the far end, all alone, desperately trying to connect with them but failing to do so.

Soon, I stopped doing my homework. Sometimes I would take it out and make an effort to complete it, but usually I would fail to get very far and, closing my notebook, would stare off into the distance daydreaming of the lush, happy life of my imagination. The pleasure would last until realities crept in—like how long it might take or how I would survive until I became a star.

I began to feel myself being jerked back and forth by my harsh mood swings. One moment I was exhilarated at the thought of becoming a star, the next I might be sobbing in the bathroom because I felt left out.

The tug of war in my head was confusing. As the days passed, I felt myself separating into two distinct persons. One observed and dictated instructions for survival like get dressed, answer "yes," put your left hand in your lap while you eat, offer an apology for not doing your homework. The other person in me was completely devoted to living my dream life—escaping to somewhere else. The struggle between my two internal selves confused and alarmed me. I knew that at times it made my behavior appear strange to others; sometimes I just couldn't figure out what to do next, so I did nothing at all while the two Melbas argued it out.

I could feel myself spinning into a space I had never ever been before. George questioned my daydreaming and the more he questioned, the more Kay assigned me tasks which she thought would resurrect my spirit and cheer me up. The more my teachers badgered me about my lack of enthusiasm about school projects, the more I withdrew from all of them and sank even further into my dream world.

I began to be frightened that I would let on to the wrong person that I wasn't really myself, not fully able to function. It was becoming more and more difficult with each passing day to pretend—to restrain the disappointment and anger I felt inside. How could I reveal my new life plan to all those people who expected me to graduate, go to college and be a teacher like my mother?

What alarmed me most was that I began feeling detached even from Kay, whom I had come to adore. She, too, now seemed to have joined the others at the other end of the tunnel. I couldn't complain to anyone about my growing discomfort, my unhappiness, my fears. I felt so isolated.

I was also alarmed at my shrinking clothes. Was the water too hot in Kay's washing machine? Why was everything I owned getting so tight? I had begun eating large quantities of junk food, but could I have gained that much weight? All the allowance sent to me by Mother Lois, which I formerly saved to buy cute clothes, was now being spent on candy bars, potato chips, Cokes and any other snacks that gave me a quick rush of happiness.

Whatever allowance remained after my junk-food shopping sprees I used for movie magazines. I also invested in copies of *Ebony* magazine to get news of Negro stars. Whenever I considered the fact that it would take time to become a star and that I might have to endure bigotry and loneliness in the meantime, I felt myself spiraling deeper and deeper into hopelessness.

"Why so silent, honey?" Kay asked me one day. "Something I can do for you?" She smiled as she patted me on the shoulder and looked me directly in the eye, as if she felt she had to fight for my attention. I could tell by her expression that she knew something was very wrong with me. She was the person I felt most guilty about deceiving. Her sensitive and attentive manner had always given me great comfort.

Under the pressure of her questions, I almost spilled the beans and talked to her about my real feelings. I thought about asking for help so I wouldn't feel so strange. But I pinched myself to remind me to pretend everything was all right, because if they knew how confused things were in my head, they might send me back to Arkansas.

I stopped going to the library and sneaked off to the movies instead, hoping to see Negro stars living in splendor on the big screen. Then I realized with some consternation that I saw hardly any Negroes in the films. And I certainly didn't like the roles they played when I did see them. And yet, not seeing them didn't quash my hopes, because I still read about them in *Ebony* and *Jet* magazines, and sometimes even in the newspaper. They were always in some pretty place, dressed beautifully, driving beautiful cars — and nobody seemed to be in charge of them. I just wanted to be that free. Had I put aside all my goals for getting straight A's at Montgomery High and going to college for a dream I could never realize? But there seemed to be no turning back even when I questioned where I was going. I had no energy left for homework. What I really wanted to do was go to bed, pull the covers over my head and withdraw from the world.

I let go of all my anchors in life. I stopped praying. After all, God had betrayed me by not answering my prayers to be a regular teenager with a happy senior year. There had been almost three years of devotion and prayer on my part without results. I decided to put God on hold.

Sometimes, when Mother Lois called, I pretended to be asleep. I couldn't listen to her words of encouragement, or let her talk of my future as a schoolteacher distract me from my life plan.

As the days passed I found myself crying frequently, spending more and more time alone and feeling utterly hopeless. Always before in my life, on the rare occasions when I had sunk into my own dark hole, I had turned to Grandma India for inspiration or Mother Lois had stepped in and turned my vision back to God. But I had never sunk to this level and neither of them were here.

Three weeks after the pool incident, my grades began to reflect my turmoil. George and Kay became very vocal about their concerns for my future. They tightened up house rules and demanded that I limit the time spent sitting around reading movie magazines. They had not only noticed my daydreaming, they now focused on ridding me of the habit.

My response to their newly implemented discipline was out-and-out rebellion. I would arrive home late from the movies on weekdays without having phoned for permission to go to the theater or stay out late. I sat on the dark back stairs with a flashlight for illumination, hiding for long periods of time in order to read the movie fan magazines they had forbidden.

"You know, Melba, we can't make your life work for you," George said with anger in his voice. It was Saturday afternoon, my favorite time for being alone and daydreaming. He had caught me in my precious hideaway on the back stairs after I had lied and said I couldn't go on a family outing because I had too much homework.

"I don't know what's gotten into you. I can't imagine that you'd let some bigot keeping you out of a pool affect you this way."

"I can't help it," I wanted to whimper, but I kept silent. Tears pushed up into my throat and stung my eyes.

"Kay and I can't stand by and watch you destroy your chances of getting into college."

"I'm not going to college," I said in a tone that I had never dared use when speaking to an adult, even though I would be turning eighteen in little more than a week.

In a raised voice that frightened me George said, "And just what did you have in mind, young lady?"

"I'm gonna be a movie star."

"Just like that, eh?"

"Yes."

He stood over me, glaring. "Overnight stardom only comes once in a decade to people like Lana Turner. Most work and study and struggle a lifetime and never achieve recognition. And who will support you while you await this stardom?"

"It doesn't have to take a long time." I felt like a deflated balloon. He had pulled the plug and drained the hope out of my dreams. I was terribly disappointed that he didn't have more faith in my abilities. I wanted him to tell me I could have my dream and that he would help me. I wanted him to have faith in me—that I could be a star.

"But you do admit it will take time and certainly we don't have that kind of money and neither does your mother." He wasn't backing down.

"I'll get a job."

"Doing what—washing dishes?"

"I'll give speeches. People know who I am. I can get on television and radio."

"It's not that easy, Melba." He lowered himself onto the stair beneath me and calmed his voice. The lines about his eyes softened but his face was still flushed with anger. "You need to focus on your studies, get your degree."

"No, you're wrong."

Suddenly, his right hand reached swiftly toward me. For an instant I thought he would hit me but it was my movie magazine that he grabbed.

"And you think this silly nonsense is gonna hold some future for you? These magazines are filled with lies, written by some illiterate who just wants to make money from people like you who don't know any better."

"But . . ." I gasped, but he would hardly let me get a word in edgewise and suddenly I felt as though I were collapsing in on myself. I heard George say, "Take the time to earn the tools you'll need to follow this dream."

"Now! I have to do it now!" My loud cry drowned out the sound of his words. I couldn't stop the tears gushing up inside me like the torrents of a raging river. My breathing was labored. My chest ached. My throat was closing.

With my body shaking uncontrollably and a shower of tears clouding my view, I stepped past George and ran to the front porch out into the cold air. There was no consolation for my despair and the anguish poured out of me in tears that seemed to have no end. I didn't feel like I had a self, only the pain in my throat, the sound of my voice hurting my ears and the racking sobs of my body. I had never cried like that. I felt like all the sorrow I had been holding deep inside from my Central High experience was coming out in the liquid fire running down my face.

Judy came out to the porch, hugging me and pleading with me to come in out of the cold, or at least put on a coat. I remembered Kay's promises that all would be well if only I talked about my feelings. None of it mattered now. I couldn't dam the flood of tears.

"Don't cry, please don't cry. Dad's just being a grouch," Judy said, as she tried again to make me put on my coat. I tossed it aside.

Then Kay joined us while Joan, Rick and Dori looked on through the screen door.

Kay put her hand on my shoulder as she leaned down to speak directly into my ear in her ever kind and gentle way. "George cares about you, that's why he said those things. Please just let us help you. Honey, it's cold out here, please let me get you a blanket if you don't want a coat."

When other family members failed to comfort me, George came out to the porch with what I figured was his professional, psychological approach. At one point he actually used the word "breakdown," saying it was good for me to cry and that he had no doubt I was crying about the past. He reasoned that now that I felt safe and rested I could finally give myself permission to cry.

In a soft, placating tone he suggested we go back to the warmth of the living room and talk things over. I could say anything I wanted and express anger at him, if I so desired, but he urged me to please go inside the house. After a long discourse he got up. I listened as he stepped inside the screen door to speak to Kay. Once again I heard him whisper the words "temporary breakdown" to Kay, who stood there with her face wrinkling in worry.

Although I was scared of that word—breakdown—I knew somehow that George was describing how I felt. But I couldn't stop crying. I wasn't even certain God could turn off the flood of tears. And I couldn't really say what I was crying about. I cried late into that afternoon. It was dark and freezing cold when I finally stumbled inside and into my bed.

The next day I awoke to a painfully closed throat, swollen eyes, an aching chest and chills, alternating with the sensation of intense heat. I had a high fever. I could hardly speak a word or take a bite of food. Kay cared for me around the clock but by the end of the week, three or four days later, I could barely move. She always entered the room with smiles, comforts and warm chicken soup. Whenever George came into the room he wore an expression of reassurance and his professional manner.

The concern in his eyes and tone of his voice told me he was worried about me—not about my physical illness but my mental state. He tried to examine my problem without alarming me. Even when I sat up and tried to eat my soup, he would sneak in silly little diagnostic questions and wait patiently for me to answer. But I was beyond caring about anything. I couldn't even be alarmed. I couldn't feel anything. I was perspiring so heavily that the bed and my clothing had to be changed two or three times each night.

"Pneumonia," I heard the doctor whisper. "Her fever is dangerously high. If it doesn't go down over the next twenty-four hours she'll have to be hospitalized."

I plunged deeper into a dark, unfamiliar space where I had no sense of place or time. Like a feather tossed on an angry wind, I was sucked into a vortex, without up or down, dark or light. "Help me," I heard a voice inside say. But there was no one to promise help.

I existed from meal to meal, from visit to visit, and I feared the awful wheezing, the perspiration and the struggle whenever I had to go to the bathroom. I had no agenda, no desires. I was conscious only of hoping to see Grandmother India once more. She always had the answers when she was alive. Now I wanted only to be with her—to be free. I was overwhelmed by the feeling that death was the only answer for me.

"You've taken a wrong turn, my child. You must go back." I heard that familiar voice that brought joy to my heart. But how could that be? Grandmother India was dead.

"What are you doing here?" I asked.

"The big question is, 'What are you doing here on my side of the road?'"

Was I somewhere different? I felt light and bouncy like a helium balloon. I almost wanted to giggle, I felt so good. I looked down and saw myself. My body was down below me on the bed, snoring and sweating. I was on the ceiling above looking down. How frightening, how funny. It was okay, I told myself. Grandmother was there, next to me. I felt a warm glow, that same warmth that I remembered when she was alive and standing near me. Every part of me could feel it was her. I'd be in real trouble if I ignored her, if I said she wasn't present.

"Grandmother, are you here?" I heard myself asking.

"I am always with you, Melba. Right now I've come to clean the wax out of your ears. You aren't hearing God's will for you too clearly these days."

"He's forgotten all about me."

"Oh, now, it's you who've let Him down by not praying and reading your Bible, and not having gratitude for the blessings you are enjoying right here, right now."

"I expected things to be so much better here but they're not, not really. They're just different."

"Things are much better here. Have you forgotten about Little Rock so quickly? Is anyone here hounding your trail and threatening to string you up? Are there midnight phone calls with ugly words? You're free to go where you please, do what you like."

"Not everywhere." I was thinking about the pool.

"Why are you focusing on the exception? Freedom is a state of mind, girl. You claim it; it's not handed to you on a silver platter. It's always in your head—in your heart. It's nothing another human being can grant you, it's your God-given right. And honey, it can never be taken away. Can't you see that?"

"No, ma'am. I thought I would have a real home here."

"Claim your freedom and your home right here, right now and it will be yours to have forever. Home is always inside your mind and heart. When you get close enough to God through prayer or your daily work or however, then, Melba, your home will come."

Her voice was becoming more distant. I could hear it now like an echo—but I couldn't let her get away. I raced after her so fast that I must have been flying.

"Grandma, please, can't I come be with you? I miss you so much." I felt tears streaming down my cheek. I reached out to touch what must surely be the form accompanying the voice but there was nothing there. The warm glow of her presence was leaving my side.

"You're gonna be just fine, Melba girl. If only you'll let the Lord guide your life and stop resisting the path He has chosen for you. Pray and read your Bible and get ready for the blessing. How can God do for you if you're always complaining?"

"Please, Grandma, I love you."

Now I could only hear Grandmother's sweet voice humming her favorite song, "On the Battlefield for My Lord," just as she had always done around the house. The voice drifted further and further away from me and then I couldn't hear it any more.

My own voice calling out to her jarred me. I was awake and I was alone, but I wasn't afraid or uncomfortable any more. Instead, I felt the burden of the fever lift. I felt cool and light as a feather floating through calm, still air. I slept through the night. The next morning I felt joyous.

"Your fever has broken, Melba," Kay's voice punctured the wonderful web spun about me and my grandma. "Let us in on the secret. It must be delightful, if the look on your face is any indication."

"I don't know, I feel better," I said. I propped myself up against the wall at the head of my bed. I could hear the classical music on the radio and see the sunshine streaming into the room. I looked out to the pasture and saw the cows peering back at me through the window as though they had been waiting patiently for me to reclaim my life.

"Well, I think you can take a larger bowl of soup today and eat it on your own," Kay was smiling. "You're gonna be just fine."

All that afternoon, I could hear myself humming the hymn I had heard Grandmother sing. I was aware of a newly discovered sense of hope—a small stream that prompted me to investigate the prospect of living.

I thanked Kay for being such a wonderful nurse. I wanted to share Grandma's visit with her, but I knew she wouldn't understand. I couldn't share with anyone the wonderful news that, as I had suspected, Grandma was not in that awful coffin the black limousine took away. She was all right, wherever she was. I couldn't stop smiling and thinking of my love for her, and how much she had always meant to me. That night I wrote in my diary:

> *It's been a whole month since my last entry. I guess I went kind of crazy. I went away somewhere and found Grandma. Now I remember that she said I can never lose my mind because God is my mind. Please forgive me for not trusting you God. Thank you for the McCabes and thank you for Santa Rosa. If you'll just let me get well I'll do my best to show you my gratitude. I promise.*

After a few days, when I felt stronger, George insisted on having one of those serious chats with me. I dreaded and feared what he would say. I was prepared to apologize to the whole family for my shameful behavior. I knew I owed them that. After all, they had done nothing to deserve my wrath. They had only given their personal best and welcomed me into their family.

"It's not about an apology, Melba." George wore one of his tweed suits and bow ties. The look on his face was solemn as he sunk down into the chair at the foot of my bed.

"What you need now is to be grounded. You've had a rough time of it lately and it's apparent to me that you're homesick."

"Homesick?" I waited for him to continue.

"Yes, for lack of a better word. You're missing the ways of living that are familiar to you. It can be unsettling to any human being to have to learn new ways of doing things and try to live up to others' expectations."

I didn't know what to say. Was he kicking me out of his house? If so, where would I go? I didn't feel ready. I wanted an opportunity to prove to myself that I could make Santa Rosa work. I felt heartsick and near tears when George continued.

It was as though he were reading my mind. He reassured me that they were my family and were not kicking me out. It was just that I needed to go home, back to Little Rock to rejuvenate myself — to reconnect with my roots. I was a tiny bit relieved when he said that maybe I would only want to spend Christmas vacation there. And when he said I might decide to stay in Little Rock, I felt panic rise in my chest.

"I promise I'll get back to my studies if you'll just let me stay here," I said. But George seemed to have made up his mind. My heart sank. The thought of going home, whether for a temporary vacation or permanently, terrified me.

In the days that followed, I rededicated myself to my studies. I was determined to show the McCabes that I could belong in Santa Rosa and in their household. Even so, my social life didn't measurably improve. I spent my birthday with the family around the dinner table. But rather than lamenting that this was the second year I had not been able to celebrate with a big teenage party with lots of friends of my own age, I was grateful that the McCabes cared enough to celebrate with me.

I had settled down into a routine as the days on December's calendar passed with whirling speed. I attended the church George and Kay found for me. They also encouraged me to spend time with a black family who lived within visiting distance. Either George or Kay would take time out of their busy schedule to drive me to their home.

My own people. Just the thought of being with them gave me a warm glow where there had been empty longing. On the first ride to their home I tried to imagine what they, the Bronsons, would be like. The Bronsons lived in an area with other Negro people, George had said. But he cautioned me that there were only a few families, perhaps three, in the entire Santa Rosa area.

Mrs. Bronson greeted me with a hug. "Welcome, welcome, child. I've been waiting to meet you. We've heard a lot about you." They all treated me as though I were family come to visit after a long absence. Being with them was like suddenly being transported home. It was magic.

But something about the first visit disturbed me, and I tried to figure out what it was as I lay in bed that night. I was uncomfortable with the size and condition of the house. It made me sad to see the makeshift gathering place in the back of the house with fading pastel-colored, metal lawn chairs, reminding me of the poor Negro neighborhoods in Little Rock. The Bronsons had set up the chairs in a circle which included two old barber's chairs.

The shadows lengthened in the yard on that first Saturday afternoon and three or four of the menfolk gathered in the circle. They laughed those same, deep, growling belly laughs that my uncles had. They sat and chatted, holding cans of brew in their hands. Their house was very small and there seemed to be no place else for the men to gather except the backyard.

As I sat quietly and watched them, I thought about living in Santa Rosa. White people didn't seem to act like predators toward the Negroes here. But whites still didn't include Negroes in the mainstream community. It consoled me to think that maybe it was more a class difference than a racial barrier, and the same thing that kept the Bronsons from socializing with Santa Rosa's white folks also separated me in my relationships at Montgomery High School. And that barrier was how we lived our lives, whether by our own choice or by the dictate of the way we worshiped our God, and by the options we saw as available to us. The Bronsons, like me, seemed trapped in the prison of poverty, trapped in not knowing what was possible. They seemed to have no less money than the McCabes, but they had a far narrower vision of what they could achieve. As I talked to them, it reminded me of being at a family dinner with Auntie Mae and Uncle Charlie. I wiped away my tears on the pillow slip and pulled the quilt that Grandmother India had made for me up around my shoulders as I mulled it all over.

I decided to dwell on the wonderful, warm feeling that filled the emptiness inside my heart as I entered the Bronson home. I loved the familiar aroma of collard greens and ham hocks coming from the kitchen. Their clothes, their words, their laughter made me feel at home. When the ladies gathered to do their hair, I sat among them listening more than talking, smelling the scent of their perfume and admiring the bright colors of their clothing.

I knew I would visit the Bronsons every chance I got. There was no substitute in the world for being with my own people. Somehow I had to find a formula for blending both worlds.

All too soon it was time to pack for my trip to Little Rock. No, I shouldn't take all my things, Kay instructed. Maybe I would come back, she said with hesitation, as we folded my belongings into two suitcases. The trunk was left behind but I knew it could be filled and shipped in an instant.

When she left the room to tend to lunch, I sat down on the bed and looked at the cows just outside the window. I had come to enjoy their presence and the classical music they came to hear. I felt tears creeping down my cheek. I was sad about leaving and sad about not knowing where I belonged. Was I really having a breakdown, as George had whispered to Kay? Had I recovered now, and if not, then how would I heal myself? Despite what George thought about homesickness, I wondered how on earth Little Rock, Arkansas, could ever be a healing place for me.

This time, entering the San Francisco airport accompanied by the white people who were beginning to feel like a strange sort of family to me, I felt less intimidated by the bustle; I wasn't afraid of the other white people, but my heart was heavy with the thought of leaving the McCabes and what freedom I had found. The McCabes were also a bit teary-eyed. After our embrace, I rushed away along the ramp to the airplane and tried not to look back until I was so far away that they wouldn't see my tears.

On the airplane I wept some more. I wondered if or when I would ever see the McCabes again. I realized, as I settled down into my seat, that I had come to care deeply for them. I felt my soul being pulled apart at that moment. Why couldn't all the people I cared about gather in one place—why couldn't my Little Rock relatives move to California?

The prospect of going back to Little Rock was now a reality. The plane took off, ascending into the clouds. Thoughts of going home made my stomach tighten into that familiar knot of apprehension, even as I longed to hug Mother Lois and Conrad. I decided to spend the time on the plane trying to hear God's will for me. Surely there must be some place I belonged. Grandmother India promised and she'd never, ever been wrong before.

Chapter 13

LANDING AT THE DALLAS AIRPORT to catch my connecting plane to Little Rock made me feel as if I were plunging deep into an ice-cold swimming pool. I didn't know if it was the slow cadence of the southern accent announcing departures over the loudspeaker, or the white faces and eyes that turned to look at me in a way that revealed exactly what they were thinking: they were in charge. I had no rights, no desires and certainly no power to stop whatever they might do to me. I broke into a cold sweat, my heart raced and my palms got warm and moist. I moved slowly, like molasses in wintertime, as the passengers whisked past, jostling me.

It was all coming back—the feeling of powerlessness, of being surrounded by an enemy, of being smothered. How could I have forgotten the utter terror this scene imposed on me? What was I thinking when I agreed to come back here? A trip right down into the center of Hades would probably have been easier.

Boarding the tiny plane with two stewardesses who spoke with southern accents added one more layer of the old reality. While they served white passengers with chats and smiles, they failed to inquire about my needs or my level of comfort. I was handed a glass of water with a smirk that dared me to ask for a refill.

By then I had a stomachache and was scooting down low in my seat, hoping to disappear before one of those hostile white people crushed me like a roach on the kitchen counter. Living in Santa Rosa had enabled me to quiet most of my awful fears. Now they were all coming back to me and I was afraid—afraid of being pointed out, afraid of becoming the target of hurtful words and the rocks and garbage that sometimes followed. But most of all, I was afraid that I would forget my "proper place," forget and look a white person directly in the eye.

I had just spent four months with George and Kay, who always said, "Look us in the eye and tell us what you want." Now, I had to obey that degrading requirement that my folks had preached to me over the years, "Keep your eyes downcast in the presence of white folks to show proper respect." Once more that humiliation and the accompanying fear that I knew so well resurfaced with a vengeance and seemed to race through my veins with sirens, warning me of danger all around.

"Watch where you're going, nigger," a man said, bumping right smack into me as I got off the plane in Little Rock's tiny airport and headed out to get my luggage. I felt my muscles tense and a lump form in my throat. Lots of ugly words echoed in my head but I said nothing. I had to remember where I was—the kind of place where Emmet Till, a black boy, was killed for looking into the eyes of a white woman. What would they do to me for "talking back" to a white man?

"Melba Joy! Melba!" Mother Lois's voice was calling out to me and my brother Conrad was just in front of her. I cringed at the thought that maybe she would notice how much weight I had gained. Of course, she looked the same—beautiful, her heavy, wavy black hair, in contrast to her pale skin, framing her oval face. Curls swung about her shoulders and down her back. People stared as they usually did because they could never figure out whether she was one of us, or a benevolent, copper-skinned white person willing to consort with Negroes.

Conrad towered over her five-foot-three-inch frame, and had to be a full head taller than my five feet eight inches. I was certain when I left that we were the same height. My baby brother had changed even in the four months since I had last seen him. Now fifteen years old, he was beginning to resemble a man. The three of us embraced and then turned to the task of getting my luggage.

"It feels so good to have you home where you belong," Mother said on the ride home.

"It scares me to be here."

"Well, like I told Mr. McCabe, I think you're safe here for now. The Klan knows only two of you nine are going back to Central to try and integrate," she replied. I knew she was referring to Carlotta and Jeff.

"Did you see the Golden Gate Bridge—what's it like?" Conrad's excited voice cut into the conversation. "Did you ride a cable car?"

I was grateful he had changed the subject. Already I could tell Mother Lois had a strong commitment to my remaining home forever. As I gave stock answers to my brother's questions my own thoughts were focused on my sadness. I wished I could take Mom and Conrad back with me to live in California forever. I wanted them to feel freedom and breathe it into their souls. Even if it wasn't perfect, it was so much better than living here in Little Rock.

I was home again—and Little Rock was a dismal place compared to the grandeur of California. Already I was missing all that I'd left behind, most especially the mild winter weather in comparison to the bone-chilling bite of Arkansas cold I was feeling now.

I had to keep telling myself that I was here for a reason—to heal after my breakdown. Or at least that's what George had said. He was certain that being surrounded by familiar things would make me feel better about myself.

We pulled up to an unfamiliar house. Only when Mother turned off the engine did I remember we no longer lived in the Cross Street home where I had grown up. We were parked in front of a new, small but modern yellow brick house on Izard Street, located just a few blocks from our old house. As Conrad scrambled out of the car and opened the trunk to get my luggage, I struggled to recall the details when Mother had announced over the phone that we were moving our home. She needed a change of scene, she'd said, after

Grandmother's death the year before and my departure for California in the fall. I had not been very concerned when she told me, but I was worried that they might damage some of the things in my room during the move.

"Well, what do you think, Melba?" I stepped through the front door directly into the living room. There was no entry hall and gone were Great-Grandma's comfortable and sturdy wooden furniture and velvet-covered chairs. The ceilings were so low. The house was pristine but small, nothing like our spacious and rambling old place. It reminded me of the homes in the magazines near the grocery store check-out counter. There was a uniform kind of look with pale green walls, pale green curtains, pale green carpet and a cocoa-colored couch made of some shiny fabric.

"Pretty carpet, Mother," I said, looking around this much smaller living room for the big, old forest-green velvet chair that had been such a comfort to me through the major events of my life. That chair fit round me and seemed to hug me during Mom and Dad's divorce and Grandma's death.

"Where's the green chair?" I asked.

"Oh, I got rid of that old ragged thing. It didn't seem to fit here."

My heart sank but I didn't say anything. I was too flabbergasted. Where was Grandma India's Tiffany lamp that always rested on the mahogany end table in our living room? And where was the carved antique clock that Great-Grandpa had given her? As I moved forward I was taking stock of what was missing in all the rooms.

There were no familiar touchstones—none of the pieces that I loved, like the velvet tapestry cloths that had rested on the dining-room table. And where was that big, old, round dining-room table? Goodness gracious, the dining room was only a small cubby, a slight extension of the living room with no dividing wall. Against the back wall of the living room, in clear sight of the front door, was a hutch, and in front of it a small, shiny, fake wood dining-room table.

I held my breath and moved through the rooms of unfamiliar furniture. Suddenly I realized my stuff was nowhere to be found. Everybody had a bedroom in the family but me.

"Remember, dear, we talked about making a den for family gatherings? But the den is also your bedroom." I remembered that conversation, but somehow it didn't dawn on me that I wouldn't have a room of my own, no place for my personal belongings.

"There's no storage, so we had to get rid of some things. After all, honey, this house is so much smaller." Mother walked ahead of me to the doorway of the den as she gave me the tour. At times she sounded like a television furniture commercial.

"See the couch bed? It's a wonderful sleeper with the most modern up-to-date springs in the folding mattress. Your Auntie Mae is loaning this to us. Isn't it nice? I rather like the large checks and cheery color, don't you?"

Choking back tears, I asked myself why this was happening to me. I had left the McCabes thinking I had some sort of anchor left in Little Rock, but that wasn't so. Even my room in my very own home had been taken away. Where was my real home?

I unpacked late into the night, fitting my clothing and the possessions I'd packed in two suitcases into the small, nine-by-twelve-foot den without any closet. All the while, I fretted. If I decided to stay in Little Rock, where would I put the rest of the things that Mother must have stored someplace: my posters of Johnny Mathis, my records, the Victrola I got for my fifteenth birthday, my huge cotton-stuffed Melba doll and my stuffed animals?

When I finally lay down, the mattress of the couch bed felt like a prickly, thorn-covered monster out to ambush me in the night. I tossed and turned and wanted to do something awful to that couch with its huge wine-and-cream-colored checks. I was only comfortable sitting up in the big, old second-hand recliner Uncle Charlie had given Mother for a housewarming present.

Through the blinds on the front window I watched that first frosty night of my homecoming trip give way to the early light of dawn and then a foggy, cold morning. All night I pondered: Where was my real home?

I thought about all I had lived through in Little Rock. It had wrestled from me my innocence, some of my dreams and much of my faith in humanity. Escaping the clutches of a rampaging mob, enduring daily barrages of hurtful words and brutal physical punishment left an imprint which made the muscles in my stomach tighten even when I heard the words "Little Rock."

In Santa Rosa I had never sat around terrified, wondering whether segregationists would single me out or shoot through my window. Now, I knew I must apologize to the McCabes for behaving as though I were ungrateful. I had gotten so comfortable with them that I expected something I might never experience—that is, total freedom and total acceptance. Right now I'd settle for partial freedom, warmer weather and my own bed in the bedroom I shared with Judy and Joan McCabe.

I started telephoning early the next morning to discover if any other members of the Little Rock Nine were home for the holidays. I was overjoyed when I found Jeff and Carlotta at home and they agreed to meet me at the Community Center the next afternoon.

Mother had insisted on driving me to meet my friends because she feared for my safety. Nevertheless, I was bubbling with excitement as I pulled the woolen collar up around my neck and tugged at my scarf after Mother dropped me off.

I felt so good hugging my dear ones. Once again I felt a twinge of anguish about my weight gain. Would they see it? Carlotta was still very slender, wide-eyed and freckle-faced with her wavy, dark brown hair framing her always cheerful expression. She laughed a lot, as usual, but when her laughter trailed off there was fear and apprehension in her eyes. She was spending her days at Central High, still enduring the real dangers that I had fled. It was enough to make a body very weary.

Jeff's height was about the same as Carlotta's, five feet ten inches. Closely cropped black hair framed his round face. His expressive large eyes reflected his sweet soul. We had always called him the road runner because he was so thin and muscular and speedy in his movements. With his dry sense of humor and quiet, kind voice, he first teased me but then dismissed the notion that I should feel any guilt for not going back to Central with them.

We reminisced about rides in the jeep to Central with the 101st Airborne driver, Sarge, and I was enjoying the feeling of familiarity—the enthusiasm as we completed each other's sentences. They were back in that school that had been such a torture chamber for all of us, but they seemed resigned and strong in their insistence on continuing at Central. I complimented and hugged them, but felt great sorrow. Wasn't it time for all of us to have joy in our lives?

The next morning I lingered in bed thinking about the visit, hoping we could soon have a reunion with all nine of us present.

"You look so uncomfortable, honey. You know, you've gained some weight. Maybe that's why the couch bed is not working for you." My mother stood looking down at me.

"No, Mother, I don't think so."

"Well, you have put on a few pounds, honey. Are you ready to do something about it?" she asked.

"Mother, it's not that, it's this mattress with the metal rod running through the center."

"Well, maybe I can borrow the money and get you a bed. I just don't know where we'd put it," she said, looking around the room. She paused to observe my discomfort as I stretched and wondered whether I'd ever be able to stand up again. "Oh, we'll find a place." At least ten times a day she hinted that I should return home permanently. I just couldn't see that happening when it made me feel so sad to be here. I was trying my best to let her down easy.

"Don't worry about it, Mother. I'm not certain how long I'm going to stay."

"Isn't that a question I will decide as your mother? You're not taking on those California ways, are you? Have you forgotten that Little Rock children respect their parents?"

"Mother, Little Rock frightens me and makes me real unhappy. George said he thinks I need a peaceful place that makes me feel safe and all right." I wondered why she never talked directly to me about what she and George must have discussed. Did he say the words "nervous breakdown" to her like I heard him whispering to Kay? And if he had, why didn't Mother come right out and say them to me? Was I still having a breakdown? I felt better now—just a bit fragile. But each day I was stronger.

"If you let the newspapers announce that you're not interested in going back to Central High, the segregationists might leave you alone. Then you can come home for good, attend school here and feel safe doing so."

"Mother, this is still a place where we're not supposed to look white people in the eye for fear of showing disrespect. I could never live here kowtowing and bowing and scraping for even an ounce of respect," I replied.

"Yes, but are we going to let white folks break up our families and send all of you packing?" she demanded.

White folks. Those two words rang in my head and stuck there. Now, the term, which I'd long defined as those in charge who could push us around and make us do their bidding, had another meaning for me. They were George and Kay and Joan and Dori and Judy and Ricky McCabe. They were white folks, too. But they were white folks who had taken a part of my heart. I genuinely cared about them. I missed them, especially when Conrad, Mother and I sat about the dinner table. It was lonely with just the three of us. Moving to a new house had not assuaged our loneliness for Grandma India, especially at mealtimes.

Besides, I had grown accustomed to a lively dinnertime filled with discussion and laughter and jokes. I loved my family in Little Rock, but having dinner with them was a poor substitute for the talk and laughter I was accustomed to at the McCabe meals. At home we constantly discussed our station in life, what we could do about it and what the white folks in Little Rock might accept without a violent response. What a waste of time. Those discussions prevented our nurturing new ideas and inventing things and thinking of how to build new colleges like George did.

Early next morning, Mother told me to get dressed and go with her to Dr. DeJenkle's office. I protested but she insisted that my weight gain must be due to some change in my health that could be corrected with medicine.

We rode in silence to the office of this white doctor who was pleasant, but never failed to make me feel like he was doing us a big favor by allowing us into his presence. As I grew up, we had alternated between seeing the Negro physician, Dr. Routen, and this white doctor, who was supposed to be some kind of specialist. He allotted a small portion of his precious time for Little Rock's more elite, educated Negroes.

As we stepped through the front door of his gray and chrome waiting room, I remembered why I hated him so much. Two huge signs clearly marked off the room. There was a colored seating section running along one quarter of the left wall of the room. The white section had different, newer chairs and decorations running along three quarters of the room.

"Good grief, Mother. This is, after all, 1959. Why should we submit to this humiliation?"

"I forgot about the seating, but folks say he's a wonderful doctor and a good man. Maybe he doesn't mean any harm. And for the way white folks have treated us — I don't mind sitting separately."

Anger was rising inside me, ready to explode. I stood and walked toward the door. "Mother, how can you allow yourself to be insulted like this and still pay this man your money?"

"We've come this far and it's certainly not the first time you've been here," she replied.

In direct defiance of my mother, I kept walking. I couldn't help myself. The expression on Mother's face told me she was astonished by my disobedience, but she got up and followed me out. We went to the Negro doctor, who said I was away from home and probably not only eating the wrong things but eating too much to quell my homesickness. He handed me a diet that prescribed grapefruit and two eggs each morning for breakfast, tuna or turkey sandwiches for lunch, and white fish, baked potato and a green vegetable for dinner.

Folding the two-page document, I placed it in my coat pocket as we drove back home. I had gained thirty pounds. No wonder I couldn't get into any of my clothes. I was saddened by the news. It was better not to know.

Later, that evening, Daddy phoned to ask me to meet with him and his new wife. I still couldn't forgive him for getting married so soon after we buried Grandmother, nor had I forgiven him for being so adamantly against my attendance at Central High. I figured that my parents' final separation was probably yet another family link sacrificed to the integration at Central. Until Mother and Dad fought over my attendance at Central, it appeared they might mend their rift and get back together again. And now look at us — my father with a stranger and expectations that I would condone his behavior.

More dreary prospects for my homecoming, I thought, as I scraped the dishes into the small sink which sat halfway along the yellow tile counter. I peered out the window wishing there were cows looking back at me. I couldn't believe I would ever miss those cows. I had disliked them so much. I also missed the pastures with the lush, tall mountain in the background and the classical music that soothed my frazzled nerves. How I hated being here in this new house.

Meanwhile, the issue that saddened me was the same as in California: the absence of other teenagers—friends to talk to about music and dates and fun and gossip. I just wanted someone to play checkers with or cards or chess and to hear laughter around the table. Another trip to the Community Center should cheer me up, I thought, on my third day back as I fished out my blue sweater and skirt from my suitcase. Once again, Mother was determined to drive me so she could insure my safety.

My excitement grew as she pulled up to the curb to let me out. What if some stranger, a boy I've never met before, flirts with me today? I smiled and even giggled as I approached the Center. I paused to look at the reflection of my face in the glass door. Yep, I had gained weight, but my face was fresh with just a touch of lipstick and a happy smile, and my shoulder-length ponytail and neatly combed bangs had come out just right.

Mother insisted she would pick me up in a couple of hours. She wouldn't let me stay any longer. She was fearful that some hungry man or woman who had lost his or her job because of the integration might blame me for their bad luck and get angry and harm me.

Once inside I saw some familiar faces, but none of them made any effort to greet me as I strolled through the room. I wondered whether they still held a grudge against me for integrating Central.

Taking a seat in the huge room filled with laughter and chit-chat and people roaming about or playing pool and cards and two board games, I looked around for someone to talk to. I began to feel just as I had at Montgomery High School in Santa Rosa. I was not part of this group. No one wanted to be with me. I sat there for two endless hours. Finally, it was almost time to go outside and meet Mother Lois when I heard a familiar voice.

"Is that you, Melba Joy?"

"In person," I said to my old friend Janis, delighted to hear a friendly voice.

We hugged and I told her how glad I was to see her. She told me she was happy to see me also, but that not everybody would share her feelings. Lots of families were suffering more than ever because white segregationists continued to put the squeeze on the Negro community, in hopes of delaying school integration until at least 1962.

"I'm sorry," I said as Janis walked me to the door. "I'm sorry for all the trouble this has caused." I was sure what we were doing would help everybody. And maybe it still would, over the long haul.

This day in Little Rock became a model for all the days that followed. I was searching for something that didn't seem to be in my hometown. I was desperately trying to open a chapter in my life that had been shut tight as a drum. There was nothing for me in Little Rock—no friends, no school, no community. I was just some despicable relic of the past, not only in the eyes of whites, but in the eyes of my own people as well.

The following Sunday, Reverend Young introduced me as a heroine, and a child of the Bethel A.M.E. Church community. I felt proud to be acknowledged among these people I knew so well. Bethel A.M.E. had been my place of worship all of my life. After the service many people smiled at me, hugged me, congratulated and welcomed me. For the first time since my arrival in Little Rock, I felt almost glad to be home. As Mother and Conrad and I walked toward the car the warmth and joy lingered. We were all smiles.

"Melba, you're not back here to start more trouble, are you? We've had enough to last us a lifetime. Why don't you go back up North? And tell your friends Carlotta and Jeff to do the same."

It was some woman in a purple hat and fake fur coat, holding onto her umbrella and pointing it in my face. Mother directed me to quickly climb into the car and I got in without a word. I suppose from that woman's point of view, it seemed appropriate to speak to me that way. How could she know how much it hurt?

I spent the following days and nights in the recliner. I would have given anything to have the old, velvet, warm hugging green chair back while I figured out where I was going and what I was to do. When I left California, the McCabes said I could come back if I wanted. It terrified me to wonder if they had said that only to get me on the plane to Little Rock.

When I phoned them, George answered. He reassured me that I could return any time I wanted. Kay said they missed me. The chatter in the background made me so sad. I missed them too. I felt torn between the two families I cared so much about.

The days spun out into a tapestry of events woven from my past. On Christmas day, we gathered at Uncle Charlie's house, and I was happy to see all of the relatives. But being together in that warm, peach-colored living room that Grandmother India had loved so much made me feel her absence even more. We sang songs and made jokes and laughed as the grown-ups recounted stories of past Christmas days spent together, though I mostly sat in a corner and observed. I noticed that whenever someone said Grandma India's name or mentioned one of her famous sayings a hushed silence followed.

Around the Christmas dinner table, I began to feel overwhelmed with that old feeling of powerlessness once more. We were plunged into talk about the set of mores and customs we observed as Negroes in Little Rock. Uncle Charlie stood to lose his job at the post office because he had been accused of "looking a white man in the eye" and "talking back." My heart hurt as they talked about whether Uncle Charlie had the right to defend himself against the white man's damning accusation.

I felt so embarrassed and pained deep inside. Why should a grown man fear to look another man in the eye because he was white? After living in California, these oppressive rules, which I and my relatives had followed all our lives, seemed ridiculous. What an insult to our souls and spirits!

I sat there listening and felt as though I were in a time warp. My aunts and uncles discussed new businesses and which ones didn't or did hire Negroes, or allow Negroes to patronize them. There was no talk about whether or not Nelson Rockefeller would give up the upcoming presidential race in favor of Nixon, or what that would mean to the Democrats.

I hadn't fully appreciated that opportunity when I left California. I had taken the McCabes' generosity and the freedom and safety of Santa Rosa for granted. How had I forgotten or overlooked the pain and degradation of living in Little Rock? It was as if I had erased the past and seduced myself into believing Little Rock could be "home," a place where I could return to my roots and feel rejuvenated. But that was fantasy. The cold, harsh reality that surrounded me now shattered any thought that Little Rock could ever be a home for me.

The next day, even before I had what I knew would be a sad and agonizing conversation with Mother, I telephoned George and Kay to ask their permission to return to their home as soon as possible. In my diary I wrote:

To come back to live in Little Rock would be to sentence myself to die.

If I am to survive to be the best Melba I can be, I need space to breathe—space to dream and have faith that my dreams might come true.

There is no hope here.

Chapter 14

"IT'S GOOD TO HAVE YOU BACK here, dear," Kay said in her kind, welcoming voice. Even though I had come back early, only two days after Christmas, the McCabes seemed genuinely glad to see me. Holiday cheer was everywhere in the house. I was delighted by the exhilaration of their celebration in contrast to the restraint of my Little Rock home. In Little Rock, the threat of being noticed if we stood out from the crowd, the desire to avoid being called "uppity" by our own people and the need to avoid arousing white folks' disapproval governed our every action. It was as though we had learned, as a people, to hold back on everything we did, for fear the white folks wouldn't like it. Even our celebrations had to be quiet and controlled and little. It was as though someone had stolen our vitality. None of that was true here in Santa Rosa.

Kay was bursting with talk about joyful rituals and plans to fill each vacation day. They were enthusiastically working their way down a list of activities that included making original, handmade gifts, gatherings with neighbors, walks in the countryside with singa-longs, hay rides, pajama parties for Judy and Joan and a buffet dinner for George's university colleagues.

As I waited for Kay to bring hangers for me so I could unpack my clothing, I slumped down into the chair next to the window of the bedroom. My mind drifted back to my departure from Little Rock. It had been a gut-wrenching experience. Mother Lois was especially hurt that I had wanted to leave before the Christmas vacation was over. It marked the first time I had ever done anything totally against her wishes. The sad tone in her voice as well as her words ran through my head over and over again.

I was filled with sorrow at the hurt I was causing her, but I knew for certain that I couldn't stay in Little Rock to make her feel better. I had spent long hours on my knees, praying, reading my verses, and I knew that this was my only answer. I had to get out; I had to save myself.

"It's as though your heart and mind have left here long ago," Mother said, clasping the corner of the chrome table as she eased down onto the chair. I stood in the doorway of the kitchen, facing her but avoiding eye contact. Then, with anger and tears in her voice she said, "You have been seduced by some California dream that I can't compete with. Those people at Central High School stole your precious junior and senior years. Now you're allowing them to steal you away from me and your family. They win, after all, because they took away the most precious thing we ever had—our family."

On that awful night my mother and I cried together for all that we had lost. When our tears finally dried, Mother was still frantically searching for a miracle that would compel me to remain in Little Rock, but I figured she knew in her own heart that I had no choice.

The departure was a grinding misery that hurt deep down inside. As the plane took off, I closed my eyes, trying to lose myself in thoughts of Santa Rosa in order to push away the pain of my Little Rock visit.

Now, as I sat in the bedroom waiting for Kay, I felt that I could taste the freedom in California, that it was almost tangible. I remembered the awful, tense fear knot inside my stomach, which had been with me the entire time in Little Rock, suddenly release its hold on me when the plane landed at San Francisco Airport. My decision to return felt so right to me. Still, I found myself grappling with the fact that this was a temporary home. It was wonderful for the time being, but where was I really meant to be, and how soon would I be going there?

"Well, that was a bountiful hunt, dear," Kay said, as she walked in smiling and displayed an armload of hangers. I stood and walked toward my suitcase to unpack. For the moment, being there with Kay hovering over me diminished the awful feeling that had come over me when I considered my future. Right now, I shared a room with the McCabe girls, and I had a bed that I called my very own, with a mattress that allowed me a decent night's sleep.

We were almost finished unpacking when the black and white cows peered through the second rung of the fence and looked into the bedroom window. Bright sun shone through the glass panes, the delicate shades of a rainbow hung suspended across the rays of light. I felt a warm glow despite the post-Christmas chill. At that moment I knew without a doubt I had done the right thing.

I will ring in this New Year of 1960 in California, I thought to myself, as I stretched to place my sweaters on the top shelf of the armoire that George had rescued from a junk heap and refinished to add storage space to our room. That old superstition came to mind: where you stand at the stroke of midnight to welcome in the New Year is where you will remain throughout that year. I wondered if that would be so for me. Would I remain in California?

New Year's Eve came, and George and Kay provided the family with blow horns, confetti, silver hats, balloons, champagne and ginger ale for me. When we started our celebration, just after dinner, I wanted to sip champagne with Judy and Joanie and the rest of the family, but I could hear Mother Lois's voice warning me I'd go straight to hell.

Judy had a date, Joanie went to a pajama party with her friends. I suppose I could have accompanied Joan but I chose to remain home. I sat alone, but not feeling lonely, in our dimly lit bedroom and peered out at the stars. That a cappella choir sang the radio call letters "K-S-F-O" in a long, drawn-out and rich tone. The disc jockey, Frank Johnstone, spoke in his deep, soothing voice.

The first time I heard those call letters sung on the radio in California, I had been stuck as an unwelcome guest in a stranger's home, feeling hopeless. Now I had a comfortable space and the small part of a plan for the future. This time I could take joy in listening. The new year promised to bring me new and wonderful adventures, college, maybe, and more people that allowed me—no, encouraged me—to be equal. I had faith that God would keep his commitment. My only question was: how long would it take to become a reality?

January classes started and I found myself back at Montgomery High School. I couldn't stop myself from staring out the window as my teachers lectured and assigned homework. I didn't belong here, that was clear to me now. Nevertheless, I took occasional notes, did the homework and was precise about following instructions. I found that if I focused, I could do the work and enjoy it. If I didn't know something, it was just a matter of going to the library and looking it up. I realized that when I had arrived in September it was appropriate that I'd felt overwhelmed. Compared to Little Rock schools, the classes here were so complex that I'd felt confused and intimidated. Now, with a clear head and more realistic dreams, I was confident that I had the capacity to do the work.

I decided not to waste time exerting one iota of energy in efforts to be included, to socialize. I was friendly when someone approached me, but I didn't seek people out or stand about waiting to be noticed. Every now and then I accepted Judy's invitations to go to the Pickup drive-in, but it was mostly to observe rather than a genuine desire to be part of her tightly-knit clique. I felt newly relaxed just being alone with myself.

I was convinced that no matter how far I stretched, I couldn't be a full-fledged Montgomery High School student. I realized that it wasn't only the color of my skin, but a difference in our mind-set. Most Montgomery High students had grown up totally free to be whatever they chose. I had been, since I could remember, coping with the fact that I was Negro. I had to fight for the right to be myself. I had been coping with fear, and all my energy had been committed to survival—every minute of every day.

Another difference that set me apart was my lack of skill and experience with music, theater, golf and the world of play. I also didn't know anything about the "big" world, beyond Little Rock— places like Europe. I might put on my list of goals to broaden my own horizons and become more sophisticated. Still, I wanted time to pick and choose what part of their world I would claim as my own. I wasn't going to rush into any major changes in my personality just to please those particular people. It was time to start pleasing myself.

Meanwhile, I faithfully followed Grandmother India's instructions. I read my Bible each morning and evening and I prayed unceasingly to know that God was my mind, my father and mother, my home and my social life. "God is all," she had said. And on Sundays, I was persistent about asking George to drive me to church. I didn't relent even on those Sunday mornings at 10:00 A.M. when he appeared in the front hallway, bleary-eyed and red-faced with his suit coat over his pajama top and his pajama bottoms showing beneath his trousers. I felt guilty knowing I had disturbed his weekend rest, but I had no choice. I always expected him to complain, but he never did. He would force a smile and tease me, asking, "Do you really think churchgoing can cover all your sins? If you have time left over, work on mine."

During a mid-January, Saturday morning breakfast, two weeks into the school term, George suddenly peered over the top rim of his glasses at me and said, "You know, I'll bet I could get you into Santa Rosa Junior College now. I think you're mature enough and maybe it would be a kick for you."

Stunned at his comment and a little frightened, I shook my head and mumbled. He must be reading my mind, I thought. I had been feeling that it was time to move beyond Montgomery High School, but I didn't know how or what to do about it. It never occurred to me I could go on to college. I smiled my gratitude and plunged my fork into a stack of buckwheat pancakes. Trying to appear calm, my heart raced.

I leapt at the chance, and in a matter of days, after withdrawing and collecting my records, I left Montgomery High School. I felt a sliver of regret because the teachers had been wonderful. Although I hadn't felt totally welcome, I realized that in time, perhaps, it would have worked out. But I didn't have time. So George took my records and presented them to the school officials. He persuaded them to take me on the basis of my grades.

I prayed for God to give me a sign as I entered Santa Rosa Junior College. If it was not right for me, I wanted to know immediately. I entered classes feeling as though I had walked into the middle of a movie in a darkened theater and there was no one to explain the plot. Once again I would be playing catch-up.

I spent only one week attending classes when I decided I could not be happy or comfortable there. I pondered the reason for my discomfort. Was it the fact that I entered late, or perhaps that the students were mostly older commuters who didn't have much time to linger and be friendly and, consequently, there was no sense of community on campus? Or was it the physical layout of the campus with classes scattered throughout several buildings, which I wasn't used to? Whatever, it didn't feel right and I wasn't willing to take lots of time trying to fit my round peg into their square hole.

Breathing a sigh of relief at my quick decision to withdraw, once again I was filled with excitement and hope when George said we should look into city colleges nearby. It only occurred to me as we drove along the highway toward San Francisco that attending any one of those colleges would mean leaving the McCabe home. Where would I live; what would I do? Now, I knew the truth: the McCabes had taken up residence in my heart, and I would never, never be able to erase them. It wasn't as though I could just move away and forget them. Most of all, I would miss the joy and freedom and ordinary times they would share with me.

At City College of San Francisco, George and I tramped along narrow walkways, up and over hill and dale, as I shivered at the large and complex layout of the campus. Once again, most of the students I saw were older men and women.

"No, huh?" George said, as we drove home. "Not your cup of tea, I suppose." He yawned.

That evening at the dinner table, smiling warmly at me, George said, "Maybe you'd like U.C. Berkeley." He winked at me as if he were wondering if we'd ever find the right place. I had read about U.C. Berkeley. It was such a big and powerful place, full of big, powerful ideas. How would I fit in there? Fear flowed into my heart. And then, as if he thought he needed to convince me, he said, "Kay and I loved it there."

The University of California at Berkeley with its huge buildings seemed like a town unto itself. The thought of attending classes there frightened me out of my wits. Besides which, George kept saying over and over again that the university was at the cutting edge of social change, which terrified me to no end. I wanted to be stable, subdued, quiet, unnoticed, and I certainly did not want some grinding machinery that stoked social change.

George could easily see that this massive campus overwhelmed me. I wanted to like it because he and Kay had attended there, but it was so far from Little Rock and so much bigger than Little Rock, that I had no idea where to begin trying to fit in. He concluded I might be most comfortable at San Francisco State College. Since he was the administrator of the Santa Rosa branch, he was familiar with its internal workings and requirements. Within a few days he had worked out a transaction that enabled me to get a partial scholarship, and to apply for a loan that might cover other expenses.

Because I was a last-minute entry on the first of February, no dormitories were available. George found a home for me through one of his colleagues who knew a Negro college professor living near the school. Over the next few days, as I packed my belongings, I once again felt frightened of the notion of moving, of going to a place with new people and new rules that I would know nothing about.

"Are you sure about this? I mean, why would you want to do this, leave home so soon?" Judy asked as she sat on her bed watching me pack. I didn't have an answer for her. Once again I was pulling up anchor with no idea of what my new home would be like, and enrolling in yet another, unfamiliar, school.

With balloons and Kay's special walnut cake, the family gave me a send-off dinner party on the eve of my departure, presenting me with a beautiful camel's hair scarf. George and Kay managed to keep things light, reassuring me that I still had a home with them and that starting college sixty miles away was a normal part of growing up. I wept into my pillow later that night because I already missed them.

The next morning we packed my things into the Plymouth and George and I headed into San Francisco. Our first stop was to drop off my belongings at my new address, a pleasant, two-story home only ten blocks or so from the college. The professor was not there but his wife, Mary, greeted us at the front door, wiping her hands on her apron. With a warm smile, the sweet-faced woman with wire-rimmed glasses and long brown hair caught at the nape of her neck directed George to put my things in the basement apartment.

The campus of San Francisco State College was bigger than I had imagined, but it wasn't nearly as large as the U.C. Berkeley campus. I estimated that the campus was about four blocks in diameter. One block bordered on 19th Avenue, a thoroughfare with trolley cars running on tracks down the middle of the street. George and I ambled along the narrow, concrete walkways, past trees and a grassy area where a few students sat on the ground, even in the February cold, and I liked the informality of the place. Right away I could see that its size was more manageable.

It was just after nine o'clock when we made our way to the administration building.

"I'm here to register my kid," George said to the clerk behind the desk. He was speaking through the open top half of a Dutch door where a sign read "San Francisco State College Registration." A woman with bushy red hair and freckled white skin stared, looking from George to me through her horn-rimmed glasses. Then her face flushed and she walked over to the door to greet us.

She looked at George and said, "Did you say your kid? Where?"

"She's right here," George pointed to me, and then grinned and tugged at his bow tie. "You should have a packet and a note regarding Melba Pattillo," he said, clearing his throat, his chin set and head tilted just the slightest bit to the left, the way he always did when he wanted to let anyone know that he was in command. The redhead didn't hesitate in her search, and after a long, silent moment, she walked back toward us with a large manila envelope full of papers to fill out. College must be a complex place, I thought, even more than I had imagined. When we had completed the papers, she handed me my class schedule.

On the stairs of the registration building, George smiled and said, "Well, Melba, it's all up to you now. You can make your life into whatever you want it to be. Kay and I are here when you need us. And you remember, kid, you're never anything less than our daughter." He was pointing his finger at me with a stern expression. "Never less than an important human being and a person who had the strength to set this country on its ear and teach it a lesson in civil rights."

With a brief hug and a hardy smile, he was off and I stood there alone. I watched him walk away down the concrete path until I couldn't see him any longer. Then, through the tears seeping down my face, I checked my class schedule and followed the directions George had given me to the Social Science building to attend my first class.

Chapter 15

I WAS REELING FROM THE THOUGHT of being alone and losing
what sense of family I had achieved with the McCabes, but I also felt
a thin wisp of excitement. Maybe San Francisco State College would
be the place where I could fit in and make a life for myself. The one
wrinkle in my whole plan was my fear of being so suddenly a "college
student." I had always dreamed about preparing for college, and
Mother Lois always talked about it being such an important thing in
your life. I thought that it would have been some huge ceremony,
where people told you what to expect, what the rules were, how to
study such big, big subjects in a college kind of way. But instead, here
I was, all by myself, with no book of instructions and nobody to ask
questions about how to be a San Francisco State student. I wiped
away my tears and began the search for the class marked on my
schedule.

There wasn't time to ponder being suddenly on my own. Finding the right classroom in the right building took all my concentra-

tion. By the time my third class of the day met, I was getting comfortable with the routine of getting lost, being frightened of asking a white stranger for help, and then deciding that the only solution was to ask the next person that came along for directions without considering the race of the individual. I held on to positive thoughts and smiled as I approached them, and the students were very nice and often accompanied me all or part of the way to the classroom I sought.

Exhausted with trotting across campus, trying to read my map, locating classrooms and memorizing unfamiliar procedures, I was very glad when four o'clock rolled around. It was time to meet the professor who was my host. Dr. Tye Corrigan would meet me outside the administration building and give me a ride back to the apartment. All I knew was that he was a dapper, middle-aged Negro man, a professor of English literature.

I spotted a stocky gentleman wearing a charcoal gray suit with a boutonniere in his lapel and sporting a nervous smile, and I waved to him. As we walked to his car, he was polite and friendly, but his smile made me uncomfortable because it never left his face even when he said ordinary things or sad things like, "So, you're on your own! Just a little girl from Little Rock. It must be difficult to come here like this without any experience of such a big place." He asked all sorts of questions about my day and my classes, making polite but distant conversation as he drove.

I crossed the threshold of his beautiful, spacious house and his wife, Mary, directed me to the basement apartment where I would live. This would be a pleasant home until I could find permanent housing, I thought, as I took stock. A single bed covered with a mint-green corduroy cover and huge throw pillows stood against the wall in one corner. A tall plant was perched on the small, round mahogany table near the windowsill. Because the house was perched high on a hill, there was a view from my window that looked out over the hills of San Francisco. In the distance was a glimpse of the bay. The mahogany chest and the table that held the television looked like antiques. The carpet was rust colored and almost clashed with the mauve walls. At that moment it occurred to me: This would be the very first time I had ever lived alone—on my own. Panic began to seep into my sense of adventure as I stood and assessed the situation.

I was accustomed to reporting to an adult, to adult advice and adult reassurance and protection.

Shortly after my arrival, the professor summoned me with a serious tone in his voice, saying we must talk. My heart pounded. What did he want to talk about? We were alone in his enormous study, a handsome and imposing room with wine-colored leather and lacquered wood surfaces. The view from the windows was magnificent, with vistas of the city and the bay beyond.

Directing me to take a seat in the overstuffed leather chair, he began talking in the tone of a classroom lecture. He told me that I must use the word "black" rather than "Negro" when referring to my race. According to him, a new wave of thought was emerging about our identity as a people. He said that if I wanted to be thought of as up-to-date, I had best study it. As a student who had helped to advance the civil rights movement with my term in Central High School, he told me that I might be called on to talk about my experiences, and perhaps to talk about the change of terminology from "Negro" to "black" and what it symbolized. On and on he went, until I caught myself biting off all the nails on my right hand.

Back home in Little Rock, when somebody referred to one of us as "black," it was considered a derogatory term. But the professor said that it was the appropriate reference term for my people. It signaled that we were claiming our heritage at the opposite end of the color spectrum from white folks and that we were proud to be there.

I nodded my head in agreement, although I didn't totally understand why he was so serious. It was as though he were accusing me of making a big mistake, or of being a country hick come to the city without proper manners. He continued to explain that using the term "black" was a declaration: we were raising a philosophical flag to claim our own space—our own territory—and that we took that stance in preparation for equalizing our position. Following that act, we were prepared to cooperate and meet white folks halfway—to participate in building this nation, but only if they were willing to meet us halfway. It would not be up to us to make all the concessions.

"So now, young lady, I want to make certain I've made my point. Can you verbalize for me several reasons why this new designation is appropriate?"

"Does that also mean that we're not willing give up being who we are to be accepted and included as equal?" I asked. And without waiting for his answer I said, "We are different in appearance and perhaps in every conceivable way from whites. And we work each moment of every day to be proud of that fact, even in the face of all the abuse we take for being different."

"Yes, yes, you're getting it," he said with a smile.

Exhilarated by his approval, I continued, "I am black and you are white and that is not now nor can it ever be the same. Wanting integration is not wanting to be white or necessarily to associate with whites. It is wanting equal access to opportunity."

I was surprised at the pride puffing out my chest and the words leaping out of my mouth. It was as though they had been secreted somewhere deep inside and now it was time for them to come out.

I enjoyed the debates I had with the professor over dinner that evening and the following evening. He showed me around the house and I saw that he had lots of signed pictures of famous people, autographed explicitly to him, which were mounted on the walls of his study and his large library. He was quite a talker, like George, pontificating and using big words and planning for the future of the nation. He was the only black man I'd met who resembled Thurgood Marshall in demeanor. He was truly free in his gut, his heart and his soul and he had a million buckets of self-confidence.

During my first three weeks at school, I lamented about my state as the only black person in my classes. As I walked across campus I saw very few black people. In one of my phone calls to the McCabes, George chuckled as he reassured me that I wasn't being called upon to integrate San Francisco State College.

I missed the McCabes. Although the professor and his wife were very nice, I often felt lonely, shut out and very much on my own. The Corrigans went to great lengths to treat me like a guest. I had expected to be accepted into their family, as I had been accepted with the McCabes.

After those first two days, I was invited only occasionally to eat my meals with the Corrigans. There was no real cook stove in the little apartment I occupied, only a refrigerator and a hot plate. I sat alone many evenings in front of the television near my bed, eating cheese and crackers while my room filled with the pleasing aromas wafting downstairs from the Corrigans' kitchen.

They didn't treat me at all the way I expected my own people should. They weren't like the black people I had left behind in Little Rock. They weren't cozy and chatty and chummy. And they certainly weren't like the Bronsons in Santa Rosa, who had been so warm and welcoming. The professor and his wife maintained a formal distance in their interactions with me.

All too often, Mary alluded to the temporary status of my stay with them, saying things like, "On Easter we plan to have my very special recipe for ham and yam casserole, but then, of course, you won't be here, will you." It wasn't a question; it was a statement of fact.

I felt frightened and insecure and I longed for someone with whom I could be absolutely honest, some dear person who would listen while I discussed my fears about certain classes, about homework and such—a person who would listen and give advice, as Kay had.

Once more in my isolation I began to eat junk food, and I started going to movies on the weekends for solace. Although I remained in touch with the McCabes and Mother Lois, I had no real family or true friends close to me. There was no one to break bread with, to spend time with after dinner talking about the things that worried me. There was no one to pass in the hallway to reassure me that things would be okay. No one like family, the kind of family I'd like to visit with each night. I prayed for peace and for comfort—for something to make me feel loved and secure and filled up inside the way the food did. But chocolate was the immediate remedy.

As I binged and gained weight, my school wardrobe dwindled down to a precious few circular skirts and oversized sweaters. There was little prospect for shopping, since Mother's budget was severely limited. She was already contributing more money than I had expected. I knew for certain she was doing without in order to keep me in the extra food and rent money I needed in addition to the money that the scholarship provided.

I began to look at magazines and pay close attention to the beatnik style of dress that was becoming the rage all around me. I discovered that one could wear different blouses or sweaters with skirts, pants or jumpers, and create a variety of different outfits and looks, with just a few basic items. I learned I could mix and match and make do. I adopted a style that Mother would never have approved, but one that nearly matched the pictures in magazines and mimicked the style of students I saw on campus.

I decided that I had to be grateful for the atmosphere at the college. Most everyone I talked to or came in contact with was friendly. I wasn't being put upon or treated unfairly by anybody. Socializing was so scattered that I didn't feel left out of anything. In the cafeteria during lunchtime, I found myself among a mix of races, and some people I could not identify either by the language they spoke or their physical features. Perhaps ten students in a roomful of several hundred were black, but I was gratified to find that most students, whatever their race, behaved in a way that helped me feel as though I were being seen as and accepted as equal.

I was most thrilled about my astronomy course. Early on, Grandma India had encouraged my interest in studying about jet fuels and rocket ships and this class seemed to fit right in. Now I learned about the planets, their relationship to each other and to the Earth.

Not all classes thrilled me. In philosophy, for example, the professor shocked, frightened and annoyed me when he said in a loud, commanding voice, "There is no God, there was no Garden of Eden. I shall prove this to you conclusively before this semester is over." I winced and felt the muscles in my body tense. How could Grandmother India, Mother Lois and all those ministers be wrong?

By the second class I was fretting, whispering the God question to myself by day and worrying about it at night. Wasn't there a God? If there wasn't, then I was in a lot of trouble. I counted on Him every moment of every day to parent me, comfort me, help me to find a place to live my life and be accepted. Even the discussion in my head made my heart pound with panic.

I felt unbalanced and very frightened. I couldn't withstand such an attack to the very core of my being. After the third week of continuous hot debate in my head, I withdrew from the class. I felt so relieved to scratch that class off my schedule; I just knew that if I kept going there I would be hell-bound. I figured it most surely was a sin to speak that way about my Lord Jesus.

In sociology, I felt as though a gigantic monster had come to cast a huge spotlight on me when my aim was to hide. The second week the professor announced we would be touching on aspects of the civil rights movement. I sat straight up in my chair when he said, "And as you will see, the 1957 integration of Central High School in Little Rock, Arkansas, had an enormous impact on shaping the direction of this movement. History will bear this out."

My stomach felt queasy even as my chest puffed out with pride. So my school year in Central High was written about in textbooks! It was being discussed in college classes! My first instinct was to run as far away as I could, but I was so intrigued by his lecture that I vowed to stay. I would simply not reveal that I had anything to do with the integration of Central High School. As I sat there quietly, I could hardly keep still while they discussed what they thought were my reasons for deciding to go to Central High School. They pondered and discussed all sorts of issues that they knew nothing about! When one of the boys said that we wanted to go to Central High School because we were paid by the NAACP to do so, I almost burst out of my chair wanting to stand up and shout, "No, no, no!" I thought how wrong he was. There was not enough money on Earth to pay me for what I went through. I sat silent for a long time thinking to myself, *You have no idea what I've been through, or what I've done.*

The first weeks of classes had turned into a month; the days were speeding by. I had so much studying to do that I didn't have time to care any more about eating with the professor and his wife, even though I still wondered why I was not accepted into their family. I did have time to be lonely on the weekends, but precious little of it. I could seldom get away to visit the McCabes. I was locked into the routine of attending classes and going to the library.

Most days I felt like a track star as I rushed to keep up with classes, do my homework, maintain my wardrobe and keep my room clean. I found myself being fascinated by the fact that even though Mother Lois was not there to watch over me, and Grandma India had long since departed, I stuck to the list of chores as if one of them would soon arrive to see: Had I really swept beneath my bed? And that's when I thought, *Maybe this is what it's like to be an adult.*

The weeks of hustle and bustle left no time for me to sit and feel sorry for myself. Compelled to focus on the tasks at hand, I didn't even have time to ponder my role as a black person in the world. I was too busy being a student.

Sometimes I awakened in the wee hours of the morning, cold

with perspiration, startled by nightmares that I was back in Central High School and reliving the entire experience. It had not even been one full year since I had left Little Rock and come to California. I continued to long for an adult to comfort me and promise me that things would be okay in the future. As always, I would listen to KSFO radio and try to think of ways to alleviate my loneliness.

I began a search for a church home. I chose to attend a nearby Methodist church and, even though most of the people were white, it felt and sounded like the church I was most accustomed to. I sat in the back pew, looking around for something or somebody familiar. There were touchstones in the songs the congregation sang and the verses they read, and every time the minister raised his voice, he reminded me of my very own Bethel A.M.E. minister, Reverend Young. Still, I was too shy to make friends and frightened of the motives of strangers who approached me.

For most of those early weeks I had sat alone in the college cafeteria, walked alone on the campus and envied groups of people who talked to each other. As time passed, however, people began inviting me to coffee or telling me about political rallies being held. It seemed that San Francisco State College was becoming a hotbed for radical activity by members of CORE, SNCC and other organizations. I listened to the fiery speeches and thought, "You California folks have no idea what you're talking about when you say you're suffering under the heel of the oppressor. Have I got a story for you! But if I were brave enough to tell it, would you all really understand it?"

By the second week in March, my sociology class was in the middle of studying the civil rights controversy in Little Rock. Our assignment was to read news clippings, dissect the issues and prepare for discussion. I figured I would breeze through that assignment. However, the more I read about The Little Rock Nine, the more depressed I got. I had never really sat down and read the newspaper articles from start to finish. Never really looked at all the pictures of us, and the troops, and the howling, rampaging mobs.

At first, I wanted to read everything, as though I had some deep hunger for all those musty clippings I was pulling out of folders. But then, after a while, I felt my heart sink, because it brought back a reality I'd tried so hard to escape. That was me they were writing about! It was as though the clippings opened wounds and all I

wanted to do was to seal them up quick, and keep pretending everything was all right. By 6:00 P.M. when the bright lights of the library
reflected images on the huge, glass windows of students bent studying over tables, I was in tears. I didn't want to read any more about
those nine brave teenagers. I just wanted relief from the intense descriptions of pain. I returned the clippings, deciding I couldn't take
any more, and I vowed to remain absolutely silent in class. I would
never, never under any circumstance let on who I was.

In late March, during a sociology class, students were deep in
the midst of the discussion. One student, a big, white boy about
twenty years old named Abe who was wearing a pooka-shell necklace peeking from beneath his brown wool sweater, demanded the
floor. His reddish brown hair was combed forward into bangs, and
the Coke-bottle-thick lens of his glasses emphasized his very blue
eyes and long, dark eyelashes. His voice sounded so angry that it
frightened me.

"Enough of this bullshit about civil rights! We all know niggers
have a place and they should stay in it!" he shouted.

"Place?" The teacher's voice was angry, too, as he almost shouted
his response. "Who designates the 'place'? What's your 'place'?"

The tall, gray-haired professor with a very young face, wire-
rimmed glasses and a tweed suit was aggressive. He walked very fast
toward the offending student. His cheeks were red and his eyes nar-
rowed as he stopped directly in front of the boy, pointed his finger
and, biting off each word, said, "We-will-follow-the-rules-to-respect-
one-another, no matter how heated tempers get." Slapping a sheaf of
papers against his hand, he strode back across the room, his bearing
commanding silence from all of us. Then he began to speak in almost
a whisper that demanded our attention.

"By understanding the past, we can perhaps avoid repeating
our mistakes, and please sir, let's not use derogatory names like the
'N' word. Let's not offend."

Abe persisted, "What's the big fuss—I mean, why are we re-
hashing this shit? Anyhow, what business was it of that Communist
President Eisenhower to get our soldiers protecting nigger students?" His voice was deep and attention was riveted on him. I felt an
icy arrow pierce my heart. I felt bombarded by the same ugly words
and sentiments that I'd fled to California to escape.

Suddenly, another white student, a girl wearing dark glasses and jeans, stood up to say, "Crazy white folks were running wild, threatening to kill innocent black people. Those Little Rock segregationists were out of control!"

"If Eisenhower had minded his own business, a few of those boys carrying ropes would have settled this issue in no time flat."

"You ignorant son of a bitch, don't you realize you're talking about killing people to keep them from going to a school?" a tall, slender, blond boy shouted my thoughts out loud.

"Ladies and gentlemen, we can debate our points without using foul language or getting personal," the teacher interrupted.

"These are people that are always wanting what they ain't got." The red-faced Abe unleashed a barrage of words. "The President of the United States got no business using taxpayers' money to send troops to protect black kids while they invade a white school."

"Those black kids had a right to be there, and the people who didn't want them were breaking the law," said the young woman who had first challenged him.

"You mean the law—or are you talking about that nigger-loving Supreme Court?" he replied, turning around and giving the young woman a menacing look.

"Clean up your language or leave the classroom," said the professor.

"I have a right to voice my opinions. That's what this class is supposed to be about. You just disagree with me, that's all. That's why you don't want me to talk," Abe replied, vehemently.

I could feel adrenaline shooting through my body like a geyser. I felt like I could have climbed Mt. Everest or lifted the very building we sat in. But something was holding me down in my seat, while my temples pounded so hard I thought they would explode.

Wait, a voice in my head spoke to calm me down. *These people aren't going to harm you. They can't get a rope and hang you. The bigots here don't have as much power as the ones in Little Rock. They aren't always in charge, and you can fight back.*

Melba, the voice continued, *you can't allow them to drive you back into your darkness.*

That's when it happened. I felt myself rise up like I'd been shot out of a cannon. My body was upright without my permission and my mouth was open speaking words that were loud and slow and clear and pulsating with anger. Each word seemed to come from a force anchored to the very deepest and most powerful parts of me.

"When freedom isn't available, you gotta seize it. It can't be something you wait for others to give you. Freedom is the right of every human being!" I heard myself gasping and shouting as I spoke. I was pointing my finger at him. "You have no idea what you're talking about, mister. Those nine people entered that school to claim their God-given freedom."

"No! No! They thought they could be white by sitting near white people," and Abe smirked at me, goggle-eyed behind his glasses.

"Hey, white folks ain't got no magical dust! Those nine black people had no desire to be white and they never thought white people could spray magical dust and consecrate them. Central High offered them an equal shot and opportunity because it provided a better education than they were getting!" I spoke with passion.

"They knew dang well they were going where they weren't wanted!" he shouted. "That school belonged to those folks who built it!" Abe was on his feet and moving toward me.

"Black parents pay taxes, so why shouldn't their children have the privilege of attending whatever school they want to?" I continued, refusing to back down.

"Those people had no claim to that school. Why didn't you build one like it if you're so smart?" He was almost in front of me. I glanced at the professor who winked encouragingly at me as he stood quietly in front of the class, refusing this time to interrupt or admonish.

"Shut your mouth!" I shouted so loud at him that my throat hurt. "What you need is an intelligent and informed grasp of the issues rather than your selfish, ignorant ranting and raving."

Abe stood before me now, we were toe to toe, and he was shouting so close in my face that his saliva was spraying my cheeks. I felt such a charge inside. It wasn't fear pumping adrenaline through my veins a mile a minute, but anger and determination. I would deal with this person and I would air my views. I felt strong and capable of fighting this battle. And for once, for once, I didn't fear the consequences.

"First off, move back, give me my space." I paused for a moment, looking straight into his eyes, daring him to refuse. He heeded me, and only when he had backed off several paces did I continue speaking.

"See here, every human being has the right to see and be seen as equal. Those people had a right to attend that school. Being wanted is not a criteria for claiming one's human rights! Being human is the only requirement," I said.

At this point many of the students shouted, "Right on!" and stood to applaud me. Shocked at their demonstration of approval and wired with adrenaline, I went on. I couldn't believe what I was hearing—my own voice, speaking things I had wanted to say for three years, at least. These words must have been trapped inside me during all that Central High experience.

On and on I went in a loud voice. At first my knees had been wobbling, but then they locked in and the muscles in my calves felt like concrete surrounding steel. I was standing with a power in me that demanded to be heard. I did not hear nor would I be able to repeat some of the words that escaped from my mouth that day. I spoke as though I were the conduit for someone else who spoke through me. Applause burst out in the room once more. My heart was pounding in my ears and my chest was inflated with pride. I felt so good about defending myself. I felt a stronger Melba rise inside me. I wasn't frightened of the racist student's white skin. There was no difference between his skin and the color of George's McCabe's skin. They were both just men—people who happened to be white—each with a different point of view.

Speaking up to George, debating George and Kay on issues, had prepared me to take this stand. Why should I fear this white man who confronted me? He wasn't carrying a rope; he wasn't accompanied by a mob of hooligans; he dared not threaten to follow me home. We stood on equal ground right here, right now. He possessed no more power than I did and certainly not as much as George.

I left the classroom feeling as though I had discovered myself. I had thoughts about joining a debate club. Who knew, I might become a politician—maybe even run for the presidency. My fantasies took off as they had when I dreamed of being a movie star. Commentators were already saying if a Catholic like John Kennedy was running for president, then a black and a female could not be far behind.

I was so full of hope that I was bursting inside. If I didn't have to worry every moment about someone treating me the way I was treated by Little Rock white people, what couldn't I accomplish? I would have time to become whatever I wanted.

Walking home that afternoon, I thought about how strong and free I was beginning to feel. I didn't spend so much time watching the white people that brushed past or walked close behind me on the way home. The fear that they would strike out at me was diminishing daily. Instead, I felt secure in having a small modicum of power within myself. Those white people had no more right or need to attack me than I did them.

As I pondered my situation, I realized what a valuable gift the McCabes had given me. I no longer needed to stand by forlorn and yearning for the freedom I had assumed I could never wrestle from those white people who seemed to be forever in charge. I knew now they were just people who happened to be white. They were people like George and Kay and their four kids. Living with the McCabes had made me see white people up close and realize they were only human—they were people, just like me.

"You don't have to be white to be free," I mumbled aloud. "White is a state of mind," I said, aloud again. White people were never endowed with some divine right or gift of freedom and royal reign. They claimed it as long as we allowed them to. And now I knew a secret: I could claim it. *I am equal—I am free, right here, right now! I can be as free as I want to be.* Even when harsh circumstance took my physical freedom away, just like Gandhi, I could remain free in my mind. My state of mind could imprison me or set me free.

Arriving back at my apartment feeling exhilarated, I was surprised and then almost immediately apprehensive when Mary invited me to come upstairs for dinner that evening. Over the dessert of lemon pudding she cleared her throat and made the announcement that brought a knot of fear into my stomach.

"You'll need to be thinking about finding a permanent home, Melba. My daughter is coming with my grandchildren for a week's visit at the end of March, and we'll need your room."

Chapter 16

I SAT AT THE TABLE MOTIONLESS, wondering what I should do next. Who would find me a home—a roof over my head? How did one go about looking? I had never thought about hunting for a home before. That was what your mother did for you. For the rest of the meal I sat pushing my food around on the plate, trying to pretend that I wasn't falling apart inside.

Back in my room I sat silent, reviewing the past weeks. Had I been so busy adjusting to school that I ignored some signal the Corrigans had given me? The thought of my next move had never entered my mind. I figured somebody else was taking care of it. Mrs. Corrigan had said she needed the apartment at the end of March, but that was only eight days away. At that moment it suddenly occurred to me: I was on my own. *Maybe they think I'm an adult.* Climbing into bed, I said it once more, aloud, "Am I an adult?" *Now, what do I do?*

My thoughts raced. Was I supposed to have been looking for a place all along? And when I failed to do so, shouldn't they have encouraged me to look? I hadn't fully realized until this moment that I was responsible for myself. I was confused, still thinking the adults nearby would automatically make decisions for me and act in my best interest. Shouldn't there be some kind of ceremony to mark this new life?

My way of coping with my housing problem was to freeze. I had little time to think about getting a home and even less time to really look. Whenever the urgency of it all rose inside me, I swallowed my panic and told myself a home would be found for me. I trusted that God would show me the way. I tried to ignore the issue. After all, Grandma India always said that my home was hidden in my relationship with my maker.

The following Friday afternoon when I arrived home from school, anticipating a restful weekend but wishing I had a social life and a date, I couldn't believe my eyes. My suitcases, along with neatly tied, cardboard boxes of my precious belongings, stood in the hallway by the front door.

"I've taken the liberty of packing for you," Mary said nonchalantly. Paralyzed with astonishment, I could only stand and stare at my things. No words came out of my mouth even though my brain formed many questions.

"No need to check the apartment," she said confidently, with a slight smile on her face. "I got everything. You're all set to go."

"Go? Go where?" I mumbled.

"Well, not every young lady has someone to pack for them. Good job, Mary," the professor said. Beckoning me toward the car he said, "Are you ready?" The rush was on. I felt as though I were standing amid a cattle stampede.

"What?" I said. Without any further words, I was escorted to the car and the professor drove me to the home of his friend, Mrs. Andrea Carson. As I sat with tears brimming just beneath the surface and feeling sick at heart, Professor Corrigan explained that Mrs. Carson's husband, a former university professor in the English department, but now deceased, had been a mentor of his. He had kept in touch with his widow and thought that I might be able to live with Mrs. Carson and assist with housework and some care as she was aging. "It'll be a wonderful opportunity for you to earn your housing and save money," he said.

I said nothing and just sat with my shoulders slumped. All I wanted was somewhere I could stay for a while and feel as though I belonged. Why did peace and joy come to me only in brief moments and then slip away as though I didn't deserve to hold them? As soon as I felt the slightest comfort it seemed to flit away.

The petite, gray-haired Mrs. Carson, a black woman about seventy years old, answered the door. She leaned on a fancy, carved ivory cane. Her bright red fingernails attached to twisted, misshapen hands clutched the cane.

"Hello," she said, drawing my attention to her huge eyes and her upswept hairdo with the false black bun contrasting in color with her own gray-white hair. "This must be the young lady we spoke about," she said to Professor Corrigan. Her voice was gravelly and she carefully pronounced each word. She spoke as though enunciation were a contest and she was determined to have first prize. Her lips smiled but her brows knit a wrinkled frown in the center of her forehead.

I stepped across the threshold into a dimly lit living room where two mauve-colored couches and all three chairs were covered in plastic. One lamp with a low-wattage bulb added to the dreary setting. I looked through the living room where a long hall led to several darkened rooms off either side. The hallway was also dark except at the far end where weak daylight crept through a window.

"So, you must be Melba. Well, you are a big, tall, strong girl," Mrs. Carson turned to me.

That's an odd greeting, I thought to myself, but I smiled at her.

"I think you'll find that you two are a match," Professor Corrigan said, in a matter-of-fact way. "She needs lodging and you need a few chores taken care of." And with that, the professor carried in my luggage, said his goodbyes and headed for his car. I stood stunned until Mrs. Carson invited me to have a seat so that we could get acquainted.

She began with polite conversation about the weather and my studies. What followed was an interrogation about my personal habits: What time did I get up in the morning? How did I bathe — shower or tub, and how often? What time did I come and go? Did I smoke? What did I eat? And what kind of company did I keep? Mrs.

Carson also wanted to know what church I belonged to. She asked me if I had a regular boyfriend and if I was intimate with him.

"I don't know what you mean," I answered as honestly as I could to her final question. "I don't have a boyfriend and I am not intimate. That happens after you're married."

"Well, that will be enough for right now. You're excused," she said as she stood. "Oh, yes, please don't assume you have the run of the entire house. Your room and bath are at the rear of the first floor. That is your domain. You may join with us in other rooms of the house by invitation only. Oh, yes, and once in a while you may ask to have a friend over. I'll grant permission for you two to sit in the living room, but only with the doors wide open while you entertain. Is that understood?"

"Yes, ma'am." It was dawning on me that this woman thought I was the new live-in maid.

"I know you southern girls are good at housekeeping and cooking and such. I hope you'll do the professor proud. He has spoken highly of you and your talents. But he didn't tell me where you were from originally."

"Little Rock," I said.

"What a big mess that was a couple of years ago. Those brave children broke my heart with their courage."

"I'm one . . ." I blurted out, hoping to bust her vision of me as a big, tall, southern girl whom she obviously thought was only fit to be her new maid. I wanted to tell her I was a courageous person, a civil rights person, a heroine. It was obvious that she had no respect for me. She was busy gauging my size and strength, evaluating how much work I was capable of doing.

Cutting me off before I could explain my identity, she said, "You're excused. That's enough for now. I get tired easily."

I had no idea what my response should be. How should I behave in a situation like this? Right away I realized that I wasn't going to be included in her family, but who were they and how many members? Was she expecting me to do household chores to pay my rent? Should I be asking her what chores? Or did somebody already sign me over to her for everything?

Not sure what else to do, I began dragging my suitcases into what was to be my new home. The room was tiny, about eight feet by ten feet with minimal drawer and closet space. The single window faced the house next door. I felt trapped. Dropping down onto the bed, I burst into tears.

I had to get hold of myself. I couldn't ask Mother about this. She might summon me home to Little Rock for good. As I tried to put my things away, I began to feel powerless again. It was that old, forlorn feeling of helplessness and fear I knew so well, taking up residence in my soul.

I decided I should call George and Kay. As I dialed their number on the phone in the hallway, I thought how absolutely astounded I was by the way I was moved around and then confined to one room without anyone asking me what I wanted.

"You can't live someplace where you're unhappy," George said. "But you can't just leave without a place to go, so start looking now. Get a newspaper and a bus map and start your search. And contact the school housing office. Maybe they have a list of available housing, and they can also counsel you about the best neighborhoods."

"You'll need my permission to use the phone." Mrs. Carson's voice startled me and snatched me from my conversation with George. I thanked George and said goodbye. I had barely replaced the phone in its blue marbleized receiver and retreated to the bedroom when Mrs. Carson opened the door.

"And we don't sit on beds here," Mrs. Carson went on. "That's a southern thing, I know, but you'll have to change your ways."

"Yes, ma'am." I hopped up.

"You may dine with me promptly at six," she said and went out, closing the door hard.

She had entered the room without knocking. That was further evidence that she had little respect for me. It was obvious she did not see me as an equal. I settled into a chair in the dim light and examined the room, looking for a place to unpack a few more things. I tried to push from my mind the fact that Mrs. Carson resembled a corpse and her house reminded me of a mortuary.

Dinner was dismal. We ate chicken that tasted like cardboard and canned peaches in another dimly lit room. I felt belittled by her conversation. She lectured me on the manners and appropriate behavior one must abide by to live with her and to be a proper "California Negro." I was beside myself trying to figure out what I should do next. Who was responsible for me? Was I a child or a grown-up, and how could I change the way I was living? Would I ever again find a pleasant home?

I cried myself to sleep. When I awoke in the middle of the night, I didn't have a radio to soothe my aching heart. In my dark misery I vowed I would do whatever was necessary not only to have a decent home where I was appreciated, but a home that I could appreciate.

The next morning I didn't know whether to emerge from my room and go into the kitchen to fix breakfast or wait for permission. I decided I would follow her rules for now. I would not eat in her kitchen unless invited. By 7:00 A.M. I was dressed and heading for the front door.

"My goodness, you're not going out looking like that. You look like one of those 'darkies' from the other side of the tracks. Casual dress is not appropriate for our young Negro women who want to make something of themselves." Mrs. Carson stood in her pink chenille robe and shiny pink slippers as she lectured me, pointing her finger in my face.

Aghast at her use of the term "darkie," I had to get away from her. That word meant the same to me as the word "nigger." In total silence I turned and walked out the front door. This woman was black but she was my oppressor. With tears stinging my eyes, I vowed I would not be treated that way by any other human being ever again.

I imagined Mrs. Carson subscribed to that southern black caste system in which fair-skinned blacks fancied themselves a cut above darker blacks. That code had been passed on by slaves who accorded the fair-skinned among them more privilege because they were the sons and daughters of slave masters. I was well acquainted with the system from living among my racially mixed family with its wide range of colors. But my fair-skinned mother had been adamant about my never, never subjecting myself to that color code. She said I should never be made to feel less than God's child by someone who practiced it. As I boarded the trolley for school I was steaming— angry enough to explode. I had to get out of Mrs. Carson's house now!

By lunch time I had talked with a number of fellow students about their living quarters. Residence clubs in downtown San Francisco were the preferred alternative to the campus dorms because they were less expensive and usually provided at least one meal per day.

Skipping my last class, I bought a newspaper and a map of the city and got transfers and change on the trolley. I was prepared to go to the ends of the earth to find my "right" home. It was the first of several evenings I spent hunting.

There was no doubt in my mind that several times I got turned away because I was black. Heartbroken, I walked away from those residence clubs and apartments thinking that California wasn't at all the place I had hoped and dreamed about. But I was determined not to be defeated by that.

I would see for-rent signs in the windows of the residence clubs, but when the clerk or manager saw me they would say, "Oh, if you'd just come Tuesday morning. The last room has been rented." Finally I got suspicious after four such incidents. I went to a corner phone booth and called the last residence club where I'd been told the room had already been rented. I recognized the voice of the manager I'd just talked to. He said, "Sure, we have an opening. Come right up."

I was reminded that while my appearance was immediately recognizable, my voice and way of talking were not. My mother, an English teacher, had demanded that I speak the "King's English" without a southern accent or colloquial or black slang.

On the fifth day of my search I got off the trolley on Market and Leavenworth outside a restaurant called "Tommy's Joint" to transfer to a bus which would take me up Nob Hill to yet another residence club. As I stood waiting for the bus, a tall, rather attractive and well-dressed woman joined me at the bus stop. She stood so close to me that I felt uneasy. She reminded me of both a teacher I'd had and a movie star in one of my movie magazines. She smiled at me. A familiar phrase popped into my head, "Don't talk to strangers."

"Wanna have coffee? There's a really great spot just over there." She touched me on the shoulder and I jumped.

"No thanks." She made me so nervous that I backed away from her.

"Do you want to come over to my place? Dinner's in the oven and ready to pop."

"No thanks." Why would I want to have dinner with a

stranger? I stepped even further away from her. Her conversation made me feel odd. It wasn't as though she was a man being forward with me—she was a woman. Even so, it all felt wrong, as though I should defend myself.

"What's your name?"

I didn't answer.

"Oh, come now, I think you know what I'm talking about."

"No . . . no, I don't." I felt panic-stricken. She was moving closer and closer to me. She wouldn't back off.

"You can let go of the hard-to-get act, honey," she persisted.

"Heeelllp!" I heard myself scream aloud. I saw a uniformed policeman come running toward me. Terrified, I kept yelling. This had never happened to me before.

"Yeah, what is it?" said the policeman, impatiently pushing up the brim of his cap on blond hair.

"She's, well . . . uh, uh, a man. She's asking me to go out with her," I sputtered. I turned to identify her to the policeman.

The woman was aghast. She stood stock still looking at me in total astonishment.

I beckoned to the policeman to step aside with me, and began speaking to him in a very low tone. "She's attacking me, insisting that I want a date with her."

"Insisting or asking?"

"She's pushing me. Besides, she's a woman, she shouldn't be doing either," I said.

"Just say, 'No thank you,'" he said irritably, loud enough to be heard by anyone in the near vicinity.

"But she won't go away," I pleaded.

"Look, say, 'I'm straight.' That's all she needs to hear and she'll back off. Say, kid, where are you from?"

"Little Rock."

"Where's that?"

"Arkansas."

"Ohhhhhh," he said, winking at me, and then he grinned, turned around and walked away.

The woman got on the same bus that I boarded, but she kept her distance. *There are strange people in California,* I thought, as I climbed off the bus at the corner of Leavenworth and Bush, grateful to escape that odd woman. For an instant I pondered if there were something about me that attracted the woman who thought she was a man. This had never ever happened to me before; I was all girl, with girlish thoughts and ways. I concluded the answer was "no" by the time I was climbing the white marble stairs up to the front door of the Mary Elizabeth Inn, a Methodist residence club.

The front entry hall was beautiful, open and light and clean. It gave me a feeling of peace to see the simple mahogany desk and cro-cheted doilies on the end tables, just like Grandmother India had in our home in Little Rock. A slender blond woman with a deep south-ern accent and huge blue eyes sat behind the desk. At first I feared her southern accent would mean my immediate rejection, but she was very kind and friendly. She directed me to the Residence Administra-tor's office.

Mrs. Weber sat behind a small desk in a beautiful oak wood room with white ruffled curtains at the windows and white doilies. Once again, it resembled a southern home. After a few questions, she handed me an application. I scanned it quickly. Yes, I had been a member of the Methodist Church. Yes, my mother was a school-teacher and I was raised a Christian.

Right away she began describing to me the small, single rooms and said I would enjoy them. I nodded my head "yes" and listened in-tently to her description. I didn't feel unwelcome, so a flicker of hope rose in me.

I wondered during the interview whether I could be happy at a residence club. Would this unfamiliar place on Nob Hill, an exclusive and elite part of San Francisco, become my home for a while? How would the other residents and neighbors feel about my being there? Could I feel at home in this place which housed so many other people?

Mrs. Weber took me on a tour and told me more about the club's features as we walked. The residence club provided two meals a day, breakfast and dinner, and a small room with a bed, chest, small desk and a closet. The bathrooms on each floor were shared. There was a main television room, a den and a library. There were seventy-five women residents. The club seemed warm and inviting during the tour and everyone we passed in the hallway smiled and greeted us. I liked the chapel and the laundry room on the top floor filled with whirring machinery and chatting women. The only black people I saw were behind the steam tables in the cafeteria, but surely there must be black residents at the club because this was California. I told myself that they were probably all at school or work. I liked the Mary Elizabeth Inn and decided to make out an application. Mrs. Weber said they would consider me. They would call my references and let me know.

I needed to call my family in Little Rock and get in touch with the McCabes to let them all know what I was doing. Mother Lois balked at my living on my own in downtown San Francisco. I called George and he knew about the residence club and thought it would be a great idea. He said he would explain to Mother that under the circumstances it might be my best option. Besides, he said that he had called up a colleague and inquired about the place once I mentioned the possibility of living there. Indeed, it was a church-connected residence.

Meanwhile, I was on edge until the phone call came telling me I was accepted. Every moment I spent at Mrs. Carson's was torture. Each day after school she was complaining that I didn't arrive home earlier. She wanted me to wait on her hand and foot, to vacuum and to wash. I wanted to talk back to her. Instead, I was showing up later each evening—too late to do anything but study. I was emphatic in saying, "I'm sorry, I don't have time for your list of chores. I must keep my grades up."

I was holding my breath, crossing my fingers and praying hard to hear from the Mary Elizabeth Inn. I thought I would burst a blood vessel, when finally on a Wednesday I heard Mrs. Weber's voice on the phone saying that I had been accepted. She said, "We'd like to have you live here on a trial basis." Then she said, "We hear you are quite a famous young lady." Immediately I told her I did not want my identity made known to the other residents. I thanked her for admitting me and as I placed the receiver back into its cradle, I drew a long sigh of relief. Finally, I belonged somewhere again. But why had she said I'd been accepted on a "trial basis"? I reasoned that maybe every resident had a trial period when they first moved in.

Once more George and Kay helped me load their old Plymouth with my belongings and moved me. It was a chilly Saturday afternoon when I walked up the marble stairs of the Mary Elizabeth Inn again, carrying two paper bags and a box stuffed with the growing overflow of my possessions. I had said a smiling goodbye to Mrs. Carson. At last the decision to move had been my very own choice. It had given me pleasure to leave her with only three days' notice. Her response was to accuse me of being ungrateful.

When the last box was inside my room, I said goodbye once again to George and Kay. It wasn't as difficult this time to let them go; I was certain, finally, that they would come if I called. And I was beginning to feel that what I wanted most was the strength and skill to survive on my own.

George and Kay had purchased a radio for me. Once again, as I unpacked my things, I listened to KSFO with the a capella singers reciting the call letters "K-S-F-O" in their sonorous tones and Frank Johnstone's smooth, comforting voice announcing the news. Putting clothes away, I realized that for the first time in my life I was about to live in a room that was all mine. I was so proud of myself. If I got through the trial period, whatever that meant, and if the rent was paid on time, I could remain forever, and no one could tell me what to do. No one could one tell me to leave unless I behaved in an unlady-like manner.

I stood and surveyed the narrow space. I decided it must be about ten feet wide and twelve feet long. I stroked the dark, ma-hogany dresser built into the wall and looked at the narrow bed cov-ered with a chenille spread. This was my domain. I touched the curtains and the window sill. Seated at the tiny desk, I wrote in my diary:

> *"Home," Grandma India said, "is the harmony of the mind set be-fore you in physical terms." My harmony is small for now but it is mine.*

That night I slept soundly on the solid and narrow bed. I was grateful for the window that looked out onto a backyard. The next morning I approached the dining room, and I was surprised when Mrs. Weber told me that I would eat my meals at the administration table with the staff. She also said they wanted to gauge the general reaction as they slowly introduced me to the girls they identified as the "best girls." The administrators defined these young women as the "God-fearing, churchgoing girls."

"But why?" I asked Mrs. Weber, after sitting down and eating some of my breakfast and thinking over her comments. That's when she said, "Oh, Melba, don't you know? You're our first and only colored resident in all our years of operation." Why hadn't they told me that before? So this wasn't really my own home yet. The truth was that I was on probation because I was black, not because every new resident had to go through a trial period. My security depended once more on the whims of white people and what they wanted. A sharp pain gripped my stomach and I could not finish my breakfast.

I had wondered why they insisted that I have a single rather than a double room. We had gone around and around about that issue. I wanted a double because it would have been less expensive. Ultimately, they had given me the single room at a bargain rate. Had they insisted I have a single room because I was the only black? I asked Mrs. Weber, wanting to know if my suspicions were correct. She admitted that they did not want to force me on one of the white residents, since I would be the only "colored" resident at the club. She said I would be allowed to remain for seven days to see if the other women accepted me. If there were no major negative responses, I could stay.

My insides quivered at the realization that once again I was on trial, and my fate was at the mercy of white people—because of the color of my skin. Had I known, I might not have been so quick to move in, but the truth was that I didn't have a lot of choices. I had to put up with their probation. All I could do was wait—wait like always to see whether white folks would accept me. It felt as though I was standing on the steps of Central High School pleading entry, except there were no violent mobs and I didn't need troops for protection. I could be excluded without preamble—without a court decision.

As the days passed, I discovered that I was spending an awful lot of time in my room trying to be invisible, hoping that I wouldn't be rejected. I didn't tarry in the front hallway or go to the bathroom or the laundry room a lot. Out of sight, out of mind. I hoped I wouldn't agitate anyone. I had to have faith that nobody would bother me because this place was affiliated with a church. At least there was no one criticizing my clothing and treating me like a maid as Mrs. Carson had. No one was lecturing me on being a "proper California Negro." So far nobody here was openly behaving towards me as though I didn't belong.

Mrs. Weber was as good as her word. She saw to it that I met the group of women residents whom she considered God-fearing and "the best girls." Primly dressed in dark suits and wearing white gloves, obviously hopelessly square, they were walking out of chapel when we were formally introduced. Although they were pleasant and welcomed me, they did not extend invitations to sit with them or socialize. I was not drawn to them at all. Still, I didn't give up hope of meeting potential friends among the other residents, maybe after the probation period was over.

After seven days, Mrs. Weber said that the other women seemed to accept me. And since no one was making a fuss about me, I would be allowed to sit at the tables with the other young women. The knot in my stomach loosened and my temples felt as though someone had released tight rubber bands from around my head. On that seventh day I wrote in my diary:

> *Dear God, I have a home. My space, my bed is mine. This time my name is on the lease, with Kay and George as cosigners. They can only kick me out if I behave inappropriately. I have some control over my home. I can take a deep breath—for now, this is a place where I can claim peace of mind, and maybe I can begin to feel I belong here.*

After that day I developed a routine. I vowed to use all the amenities offered. I would use the laundry room, the TV room, the library and the chapel. I would claim my dominion rather than hiding in my room to keep out of people's way. Most evenings, after dinner, I would go to the large sitting room at the front of the building. From there I could see what was happening outside on Bush Street, watch television news or sit in one of the comfortable chairs and read a newspaper.

I was beginning to be aware that blacks weren't the only ones who suffered the brunt of prejudice. One of the girls asked me how I managed to get a single room as a newcomer to the residence club. She followed her question by saying, "Did you jew them down?"

"What do you mean," I asked, "'jew' them down?"

"You know, like a Jew does," she replied. "They're always looking for a cut rate—always hoarding their own money." I was shocked but I didn't know how to reply. I shook my head and turned away from her, swallowing the words "narrow-minded bigot."

It was April 1960, and a big topic of conversation was the Catholic candidate John F. Kennedy's bid for the presidency. That discussion was the very first time it dawned on me that there was also real prejudice against Catholics.

"What's this country coming to when a Catholic can move into the White House?" a redheaded woman asked one evening after dinner as we sat in the TV room.

I wanted to say something to her, but decided I couldn't reform all of the world's bigots. At least she was willing to sit in a room with me, a black woman. Maybe we could start from there. As I walked back toward my room, the redhead who had spoken out against Kennedy stopped me in the hall. She had the face and hypnotic violet eyes of my favorite movie star, Elizabeth Taylor. She was a little thing—thin as a rail and no more than five feet tall.

"My name is Teddy," she said. "I haven't ever met any colored people but I've read *Ebony* magazine a few times." She said she was from Fresno, California. She continued, "I don't especially like colored people, but you seem so nice and so pretty." I had seen Teddy socializing at dinner. She was very popular. Even after what she had said about black people, I was excited that she'd noticed me.

At the end of my first week, after meeting Teddy, I had been introduced to six friends of hers who met to eat meals together. I felt like this odd little family was considering me for adoption. It was beginning to dawn on me that while I lived on my own, I yearned to be part of a family. I hoped that this group might become a workable substitute. Maybe with their help, I could even enjoy being a young adult.

My social life began to blossom, as my new friends and I went to movies, restaurants, to Golden Gate Park to listen to the music and for walks along Market Street, taking in the sights. Teddy and her friends were a few years older, and for the most part worked in offices as dental assistants, bookkeepers and secretaries. Teddy was the undisputed leader of the group. Then there was Wendy, a twenty-two-year-old tall, stocky, Fresno farm girl, and Alison, a twenty-six-year-old, dark-haired secretary with a lisp and horn-rimmed glasses. This dark-haired, matronly young woman played the role of den mother in our group. And what a wild den mother she was! It wasn't as though she gave advice on toeing the line or how to be ladylike. Instead, she read passages from her book on how to please a man and told us to remember, you only live once. Mandy, petite and quiet, was from Hawaii and worked as a secretary for the federal government. Zoe was a dancer, a willowy blond who ironed her underwear, "because you never know where you're gonna end up." Then there was redhaired Kerry Lynn, a tall and slender Indiana intellectual. Her father was a scientist and inventor. In just two weeks Kerry Lynn became my best friend. We seemed to share the same small-town American values. We loved to talk about the news and absolutely everything else.

Kerry Lynn and I spent hours talking about her father's science project. She told me about the Indiana farm where she grew up and I told her about growing up in Arkansas. We talked and talked. I never mentioned to her that I was one of the Little Rock Nine. But I felt very comfortable with this white person and, for the first time, I told my secrets to a white person. I revealed that perhaps I had had a nervous breakdown. And she said she thought she'd had one also. But she reassured me by saying I couldn't be certain because no one ever really knew about such things.

For the most part, my class time and my after-school time were uneventful. Finally, I was beginning to feel like an ordinary person. My only problem was that my new friends weren't going to school and hence didn't have homework. They could visit with each other, party, watch television and chatter until all hours of the night. After the first week of going everywhere with them, I realized I had to discipline myself. Mother had been right — study and bed down early on school nights or your grades will suffer.

Over the next few months I started to relax. I ate less junk food, quit biting my nails and began to sit in chapel just enjoying the stillness and the silence. I hoped to hear what God's will was for me. My schoolwork improved and I began to take a close look at people and the life around me. I felt truly blessed. Finally, I had a space to call my own. As cramped as my tiny room was, especially when it was cluttered, I felt safe there.

As I logged more breakfast and dinner meals in the dining room, I became comfortable not only with eating and laughing with my group, but also occasionally sitting at random tables and introducing myself to other people. But I wasn't totally comfortable with the fact that colored folks cooked and served the food from behind the steam tables. Over and over again I wondered how I should behave around them. The other residents treated them as though they were invisible, as if nobody were on the other end of the large silver spoons that served their food. But I decided I should speak to them. I was feeling guilty because maybe they thought I was trying to be uppity with them, as others had been to me.

As I passed through the line one Saturday morning in late May, adding scrambled eggs to my stack of pancakes, I felt compelled to call out, "Good morning. My name is Melba Joy, what's yours?" to the woman serving the eggs. She smiled back at me but did not speak. The girl behind me said, "Oh, we don't talk to them. They're, uh . . . oh. I guess they want you to talk to them . . . well, uh, I guess it's none of my business."

"That's right," I said without hesitation, "none of your business."

As I settled down to eat with my friends, I felt so free, filled with probably more joy and freedom than I had ever experienced in my entire life. And I felt proud of those black people who had jobs, even if they were behind the steam tables. After all, they were working and not stealing, and they were my people, and I saw so few of my own people.

The big topic of conversation over dinner was Elvis Presley's discharge from the Army and Paul Anka's song "Puppy Love," which was at the top of the *Hit Parade* charts. Bomb shelters were also being discussed. Who had built them, who was building them and where we would go if we needed one. Two years before, white students at Central High in Little Rock had discussed bomb shelters, but it was a topic I had never heard my own family or our friends mention. Listening to the talk, I reasoned that, since we could barely afford the roofs over our heads, bomb shelters weren't much of a concern for poor, black people.

I was pleased to see on the television news that the sit-ins staged by black people that had begun in February in the Greensboro, North Carolina, Woolworth store were in full swing. In Little Rock's Woolworth store, I had been made to feel like I was some kind of freak by being forced to sit at the lunch counter behind a railing in a small space on tacky stools. Meanwhile, white Woolworth customers spread out along the counter, taking up eighty percent of the space, relaxing on their nicely upholstered stools.

Lunch counter sit-ins had now spread to fifteen cities in five southern states. Three hundred fifty students had been arrested and still those sit-ins continued. One evening, as I heard myself say, "Right on!" to the news commentator on the television, I was reminded that I was the only black person in the Inn's large sitting room where there were more than twenty-five white people. A couple of the women looked at me as if they wondered how I dared express my happiness about the sit-ins. One of those women asked me in a huffy way if I wanted to make a statement, but I calmly told her that I had nothing to say and smiled. I wasn't about to get into a debate with her. I figured those people sitting in were saying it for me.

As I walked back to my room Teddy came bouncing up to me in the hallway. She was obviously excited. "Do you wanna come with us? The Fleet's in town!"

"The 'Fleet'?" I replied. "What's that?"

"The Navy has landed and it's time to have some fun!"

Chapter 17

LATER THAT AFTERNOON TEDDY STOOD in my doorway and said, "Get dressed. Put on something that says you're willing." She tossed her bright red curls about her head and winked at me.

"Willing?" I wondered what that meant, but the sound of her voice and the twinkle in her eyes intrigued me. I knew from the anxiety flooding into me that I shouldn't be following her advice, or accepting her invitation to welcome the Fleet. For an instant I considered calling Mother Lois or Kay or George to ask permission, but something told me that wasn't a good idea. Then whom should I ask? I felt guilty about making a decision like this on my own. But I had a real yearning for excitement and I didn't want to be left out.

I was really curious about my newfound friends. Wendy, the Fresno farm girl, was racing back and forth—frightened to go but more frightened about being left behind. After quickly washing her hair with some new, fancy shampoo, her curly brown mop had friz-

zled and she looked like Little Orphan Annie. She was furiously trying to straighten it. She wondered if I had a hot iron. I told her that I
didn't, and she said, "Don't all black people have hot combing irons?"

I said, "No, not all black people have kinky hair. Mine is curly,
and I only use a hot iron if I want it to be really straight." She was so
disappointed. Then she whispered to me that she'd never even had a
date.

Alison seemed so much older to us at twenty-six. The others
were aged twenty-one to twenty-three. She frankly admitted she
wanted male attention and a husband, and she said she adored
sailors. She had been on these kinds of excursions with Teddy before.
Alison was such a grown-up in our eyes—giving us advice and quieting our fears.

Even Mandy was getting ready to go with the rest of us, her
large, brown eyes perpetually filled with tears as a result of chain-
smoking cigarettes. She was overjoyed at the opportunity, sure it
would be a real adventure.

Zoe looked wonderful in her skin-tight purple slacks and
blouse. She tended bar and danced somewhere during the day, and at
night she always went out. Zoe would never reveal her age, but she
seemed like a woman of the world.

More and more I realized that Kerry Lynn was different from
the others. She sat reading the *Examiner*, a San Francisco daily newspaper, and wondering aloud if we would get into trouble. She had
some of the same trepidations I did. With her huge blue eyes and
waiflike appearance, she resembled a twelve-year-old. I realized that
I liked to be with Kerry Lynn most of all because she was interested
in something besides boys. She was saving money because she
wanted to go back to school. She thought she might become a doctor
as soon as she'd saved enough money from her clerical job to finance
her education.

What could Teddy mean when she kept repeating, "The Fleet is
in and we are gonna have fun?" Whatever we were going to do was
giving my friends the giggles and I longed to have that much fun. It
was something I had done without for a long, long time. The prospect
of boy-girl fun made it even more irresistible. After discussing the
pros and cons, Kerry Lynn and I agreed to give it a try, this "going
out to meet the Fleet" thing, but we vowed to watch out for each

other. Maybe I would meet a black sailor—the man of my dreams—and be married at sea.

For an hour of madness we rushed back and forth in the hallway, borrowing each other's makeup, clothing and perfume. I did a lot of the borrowing because I had few things that were apparently so necessary. Lipstick had been my only makeup, but Teddy insisted I needed to highlight my eyes. "And wear this blouse. Give 'em a peek of your womanhood," she'd said. I stood in front of the mirror for one last look at the soft, see-through, black lace blouse with the drawstring on top which Teddy had loosened until the neckline was well down on my shoulders. As I reached for the black shawl that had belonged to Grandmother India, I could almost hear her voice saying that I should stop and pray about where I was going. I ignored that voice, telling myself I didn't have time. I would pray about it later.

The six of us were chattering nonstop as we walked out the front door. Mrs. Quella, the night supervisor, stared at us with curiosity. Her expression betrayed her desire to give us a long lecture, but she only said, "Remember, curfew is midnight, girls. The front door is locked then, but you can ring the bell. You know we prefer you to abide by curfew."

"Yes, ma'am," I'd said, wondering why she thought we needed that information. I had never been permitted to stay up and certainly not out past 10:30 at night by my mother. And there hadn't been any occasion at the McCabes for me to stay out later. All of a sudden, after Mrs. Quella's admonishment, I realized that I'd taken another step into adulthood. I could stay out later than my mother had ever permitted me! But, of course, we'd be home long before midnight.

I was anxious and chilly after a few blocks in the cold night air wearing the thin blouse, and I felt too forward, unladylike, even sinful in my outfit. I had never worn that much makeup or anything so revealing before. I knew very well that Mother Lois or any other adult I respected would not approve of my clothes. I brushed back strands of hair from the clump of curls cascading over my right eye and down around my bare shoulders, styled following Teddy's instructions. "The 'Jayne Mansfield look' is what you're after," she had said.

Walking down the hill in Teddy's three-inch heels hurt my feet. It was my first attempt at balancing on such high heels and after a while I had to carry them. Finally we came to a halt beneath a green, flashing neon sign that read "Roaring Turtle." Loud music was blaring from inside as Teddy gave us the order: "Perk up, smile and push your chests out." I slipped my shoes back on and stepped across the threshold into a dimly lit room. Gosh, it was a nightclub. I'd never been to that kind of place before. Mother Lois and Grandma India would say this was the kind of place a person never went, or if they did, they had to be twenty-one years old and escorted.

At first I couldn't see through the cloud of cigarette smoke and I choked as I strained to get a look at the room. Crossed swords and large gold shields hung in lighted alcoves along the walls painted to resemble the stones of a castle. Thin lines of neon lights flashed along a hood that stood above the long, mahogany bar and reflected on brass-topped tables placed closely together, covering the center of the room.

Most intimidating were the men with white faces and Navy uniforms seated along that mahogany bar that extended the full length of the room. When we walked through the door, the men at the bar turned to look at us, appraising us carefully. They looked us over as if they were shoppers at some store sale, examining bargain merchandise. Their eyes danced up and down our figures, a probing inspection that made me want to turn and run. I glanced at Kerry Lynn. She had a strained expression on her face.

A few couples were seated at the small, round brass tables. The place was so packed with people there was hardly enough room to maneuver across the floor. The combined smell of perfume, cigarette smoke, body odor and strange foods blended into a smothering aroma. Santo and Johnny's "Sleep Walk," one of my favorite songs, was playing on the jukebox, but the music was so loud that I had the urge to put my hands over my ears.

"Smile girls, we're up for bids," Teddy shouted. "Hey, Melba, don't look so serious, I'm betting you'll be one of the first to go up."

"Go up"? What did she mean? But I nodded, pretending agreement, and even managed a pleasant smile, as though I fully understood. The truth was, I had absolutely no idea what she was talking about, but I wanted to belong so much that I was determined not to reveal my ignorance.

"What's 'go up'?" I whispered to Kerry Lynn.

"You got me. But I'm not certain we want that honor," she replied.

Just then a blond-haired man in civilian clothes called out to Teddy and we followed her toward his table. We made our way through the crowd to a table that was not quite big enough for all six of us, let alone the addition of the two guys already sitting there. Squeezing in, I almost sat on the lap of one of the strangers, a white man who wasn't in a uniform. With a great deal of effort, eight of us finally fit around the brass table meant for no more than three.

"Hey Wally, meet Melba," Teddy said, nodding at the blond-haired man. "Oh, yes, and Stevie, his buddy Stevie."

"Where're your uniforms?" Wendy blurted out.

"We're not water babies, we're real men," Stevie said and took a drink of beer. His dark hair combed back into a ducktail and piercing brown eyes reminded me of the James Dean look on Central High's hooligans.

"We don't need uniforms," Wally said, lifting his glass.

I was uneasy. I knew very well that I shouldn't be in a place serving alcoholic beverages. *If you love the Lord, get up and leave right now,* a voice said in my head. I tried to ignore it. As my eyes grew more accustomed to the dim light, I was disappointed that there were no black sailors in the room. And how could I heed the voice still urging me to get up and leave, when I wanted to wait and see if black sailors would arrive? Besides, I was afraid to walk back home by myself, and if I did go, how could I get away without either making a fuss or disappointing Teddy?

"I didn't know they let them in this place," Stevie said, sneering at me with a look that reminded me of Little Rock bigots.

"Oh, come on, boy," Wally sputtered through his beer, "This is California. We ain't up for race mixin' but some folks are doing it even all the way down the aisle."

My heart skipped a beat. I had to get out of there. Those familiar questions had come up: what was I doing in a place where there were none of my people and how safe was I?

"Don't you fret, little gal, keep your seat and make yourself to home. Besides, you're a pretty thing," Wally said. I smiled at him, breathed a sigh of relief, decided to ignore Stevie and looked around the room. The other women seemed to be at ease; they were laughing and chatting, tugging at their dress straps and repairing makeup. They were dressed like our group, only with more flash. Nevertheless, I wasn't comfortable and I knew I didn't belong. I would get up, pretend I was going to the bathroom and from there head for a doorway to make my escape. I'd find the courage to walk home alone if need be.

I eyeballed Kerry Lynn, whose expression showed real stress, the kind I was feeling. I decided I would head for the restroom and beckon her to go with me.

"Teddy," I whispered, "where's the ladies' room?"

"Upstairs and down the hallway, but you go at your own risk. Don't call on me when trouble calls on you."

What could she mean by that remark, I wondered, as I stood and squeezed past Wally. I glanced over at Kerry Lynn, but now she seemed to be in the clutches of some tall, string-bean sailor. They were dancing. I glanced up the staircase and wondered if there was an escape, an exit out a rear doorway. Whether Kerry Lynn came with me or not, I was leaving. Suddenly, all the wind was knocked out of me as hands grabbed me around my waist from behind. Breath was hot on the back of my neck and I heard a man's voice with an accent I didn't recognize.

"Ooooooo, zat ees chocolate eef I ever saw eet, zo zmooth and zo zweet." I looked around to see a very blond sailor who was holding me with an iron grip. I struggled to break free without success.

"Relax, you don' wanna get away from me," gushed the huge sailor towering over me. He handled my body like a rag doll, turning me about to face him and giving me a goofy smile. His skin was so white that the blue light from the neon bar sign gave his face an eerie glow.

"No thank you, I don't want to dance," I said, still trying to push him away.

"Oh, no, you cannot refuse Hans. I'm een love wit you. I been waiting to meet a chocolate babee like you."

I called to Teddy in a stressed, pleading voice, but she responded, "You're quick, Mel. You've got bingo already." I couldn't count on her for help.

"I like thees song," Hans said, breathing his alcohol breath on me. "Relax, relax and let it happen." His grip tightened. I could hardly breathe.

I'd never been in a spot like this. What was I supposed to do? My first instinct was to scream for help, but with the music so loud maybe no one would hear me. Besides, the other girls from my group were looking at me as though I was lucky to have been chosen. Even Kerry Lynn appeared momentarily satisfied with her sailor.

I pretended I wanted to dance. It would give me time to figure out how to negotiate. The huge sailor was slobbering all over me, talking into my ear about his dream of meeting someone like me, someone my color, and how just being near me excited him. I wanted the music to be over and someone to open the door for fresh air.

Nothing about Hans excited me. First of all, I didn't want to date or dance or cuddle with white boys. And secondly, he was crushing me. I tried to loosen his grip so I could breathe more freely, but Hans pulled me closer, tucking my head beneath his chin, and pressing his huge hand on my back to hold me near. I felt hopelessly trapped. As he turned me on the dance floor, I could see my friends teaming up with other sailors.

"Do you feel what I feel?" Hans whispered in my ear midway through the Everly Brothers song "Wake Up Little Susie." We had danced for three songs and I wanted to sit down.

"I don't know, tell me," I said.

"Oh," he said, chucking me under the chin with one huge, rough finger, "you're shy. I'll say eet for you and for me. We go upstairs and get to know each other."

"Upstairs?" I looked over at the steps at the rear of the room. They were painted red—a flashy red. I would go over and ask Teddy what was up there. Then I saw her climbing the stairs with a sailor behind her, pulling her back toward him and trying to kiss the nape of her neck.

"Upstairs, oh no, no, thank you." I said it so loud that I was certain every person in the bar could hear me.

"I have no time for games," he said, as he dragged me toward the stairs. "We ship out een a few hours," he said. "I'll be back soon though. You will wait for me, no?" He had a death grip on my arm. I wanted to scream as I looked around in panic.

I tried to wrestle away from him, but he giggled and said, "Oh, you only make me want you much with playing hard-to-get act." He pulled me along and then when he finally shoved me up the top stair, I could see that the upper floor resembled the room of a Western hotel in a cowboy movie. The main room was wallpapered in red velvet brocade. Red velvet overstuffed armchairs were grouped along the walls, interspersed with red vinyl chairs. A hallway with closed doors on either side opened off this room and couples were disappearing down the hallway.

"Wow, you made it, Hans," said a short, stocky sailor with huge eyes and red hair. "Take a number and wait your turn. The line forms to the right." The guy handed Hans a plastic card with the number "23" inscribed on it. Why was he snickering and what was the number for?

"It's the number of moans you'll let out while you're in heaven," Hans said in answer to my question, putting the numbered card in his pocket. Heaven? I thought. What could he mean? Whatever it was, I wanted no part of it.

Several empty armchairs rested against the red walls of the room. In other armchairs couples were clinging to each other, sharing their drinks and one group was passing around a single cigarette. The aroma of the smoke was different, I couldn't quite identify it—somewhat like sage, but not really. I wondered why there was just one cigarette for everybody. Couldn't they take time to get another pack downstairs or at the corner store?

Hans ushered me to one of the velvet armchairs near this group and sat down beside me, never once releasing his iron grip on my arm. At least the music up here wasn't loud enough to hurt my ears, and I spotted my friends from the residence club with their fellows. Kerry Lynn seemed ill at ease. She was sitting up very straight in her chair, not looking at the sailor who held her hand and leaned toward her whispering in her ear. The others seemed to be having a good time. They were either sitting on the men's laps or cuddling very close, even quiet Mandy was snuggling with a sailor. Not very ladylike behavior and especially in public, I thought. I was definitely in the wrong place and I began to panic again because they were behaving in a sinful way. I didn't want to go to hell. I also didn't want to be Hans's prisoner. This whole escapade had long since stopped being fun. My mind was racing, searching for a dignified way out, when Hans said, "Take a drag, eet will warm you up."

"A drag?" I looked down into the elephant-shaped ashtray he'd handed me.

"Yeah, you know, inhale the smoke."

"I don't smoke," I said. I had watched them pass the cigarette along from person to person, giggling. I could imagine all the germs that cigarette carried. I took it from his hand, wheezing and coughing at the odd-smelling smoke curling up into my nostrils. With a vengeance I mashed it out in the ashtray.

Even in that dimly lit room I could see the astonishment on the faces of several people. Hans began speaking in a foreign language under his breath; he was fuming with anger and then he shouted in English, "My God, look what have you done. Are you crazy?" He began digging furiously in the ashtray, trying to rescue the cigarette I'd smashed. I couldn't figure out his problem, but I thought he was the one who was crazy. Nor could I understand why Teddy and the girls couldn't stop giggling. Only Kerry Lynn wasn't laughing. She sat stiff and still, as if frozen in her chair.

"Why are you all smoking one cigarette?" I asked. "I'll be glad to go downstairs and get another pack out of the machine."

"Jesus," one guy said. "Is she kidding?"

All at once they were all laughing aloud at me. "What farm did she come off of, Hans?" one guy shouted above the laughter.

"You dummy, this is grass, weed, marijuana," someone said.

"Marijuana," I mumbled. "What's that—so what?" I blurted out. I sat there for a long moment while the laughter continued to flood the room and the people pointed at me. Finally Hans told them to stop. He said he liked them innocent so he could train them in the way he wanted them to go.

I decided not to ask what he meant, but instead to concentrate on getting out of there as fast as I could. I was beginning to fear for my safety.

"Hans, please excuse me, I'll be back in a moment. I have to go to the ladies' room," I whispered in his ear and smiled and winked at him, trying to seem flirtatious. Maybe he would let me go, or maybe his pride was hurt because I was so ignorant. Some of his buddies were still getting a hearty laugh about me and the joint.

"You're so sweet, so gentle," Hans patted me on the behind as I got up. I couldn't believe it. I wanted to tell him how much he embarrassed me. I wasn't that kind of girl. I tried to catch Kerry Lynn's eye, but she had turned sideways to say something to Alison, who was sitting beside her. I was on my own. I pretended to go down the long hallway toward the illuminated sign that read "Mademoiselle."

"You come right back here, chocolate girl, so we can know each other better before eet's our turn for a grand slam." I heard his voice as I headed toward the hallway. My heart was pounding. I was afraid that he might follow me. Looking back I saw that he was preoccupied, talking to the man next to him. I snuck past the hallway door and scampered toward the main stairway that led downstairs and to my freedom. I would be out of there in an instant.

As I stepped down the first stair, I heard loud voices below. Suddenly people were running up the stairs toward me. They behaved as if they were being chased; some sailors were taking the steps two and three at a time. They came scrambling towards me.

"Cops! Cops! It's a raid!" I heard the shouting but I didn't understand. A raid? What was that? I didn't have time to wonder. The thrust of the panic-stricken crowd pressed me back across the hallway toward the living room. People from the living room were also trying to crowd into the hallway. I was being crushed against the wall. I heard my voice crying out, "Help. Help!" I was being buried beneath an avalanche of human beings. Suddenly I felt someone tugging at me.

"Hey, little lady, take my hand. You gotta get out of here." Before I could say a word, Wally and his friend Stevie shoved me past the living room, through the crowd and to the window at the back of the hallway.

In the midst of our scramble to escape, Wally asked, "How old are you?"

"I'll be nineteen years old on December seventh."

"Good God almighty, you can't be caught!" He was hurriedly releasing the creaking, rusting metal stairs outside the window and directing me to climb down, reassuring me that he would follow me down into the dark abyss below. He said the stairs led to an alley that would take us to the street.

"Get on down, girl. The police are just a minute away from grabbing our asses."

I was climbing down as fast as I could. The stairs felt fragile beneath my feet. I looked up, thinking I might go back, but not only were Wally and Stevie climbing down directly behind me, other people had also climbed out of the window and were following us down. I could see Kerry Lynn coming down in the crush of humanity above me. I was afraid the rusting metal stairs wouldn't hold our weight. Breathing hard, I climbed down even faster. When my feet touched the ground I was thrilled but then I stopped short, remembering that I'd left Grandmother India's shawl and my purse behind.

"I have to go back!" I said in a panic.

"Back? Back is jail. Oh, no, you keep going," Wally insisted and we picked our way through the darkness, trying to avoid metal garbage cans and tripping over cardboard boxes. Huge, black, iron doors marked the alley service entrances to the various businesses. The smell of rotting garbage was nauseating.

"But I left my things up there," I insisted, stumbling alongside Wally.

"I sure hope they didn't have identification cards in 'em, 'cause they'll track you down and hunt you up like a dog."

I was horrified at the thought of being arrested, but devastated at the idea of leaving my grandmother's shawl in that place. Finally, as we lurched forward through the dark, I saw street lights and then we came out onto the sidewalk and there was the green sign at the front of the Roaring Turtle. There were police cars and hordes of uniformed officers milling around. I turned to run back into the alley but Wally grabbed me and dragged me back to his side.

"Take my arm," he demanded. "We're gonna walk right through the cops and past the place just like we owned that sidewalk."

"But I wanna . . ."

"Go back and they'll chase you 'cause they'll know where you came from. Do as I say."

Two officers glared at us as I took Wally's arm. I didn't know how I could look nonchalant. My knees were shaking and I had a pounding headache.

"Halt!" one of the policemen shouted. "Well, well, well, I don't suppose you two lovebirds came from the back end of the Turtle, did you?" Just then I looked beyond the policeman shouting orders and saw Hans. He was handcuffed and being shoved into the back of the police wagon. I drew my attention back to our immediate problem. The police were on us.

"No, sir," Wally said.

"No, sir," I chimed in, trying to calm the quiver in my voice.

"Can I see your identification?"

"Right here." Wally had his wallet out in an instant. "Uh, officer, that's why we're walking so fast. My lady here left her purse back at home . . ."

Cutting Wally off, I said in a quavering tone, "Yes, at the residence club!"

"I'll have to have identification—a driver's license, something, before I can let you go, young lady." The officer winked broadly at me and looked so self-satisfied that I knew he had me in his grasp. My knees shook so hard I thought they would buckle.

"Yep, I'll need to see an ID," he echoed his own words.

Chapter 18

"YOU LEFT YOUR PURSE ON THE FRONT DESK," Kerry Lynn said, as she suddenly appeared out of the darkness and slammed the purse into my hand. With an iron grip, she was holding onto a sailor boy in dress blues. I wanted to ask if she had found Grandma India's precious shawl but I knew that would tip off the officer.

"Front desk, what front desk? " With an inquisitive expression the officer glared at us. Kerry Lynn stood silent, holding tightly to the sailor.

It was Wally who spoke up. "Oh, they live up the hill. You know . . . in that Christian women's residence club. Kerry Lynn was kind enough to come after us and deliver the missing purse."

"I don't know how you got out, but I'll bet you my badge you were in the Turtle with the other creeps."

"No, sir."

"What's a 'Turtle'?" Wally said with a straight face. And then he said, "Uh, the French Catholic church has Mass at this time of the evening and we always walk back and forth this way."

"Remove your identification from your wallet, please," growled the officer.

My heart pounded in my ears. He was pointing to me.

With perspiring hands I retrieved my San Francisco State College student identification card. I did not have more official identification like a driver's license, which did not please the grim-faced man. However, despite his persistence and the other officers' malevolent grins, embarrassing questions and endless insinuations, Wally and I managed to keep our cool. Our answers must have been pretty good because finally, after an exhausting number of questions, he let us go.

During that gut-wrenching experience I wet my pants. I was mortified that Wally and the others would find out I had soggy underwear and a dripping hemline. I said, "Goodnight," and raced back home, up the steps, through the front door and past the desk without stopping. I just wanted to get cleaned up, hide and find some way to erase the events of that evening from my memory. If I could have put my hands on my Grandmother's Bible that night, I would have sworn on it that I would abandon Teddy and her sinful and nerve-racking social life.

I sat and thought over the fact that I had not really been following the Christian values that Grandma India and Mother Lois had tried so hard to instill in me. I wondered if maybe in California there was a different definition of sin. Maybe white people had a different idea about sin. What if there were different degrees of sin—some acceptable, some not? How could I know for sure? What was certain was that my sinning had caused the loss of Grandma India's shawl. It was gone for good in the raid at the Roaring Turtle. I couldn't imagine a more shameful place to lose it than a bar—Grandma India would have called it a "honky tonk." I knew I'd be regretting the night for years to come.

Weeks passed and I plunged into preparation for finals. My routine was straightforward, even dull. Kerry Lynn and I had promised ourselves that we wouldn't go on any more excursions with Teddy that might get us into trouble. That promise meant that we spent a lot of time by ourselves. On some days I was delighted and grateful to finally live uneventfully. An ordinary life without drama had been my dream for so long, and it was especially sweet after the hideous experience at the Turtle. On other days I missed the excitement of being a participant in Teddy's group and the sense of belonging it gave me.

It had taken nearly all my energy that semester to learn to be normal, to walk around on a campus as if I had a right to be there and not look back over my shoulder. At the same time, I was learning how to live the fast-paced lifestyle of the North that others took for granted. These girls thought it okay to date a boy without waiting to be introduced to him by an adult from the community or church. They were already going out to bars and clubs when Mother had said that was something a woman of thirty might do occasionally—but only if accompanied by her husband or a gentleman friend. My new-found friends seemed not to take time to view their decisions through the eyes of God. Things moved so fast for me and there were always too many choices to be made.

My exam grades were good and I continued to think of myself as a future teacher, a profession approved by both Mother Lois and George. Yet, despite my success at school and my ordinary, uneventful schedule, I was not satisfied. Kerry Lynn and I remained good friends, but loneliness was taking over, eating at my heart. I kept my word to myself and did not go on many outings with Teddy and her group. We watched them get dressed, giggle and go out almost every weeknight and especially on weekends. All the while we remained behind at the residence club, at least for the most part. Now and again, we joined them for daytime adventures—shopping at the Emporium or lunching on Powell Street, or going to Playland at the beach for rides on the merry-go-round. I wanted to be part of a real, full-fledged family again, and join in their fun. After all, I had missed the fun of being a junior and senior in high school because of the integration at Central High School. I had sat at home in Santa Rosa on weekends and watched fun life pass me by. How long was I to give up fun? Didn't I deserve to have a good time?

Besides, they were doing things I had never done and could never do in Little Rock. There were no clubs, restaurants, movies, tea rooms, no amusement parks or mini-golf or bowling alleys open to blacks in Little Rock. I had been exposed to a few of those things in

Santa Rosa, but here and now I had a chance to experience it all. I felt so confused. What was right and what was wrong for a Christian girl? How could a Little Rock girl like me, with so little experience in having fun, make the right choices with so much available? How could a body find the people who took the Christian approach to fun? I felt left out and wondered what I was to do.

I had enrolled in summer school and was nearly finished with my courses. The United States' U2 pilot, Gary Powers, had just been sentenced to ten years in prison by the Soviets for his supposed spy mission, and everyone was hopeful that the new oral polio vaccine would mean that more people would take it and that ugly disease would go away. As time passed, I must have blocked out all the torment that evening at the Roaring Turtle with Teddy had caused. Late one afternoon in August, I found myself with Kerry Lynn riding a cable car at Teddy's invitation, along with the four girls with whom she usually traveled. Anxious to break out of my self-imposed isolation and associate with other people in addition to Kerry Lynn, I had said a hasty "yes" when she asked me to go with them.

After accepting Teddy's invitation, Kerry Lynn and I fretted about the probability that if we elected to go with Teddy we might get into some sort of trouble. However, we decided there was not a lot of risk involved this time because we would be in public and in broad daylight on the cable cars.

At 5:30 P.M. we had stopped to have ice cream sundaes at the cable car turnaround at the bottom of Powell Street and Teddy invited the six of us to join her for a very special birthday party not far from downtown. Kerry Lynn and I declined immediately. But Teddy argued persuasively. We would meet wholesome, single young men who, because of the way they lived, didn't meet many ladies. We would be in a private home, a safe setting with decent people, and although alcohol would be served it would be in limited amounts.

The first alarm bell went off in my head when we found two late-model, four-door Ford automobiles waiting for us at the end of the cable car line where Powell crossed Market Street. Who knew all of us would decide to go, thereby requiring two cars? The drivers were older men with hardened, fish-belly white faces, as though they never saw the sun. They did not smile. Their bulging eyes matched their protruding bellies. Who were they and where did they come from? We rode for about thirty-five minutes. Clearly the birthday party house was not anywhere near downtown San Francisco. But Kerry Lynn and I agreed it was too late to turn back.

The second alarm bell went off when I saw the motorcycles parked outside the birthday house—more motorcycles than I could count. When I asked Teddy about them she said in an offhand manner that we would be joined by some famous men, rough riders from the Hell's Angels club.

I didn't know any club by that name. Kerry Lynn said she didn't either. The way Teddy was snickering at us made me shy about asking any more questions. Kerry Lynn and I held hands as we made our way up the sidewalk to the front door. The house was orderly and quite modern, reminding me of the pictures I had seen in interior design magazines. The atmosphere and the tempting aroma of cooking food quieted some of my fears. And the men didn't look like rough riders to me. They were casually dressed, but they were clean enough and their hair was neatly cut with the exception of a few wearing long hair in ponytails. I had hoped to see a few business suits, but there were none.

As the evening wore on and everyone was full of wonderful food, people coupled up and the lights began to dim. Kerry Lynn and I sought each other out and found a place together on the couch in the main living room where the singles were gathered.

As I looked around, I realized I was once again the only black person in the group. One dark-skinned man I had thought was black turned out to be Mexican. He ignored me in favor of a slender blond. So there I was again, in a strange place, surrounded mostly by strangers and hoping for fun but instead getting a belly full of anxiety.

"Hi, what's your name, baby."

"Uh, Melba, and yours?"

"Napa Joe." He spoke with a very deep voice. A thin, dark line like the scar from a razor slash ran diagonally across his right cheek. Otherwise he was very handsome, with dark curly hair, deep-set blue eyes and an appealing grin.

"Why do they call you 'Napa Joe'?" I asked

"'Cause I was in Napa for a while. Does that frighten you?"

"Uh, no, no. Why would it?" Napa was a city north of San Francisco. That's all I knew. Was there something special about the place?

"Then never mind. Let's move over there and get acquainted." He reached out to take hold of my hand.

"Uh, no thank you," I muttered, grabbing the arm of the couch to anchor myself.

Ignoring me, he grabbed my free hand, pulled me up and dragged me across the room toward a hallway. I wanted to yell for help but instead I turned and called out, "Kerry Lynn!" I winked at her and said, "Let's go home, now." She must have heard the distress in my voice because she got up to follow us. If it hadn't been for the skinny, dark-haired man who grabbed her, I'm certain she would have come with me.

Joe took me to a couch at the end of the long hallway, where we sat and talked for twenty minutes about our families, birthplaces and hopes for the future. Napa Joe sounded pretty normal. Still, I didn't cotton to dating white boys. I tried to remain calm while looking for a way out. Then the music started—slow, mellow music. It was Paul Anka's "Put Your Head on My Shoulder," a song that invited people to snuggle.

Napa Joe was not subtle about his intention as he grabbed me without asking my permission for the dance. As the song was about to conclude he started caressing my hips and getting far too familiar. I rejected his advances, but the more I squirmed away the more he insisted on exploring other, more private parts of my body. I was frantic, pushing and tugging, but his strength made me feel as helpless as a child.

"No, stop, stop now," I yelled at him.

My cries for help sparked the most incredible display of temper I had ever seen. At once he was like an uncaged, mad dog, an animal, some predator gone wild. Ranting and raving, calling me a "prick tease," he demanded that I go with him to the next room where I should give him what he said I had promised. My instincts told me I was about to relive the nightmare with Hans at the Roaring Turtle, or something even worse. That possibility energized me to try harder. I thrashed against Napa Joe with all my might. When I finally got loose I ran toward the door shouting, "Keep your hands off me, or I'll call the cops!" I was yelling loud enough for Mother Lois to hear me in Arkansas. The lights came up bright and people began to gather around Bob and his raging antics.

"Did Joe take his medicine?" one guy asked. At that moment, Kerry Lynn rushed up to me with our coats and we headed for the door. It didn't matter that we didn't know where we were or how to get back home, somehow we would make our way across the city. At first, we held hands as we ran through this dark, unfamiliar section of town, and then there was the welcome sight of clustered neons and an open store. The clerk directed us to a bus that got us to Market Street in downtown San Francisco, and then a transfer connection bus to the Inn.

The next morning Wendy rushed up to me and Kerry Lynn at breakfast and took a seat. She said she was frightened of what might have happened to us. And then she said things that alarmed me even more.

"When he said his name was Napa Joe, he meant that he had been in that place, you know."

"No, we don't know," Kerry Lynn and I chirped simultaneously.

"Napa is the state asylum for the mentally ill in California. He spent three years there. That's why they call him 'Napa'—he gets a little crazy sometimes. But Glen promised that he was fully okay. I mean, the doctors let him out and said he was all well," Wendy explained. Wendy was also worried because she had heard that the Hell's Angels was a motorcycle gang—a violent gang that treated women like devalued possessions.

When Teddy joined us I said angrily, "You have no right to expose us to those kinds of people." Even though I let my anger show this time, I was careful to temper my rage, because the bottom line was, she was white and could sway the others to exclude me if I alienated her.

Kerry Lynn's flushed face was full of anger as well. "You could have gotten us killed!" she blurted out with a pointed finger.

"No harm done," Teddy said nonchalantly, dismissing our concerns.

No harm? I thought to myself. But I decided to wait to speak my mind to Teddy.

"What I wanna know is, what's the Hell's Angels club?" I asked.

The answer to that question took twenty minutes and during that time my stomach got so tight, I couldn't say a word. Kerry Lynn and I just sat and listened and if my eyes were as wide as hers, we must have looked like a pair of deer caught in the headlights. Night riders, mamas, renegades, oh, my Lord, the words just poured out of Teddy's lips and all the while she had the most evil smile on her face. She spoke as if she were proud that she knew these people and that she obviously considered herself someone special because they had invited her to their party.

After her explanation, I realized the horror of what I'd been exposed to, and I decided to heed Wally's advice. He had dropped by the residence club a couple of times to sit and talk with me. He had warned me that I ought to separate myself from Teddy's social schedule until I was more mature in the ways of the world. He said I was so naive that he would donate some advice and some of his time in order to make me "hip." "Otherwise," he cautioned, "you'll be dead or disabled before the new year."

For the next several weeks, I only spoke polite hellos to Teddy in the hallway and at the breakfast table. During dinner, Kerry Lynn and I sought out a new group to eat with. We didn't want to expose ourselves to the slightest possibility of being drawn into another one of those bizarre and sinful adventures.

Despite my yen for excitement and fun, I tried to remember my connection to the Lord. I had continued going to church. I would go to any black church, but mostly those in the Fillmore district, to see my people and hear the music, some of which reminded me of home. What was most comforting was the sight of the vibrant print dresses of brash yellow, turquoise, magenta and rose that the church ladies wore. The shiny fabrics and wondrous hats with mesh veils, feathers, flowers and satin bows made me smile and remember home. I loved the way the women sashayed up and down the aisle with their dresses rustling, bending over to speak to someone every now and then. The organ music was loud enough to touch the soul, whether you wanted it to or not. After a visit there I felt as though my spirit had been rejuvenated. It helped me to remember who I was and what really mattered. I was here in California to get an education, to make the best of being free.

California black people were free. They behaved differently, unaware of the limitations I felt; they had no experience with the kind of segregation that every black lived under in the South. They weren't always looking over their shoulder for permission. It was a comfort to worship with them. Afterward I would often go to the church dinners where collard greens and cornbread, corn and okra casserole, and sweet potato pie were served. The food and chatter made me miss Mother Lois and my family in Little Rock.

I found some problems trying to make friends among black people. If I sought out the intellectuals, those committed to change, and told them who I was, they immediately expected me to march and protest. San Francisco issues, like equal jobs and housing, were heating up. If I sought out the more complacent black people who seemed satisfied with their lot, I was bored. I decided to stop trying to meet black people. It was easier just to let things be.

I'd completed my second semester at San Francisco State and I felt comfortable on the campus. I'd become well adjusted to the fast-paced lifestyle. My best friend was still Kerry Lynn, and she and I were close once more with Teddy's group, but we didn't accept any social invitations that were the least bit suspicious.

I was going to the McCabes to celebrate Christmas. Mother Lois complained when I told her I wouldn't be home for the holidays, but I couldn't stand the heartache of Little Rock so soon. I felt like a fledgling bird just learning to fly and I didn't want to be dragged down. Finally, she seemed to be getting used to the idea. She even spoke of coming north for the holidays. When she couldn't manage, we talked on the phone every evening for a week for six minutes. That was our Christmas gift to each other.

When I went to Santa Rosa for Christmas, Kay and George and the family had moved into a new house. George was thinking of running for Congress, but then decided to wait until the college he was helping to erect was well on the way to completion. I was transfixed as he talked of his dream college becoming a reality. It inspired me to know what was possible for one individual. We laughed together, ate, sang, traded stories and exchanged gifts and thoroughly enjoyed ourselves. It was especially wonderful for me to be in a household once again where ideas and issues were frequent topics of conversation. I'd missed that so much at the residence club where the focus was always on men, men, men.

I was glued to the television set the following month for Kennedy's inaugural speech. In my diary I wrote:

I'll bet we remember those words of President Kennedy's inaugural speech, "Ask not what your country can do for you, ask what you can do for your country." Already the press is making a big deal of them.

I feel I have already done all I must do for my country. I need somehow to learn to do for myself—to make me a real person—to learn how to love, to work, to be an ordinary human being. I have a lot to learn.

I feel guilty for not marching in Berkeley—and on my own campus for the ideals like free speech and equal job opportunity and equal housing that trigger others to howl and shout and protest. I feel as though I should be quiet and creep within myself.

By the third week of February 1961, Teddy's group announced they would be moving out of the residence club. They thought they were ready for more freedom and they wanted space to cook decent meals and to entertain friends whenever they felt like it. They invited Kerry Lynn and me to go with them. Their reasons for moving appealed to me, but I couldn't help wondering how I would handle homework without any rules. Curfew, precise mealtimes, set hours for worship and a television room open only for specific hours all helped me schedule my time for studies and helped to discipline me in almost every other aspect of my life. Was I now ready to let go of all these guidelines? I was just becoming accustomed to the notion that no one would parent me.

I was thinking that maybe the residence club was the best place for me, now. Kerry Lynn, on the other hand, decided she wanted to get an apartment too, separate from the group. She and I talked for hours about the prospect. A few days before Teddy's group was due to move out, Zoe declared she would remain behind. I had noticed as we rode the bus together down to the trolley cars running along Market Street that she was changing. Before she had worn gobs of makeup and left every weekend with an overnight kit and a boyfriend. Lately she had been staying at the club on weekends. And now, she was remaining behind when her friends moved out. Her face was clean of makeup and she talked of giving up cigarettes.

A conversation with Zoe convinced me that I should stay behind with her. She was already a good friend. Later that week when I told her of my decision to stay, she announced that she would not be living in the residence club much longer. She was going to become a nun. We hugged as I congratulated her for deciding to serve the Lord. I would wonder all my life what had converted her from a person I judged to be a true "good-time girl" to a nun. Whatever the miracle, I hoped it would bless me as well. I wondered if I should consider becoming a nun, but decided not yet, at least not until I had some small amount of the good times.

I was just beginning to feel more comfortable about living in the residence club, in large part because of the group that had befriended me; I felt like I belonged somewhere at long last. But with Teddy's gang moving, I wondered whether I would make new friends. Now, I felt included, accepted by most of the residents who did not make my race an issue. But would newcomers accept me, a black person, as readily as the residents already there had when I arrived?

Still, I had definite doubts about living with Teddy. I was certain that I would go to hell with her if I lived her way. And yet, I couldn't bear the thought of being left behind. I needed and wanted to stay connected to familiar people and routines. Living with Kerry Lynn might be a good compromise, if we could live separate from the others.

Finally, after hours of pleading and cajoling, Kerry Lynn convinced me that we should move out together to an apartment separate from but near Teddy and the faithful four.

When I told my plans to Mother Lois she was adamant that I should not move away from the residence club. Kay and George were also hesitant, but willing to discuss the pros and cons. After the barrage of words exchanged by all the parties, I sat down quietly in my room to make my decision.

Each day for the past few months, I had sat in my room, looked at the dark, mahogany-colored wood that paneled the narrow space, and missed the sunshine. My window looked out on the back of the building and my bathroom was down the hall, shared by at least twenty-five other girls. It would be so nice to have a larger bedroom and share a bathroom with only one other person. And maybe we could find a bright place where sun shone through the windows at least part of the day.

When I told Mother that I would stay in church and would move only a few blocks from the residence club, she was a little more open to the idea but she said she wanted to think it over. Meanwhile, I borrowed money from Kerry Lynn and Wendy for the first and last month's payment, and I gave notice at the residence club. I would miss the chapel and ready-made meals, but I would not miss the stringent rules and the feeling of living in a large institution.

I never stopped to think about my skin color when the issue of apartment hunting was discussed. I'd had difficulty when I searched for living quarters before, but surely my experience wouldn't be repeated. After all, this was California in 1961. However, time after time Kerry Lynn and I were turned down with a polite but firm refusal, "We don't have coloreds living here and we suspect our other tenants would object." The wall of prejudice was harsh and solid.

Finally, Kerry Lynn decided to hunt for an apartment alone and not tell the landlords that I was black. We decided that when she found a likely prospect I would merely show up on moving day. She finally found an apartment for us two blocks away on Sutter Street. On the day we moved in, the Australian couple who owned the building met us at the curb. They wanted to know who I was. Kerry Lynn said I was the roommate whom she had discussed with them. The couple told our movers to halt—not to unload the truck. My heart pounded in my chest. I was officially moved out of the residence club. Was I going to be homeless?

Chapter 19

THE LANDLADY AND HER HUSBAND DEMANDED that I follow them into their apartment. I looked back at the movers, whose expressions showed their frustration. My knees wobbled, my palms were sweating.

"I have a black janitor here with me whom we brought over from Australia. Ben would walk through fire for me," the woman directed her conversation to me and continued, "so I'm letting you know if I turn you down it's not because I'm prejudiced against your people and their plight."

"Yes ma'am." I could hear my heartbeat pounding at my temples.

"But I'll need to know the kind of person you are because I can't afford to anger my other tenants," she said.

She kept the movers and truck waiting at the curbside for forty minutes while she probed. Did I drink, smoke, entertain strange men, give carousing parties, talk nasty, take baths and on and on and on. I was so angry at her questions and so incensed at their derogatory nature that I could have choked her. But I realized I couldn't give way to my anger. She held my future in her hands, and I was determined to be as sweet as honey. I needed a roof over my head.

Just when I started to shake uncontrollably with fear and anger, afraid everyone would notice, she said we'd give it a try, but warned me that if I turned out to be a noisy tenant I'd be out. She would only rent the apartment to Kerry Lynn with me as Kerry Lynn's lessee, even though we shared the rent equally. That way, the landlady informed me, she could get me out with twenty-four hours' notice if need be. It hurt my feelings that my name was not on the lease. But I trusted Kerry Lynn and I had to make the best of this deal, because it was all I had. We were both weary of looking.

Entering the living room, I looked around to see a forest-green couch made of strange, shiny mesh-like fabric. In the corner was a large, lush green velvet high-backed chair that resembled the one Grandmother India had had in our living room, and I knew this was home.

Just off the living room, through a sliding glass door, was my bedroom. It only had one window but it looked into a garden. Kerry Lynn's bedroom was to the right of the living room. We squealed with delight at the kitchen with its narrow four-burner cook stove, yellow counters and moderate-sized refrigerator. It was full of sunlight. We were now officially grown-ups and this was our first home.

During the next three weeks I was obsessed with not antagonizing the landlady, which took a lot of the excitement and sweetness out of being in my first apartment. How I hated tiptoeing along the hallway and fretting over whether our radio or television was too loud. Teddy and her group lived in an apartment nearby and visited us frequently. They could have cared less about making noise so I became the policeperson. I was always turning down music and shushing up people during their endless visits and frequent parties.

Girl talk about finding the right boyfriends, advice on dating and the newly developed birth control pills were the primary topics for our group. Sometimes I longed to bring up subjects that we were discussing in class, but none of the other girls attended school or seemed interested in current affairs. I wanted to talk about the hearings that the House Un-American Activities Committee was holding in San Francisco's federal building, which had been the catalyst for all the marching and shouting protestors; the attack on Cuba at some place called the Bay of Pigs; or the execution of Caryl Chessman, which sparked so much debate and so many candlelight marches. But my friends would have none of it. During the constant visits back and forth between the two apartments they only tore themselves away from the subject of dating when there was information to exchange about baking, kitchen utensils, Lucille Ball divorcing Desi Arnaz and how to make the next party work better. Parties, parties, parties were the themes for those days of 1961.

While I liked having my very own bedroom, a nice, convenient bathroom and even the responsibility for my own apartment, I began to loathe all the parties. I had read a statistic in the newspaper that said Americans had increased their gin drinking from six million gallons in 1950 to nineteen million by 1960. Certainly, the young ladies in my circle contributed to that increase.

One of the reasons I decided to enroll in summer school that year was to be with people who shared goals similar to my own. I needed the intellectual stimulation, and I wanted to be around the chatter and debate about current national and world affairs. And, also, increasingly I felt torn between the values I had been taught all my life and what was going on all around me, even in my own living room. Kerry Lynn understood why I wouldn't touch liquor—she knew it was against my religion and respected my decision to avoid it—but the others did not. They persisted in teasing and challenging me to join them in their gin and tonics or margaritas.

One Friday evening in July, I opened my own front door to the surprise of a party going full blast. I refused when Teddy offered me a glass of red liquid over ice. She insisted it was just like strawberry soda and even though it contained a little alcohol, it didn't make you drunk. I said, "No! Absolutely no!"

It was 6:00 P.M. and my major concern was the noise of "Alley Oop" blasting from the stereo. I wanted to unwind, find a comfortable place to park my aching feet and quiet the awful noise so I wouldn't be kicked out. Once more I questioned the wisdom of my move from the residence club with all these people who were so un-like me. Although only Kerry Lynn lived with me, it was as though they all did. We were all together so often and we all had the run of both apartments. When Teddy found a new love interest and wanted to test his talents, she sometimes used my bed. I would arrive at my very own home, turn the key in the lock and find the chain on. I could hear Teddy mumbling, "Busy, busy, go to the other crib for a while till I finish."

On this foggy, chilly evening, cold and tired after studying late, I would have loved a fireplace with a fire burning cozily, and a re-laxed evening listening to soft pop, western music or even the Everly Brothers singing "Cathy's Clown," interspersed with some classical music, maybe Chopin. Most of all I yearned to be with a group of col-lege people discussing Fidel Castro's takeover of our oil refineries, or the outcome of the Kennedy and Nixon debate—anything but the endless, empty chatter all around me. I was out of luck. We didn't have a fireplace and the group was gathered there for the familiar group festivities. The cigarette smoke made me sneeze and cough. The food aromas blended with the smell of liquor and made me nau-seous. I stepped across the bodies crammed into the living room. I ig-nored the greetings, people calling out, "She's home." I responded with a grunt and a grimace.

I sensed the others were beginning to feel my irritation with their constant parties, which all had the same theme, the same do-nothing activities, the same dead end, with bodies slumped all around. After the first hour when everyone got sloshed, I discovered that being the only sober person in the room was quite a bore. I would usually leave, go to church, see a movie or just walk around until I felt sleepy. Tonight I wanted my home and my pillow. Now here I was again, confronting the biggest party I had seen to date, complete with loud music that jeopardized my tenancy at the apartment.

Twice I went over to turn down the knob on the stereo. Twice someone else turned the volume back up. I heard one of the sailors in the room say, "Who's that colored girl? She's cute but we gotta calm her down. She's a wet blanket." Amid all the chatter and activity, Al-ison offered me a soda, saying, "Take a sip. You'll like it." Frustrated and unfocused, I grabbed the drink and began gulping the cool liquid

I thought was strawberry soda. Alison was a good person who would never harm me, I reasoned.

I don't remember much after that except that the soda turned warm going down and it eased the knot of apprehension in my stomach. I felt giggly good. I was happy and all of a sudden so much a part of the group. I heard myself laughing at jokes, I stopped worrying about the music being so loud. They were playing a game of dice and everyone was taking off their clothes. I joined them but when I threw the dice and was supposed to take off my panties and bra, I refused. "Even dead-head drunk, this girl has morals, I'll swear," said the sailor on my arm.

When he tried to push me into my own bedroom and lock the door behind us, I broke away and headed through the front door of the apartment and climbed the stairs up to the roof. I went out onto the ledge that spanned the front of the building. It was about three feet wide. Often when we had sat on the roof, we girls had talked about what it would be like to walk along the ledge. I told myself I needed a walk to clear my head and then I could go back down and take care of myself. *I might even kick all those people out,* I fantasized. *Why shouldn't I?* Kerry Lynn was away with her new South American boyfriend and the apartment was all mine.

I remember feeling chilled, then I was freezing. I stood on the ledge and realized that people were calling to me from below. I heard Alison and Teddy behind me on the roof. They were peeking around the little shed that housed the generator and calling to me. I could see all the cars and neon signs below. People down on the street looked like ants, their heads bobbing as they walked. Suddenly there was a fire truck with sirens screaming right below me. "Was there a fire?" I wondered.

In a few minutes a blinding light from the fire truck was in my eyes. They had trained a high-powered spotlight on me. Some firemen rushed to the sidewalk beneath me and they were holding onto something that looked like a round blanket.

"Don't jump," a calm voice said behind me. "Nothing is as sacred as human life."

"Oh, how sweet . . . you must be a minister," I said, looking back at the man wearing the collar of a priest who was suddenly standing behind me. I wanted to talk to him. I definitely needed more guidance in quieting my friends. Maybe he could help me stop the incessant parties in my house.

"You don't have to do this." He looked at me as though I were to be pitied. I glanced back over the ledge. Meanwhile the firemen were quietly perching their ladders up against the building. Two firemen were beginning to climb up toward me. Why? My head was whirling, my vision cloudy.

My goodness, I thought to myself, were they all here for me? And then I looked down at myself: Oh, no . . . and me in my underwear. They'll see me without my clothes. All I had wanted on the rooftop was some air and an opportunity to calm down.

"Won't you come with us? Surely there is an answer to whatever is troubling you," the priest said, his hands reaching out toward me.

"No, thank you. I have a home. I just needed some peace and quiet. My thinking was getting confused." My head was aching and I felt as though I were reeling. It must have been something I ate, maybe those cheese puffs and tuna bakes hadn't agreed with me.

"We all want you to be safe. Won't you come with us?"

There it was again, that condescending tone as if I were a nut case. Why was he talking to me that way? What did he mean—all? We all. Looking around I could see that everybody was coming toward me, and once again they were shining that blinding spotlight in my eyes. I could see people gathered down on the street. They were pointing up at me. Well, no wonder, it was that silly light. That did it. I had to get back downstairs to the apartment.

Feeling very, very dizzy as though I might throw up that strawberry soda, I turned away from the front of the building and started to walk as best I could manage. I put my hands over my eyes as I brushed by the priest, thinking that if I covered my eyes he wouldn't be able to see my nakedness. Then someone grabbed me from behind. Suddenly several other men in white coats popped into view and clutched at me. I felt a pinprick in my arm and then a black curtain dropped over everything.

.   .   .

AYLIGHT STREAMED IN through white blinds, beckoning me to open my eyes. Everything was a shadowy blur. I propped myself up on my elbows to look beyond the bed I was in. I was in a place that was all white—white walls, white sheets, white doors. My head felt as though someone were pounding on it with a hammer. The footsteps I heard in the hallway outside the room were magnified; they sounded like the thud of marching army troops. I fell back against the pillows and the room reeled at my sudden movement.

A hospital! It had to be. But what was I doing in a hospital? Had I been in an automobile accident? Was I hurt? My head was pounding and my right leg hurt, but I hadn't seen any bandages. I closed my eyes.

"I'm Dr. Ralston and I'll need you to answer some questions," I heard a deep male voice. It sounded like he was talking through a megaphone. It made my head pound and ache even more intensely. I opened my eyes and saw a tall, lanky, dark-haired man in a white coat standing beside the bed.

"I need you to answer a few questions for me," he repeated. He pulled a chair to the head of the bed scraping its legs across the floor as though he were deliberately trying to hurt me. Taking a seat, he looked directly into my eyes.

Even though I seemed to be having trouble focusing I could see that he was youthful in appearance, except for the gray sprinkled at his temples. Brown eyes peered at me through black, wire-rimmed glasses. His expression was noncommittal.

"What happened to me? I think I'm in a hospital, but am I hurt? Am I okay? How long have I been here?" The questions tumbled out. My head pounded even more as I spoke. I felt nauseated.

"You're going to be all right. You've had a close call, but you'll be fine," he replied.

"What happened?"

"First, let me ask you some questions." He drew his chair closer and looked into my eyes with a sympathetic expression.

"Why did you try to take your own life?"

"Who, me? I didn't."

"You were at the very edge of the building preparing to jump off, or at least that's what it looked like."

"No, no, I wasn't—I just wanted fresh air."

"Well, Dr. Pasmarian, the psychologist, will talk with you in detail about your intentions. Meanwhile, I have some other issues to address."

The doctor pressed and pressed me to remember my activities of the past few days. I had trouble concentrating, my head felt like oatmeal. He also persisted in asking me about my parents or guardian. He wanted to know why a responsible adult had not come to the hospital to check on me. I dared not give him the phone numbers of Mother Lois or the McCabes. I had gotten myself into this and I'd get myself out of it and make it right. Besides, why should I ruin the trust that Mother Lois and the McCabes had put in me? Why break their hearts?

"Do you have any idea what kind of alcohol you drank?" he asked me over and over.

I insisted that I did not drink. Why was he asking me repeatedly about drinking? It frightened me, and finally, it made me angry. "I don't drink!" I nearly shouted at him, which only made the pounding in my head worse.

"It's okay, Miss, uh, Pattillo. I believe you. But, young lady, someone must have stuck a funnel into your mouth and poured gin into it, because that's what we got when we pumped out your stomach: gin." His eyes were piercing as he continued, "If those firemen and police hadn't brought you right here . . ." His voice trailed off and then he said, "You almost went into alcohol shock. And, of course, you know what that could mean."

"I have no idea."

"Death," he said in a low voice. I stared at him, digesting that information. After a long pause he stood up and went over to the window where he propped his clipboard on the sill and began writing. Death? Me—alcohol? I couldn't believe it.

"I swear to you that I don't know what happened. My friends offered me a strawberry soda and I drank up."

"How much did you drink?" Dr. Ralston had turned from his writing and walked back to the bedside.

"I only remember the first swallow tasting kind of funny for a strawberry soda. But it was so good and once it went down it turned warm in my stomach and made me relax. I hadn't felt that good in a long time. Oh yeah, I did go back for a second glass. You know, like in one of those large iced tea glasses, maybe ten or twelve ounces. Over ice, of course."

"Oh, of course," he replied, his eyes twinkling a little.

Some of the events of that evening were coming back to me, and I was mortified. I was on the roof, standing there in my underwear, in front of everyone! A voice in the back of my head began whispering, *Sinner, sinner, sinner. Repent, for you have sinned.* But it wasn't my fault! I tried to explain to the doctor about being offered a drink and then refusing at first, but he just shook his head and a slight grin came over his face. "You've been had," he said. "Nevertheless, you can't get out of here unless someone over twenty-one signs for your release."

He left the room and I tried to make myself comfortable. Nothing about my body felt normal. My head continued to pound and ache and my arms and legs felt detached. I didn't feel like I could ever eat again. I searched my mind for an adult whom I trusted who would check me out of the hospital. It had to be someone who could keep a secret, someone who would never reveal what had happened. Maybe I should telephone Alison at her work and ask her. But how could I? She was the one who gave me the drink. She must have known exactly what she was doing, otherwise she would have visited, right? Besides, if I telephoned her at work I'd have to wait till the end of the day when she got off.

Wally! That's it, I thought. Maybe he'd be off work and home, or maybe his construction job site was near the hospital. Wally's phone number must be somewhere in my purse. In spite of my splitting headache I found my purse and dumped its contents onto the bed. I prayed that he would rescue me and not tell another living soul what I had done. Of course, the girls at the apartment would know, but they wouldn't dare say a word because it was their nasty prank that had landed me in the hospital.

I couldn't find his number anywhere. I examined every piece of junk I had accumulated in my purse. I had to call Wally. He was my only hope. He'd always said that if I needed him I shouldn't hesitate to telephone. Although he often referred to me variously as "naive," "fresh corn" and the "Vestal Virgin," I felt I could trust him because he had never behaved inappropriately with me, never made any sexual overtures. Over and over again he had said he felt sorry for me because I was out of my element and needed help.

Several times in the year that followed the raid on the Roaring Turtle, Wally had stopped by the residence club, announcing that he'd come to check on me. We had sat across from one another at the cocktail table in the visitors' room, awkwardly making conversation. Some of the other residents had stared at us. They wondered if he were my boyfriend, but more often they would wonder aloud to me how they could get him to be their boyfriend.

Wally had stayed connected with me and with Teddy and the group after we'd all moved out of the residence club, stopping by to party now and then. I went over my situation again, wondering if I really should call him. Then I decided he was my only hope. I'd get in touch with him somehow. And I decided that if I still hadn't been able to reach Wally or come up with another solution by late afternoon, I would break down and phone Teddy.

My headache had subsided enough so that I could watch *As the World Turns*, my favorite television soap opera, and simultaneously I sorted through the contents of my purse for the umpteenth time. I finally found the phone number on the small, green slip of paper Wally had given me. It was the number of his company where he could be reached in the event of an emergency. Even though the paper was crumbling I could still make out the numbers.

Reaching for the phone, I fretted about what I should say to him. I knew I had to get myself discharged from the hospital before Mother Lois discovered my awful sin. If she knew what I had done, she would order me home to Little Rock immediately, and there would be nothing I could do about it. I couldn't survive on my scholarship money and the few odd typing jobs I occasionally took. I needed her support in every way.

I telephoned Wally's company and the company receptionist said that she would contact him at the job site. He called me soon after, and as I explained my predicament I could hear Wally draw a long breath and then let out a loud sigh. Nevertheless, he agreed to come right over. There were tears of gratitude in my eyes and the knot in my stomach loosened just a little. "Thank you, God," I whispered over and over again as I got out of bed carefully to avoid jarring my head. Tossing off the skimpy, white hospital gown, I pulled on the weird pieces of clothing provided by hospital volunteers, all the while being very careful to guard against any sudden movement that might start the furniture whirling.

It took Wally only a half hour to get to the hospital. I had barely gotten myself together when I looked up and saw him standing in the doorway of my hospital room, tall and lean and tan. He was working as the foreman of a construction crew nearby, and he had dirt smudges on his face and streaks of dirt on his shirt. He carried a hard hat in his hand. His huge brown eyes were steely and probing as he looked at me. During the discharge process he was quiet and caring, answering all the doctor's questions. In order to be permitted to check me out he spun some tale about our parents being church friends and his being asked to see after me in the big city. But when we got outside things were different.

"For a Christian girl from Little Rock, you've really strayed off the straight and narrow." Those were the first words he said to me since arriving at the hospital. I got into his red 1959 Corvette and he climbed into the driver's seat.

"Now you got me signing a stack of papers saying I'll make sure you're okay." He was angry as we drove away.

"Thanks a million, Wally, I really appreciate your coming and so fast."

"What the hell did that doc mean when he said, 'Make certain she doesn't drink'? You told me you didn't drink! How many times . . ."

"I don't, Wally. Honestly, I don't drink!" I heard my voice get shrill and loud. He glared at me and I calmed down, modulating my voice to a pleading tone just above a whisper. "It wasn't my fault. I mean, it was an accident."

"Accident? When is getting drunk ever an accident?"

Tears stung my throat and my eyes as I hunkered down into the seat, trying to think of an explanation that would sound believable. As the words came out, I thought, who in the world would believe I could be so stupid, so naive? Who would believe I got drunk from a strawberry soda? I did my best to explain, but as we sat in the car outside my apartment, Wally's expression told me he was disappointed in me.

"Tell me the story once again and we'll start from there." He spoke in an angry, disbelieving tone.

"I swear to you, Wally, I don't drink. It wasn't my fault. I mean, they offered me a drink — strawberry soda, that's what they said." On and on I went, recounting the story as best I could.

"And how did the strawberry soda taste?" he asked.

"What do you mean, taste? It was like strawberry soda."

"Was there anything different about it?"

"Yeah, there was. It was thick and kind of like syrup. And once that sweet, sweet taste went past my tongue and down my throat it got really warm. Like I told the doctor, first it warmed my stomach and then every other part of me. And I felt so relaxed."

"Sloe gin. That wasn't any strawberry soda you got, Miss Hershey Bar. You got ahold of the kind of gin that will kick the ass of the biggest mule with just a few ounces. And you say you had two glasses of the stuff, one right after the other? You're due to be dead."

"I felt dead there for a while," I said.

"Jesus, you're like a lamb set loose in a den of wolves. I'll tell you what, girl, with friends like yours, you don't need enemies."

"Promise you won't tell Teddy," I said as we climbed up the third step to the front door. "You know . . . about how sick I was and everything."

"I'll check with you in a few days," he said as he bent over to chuck me under the chin. He towered over me at six feet four inches with his blond hair cascading down over his forehead. His huge brown eyes looked down at me with amusement and kindness. "Kid, you take care of yourself. Ain't nobody else gonna do it if you don't."

As I entered the apartment on that Monday afternoon following two nights in the hospital, it occurred to me that none of the friends I treasured, the young women from whom I'd craved acceptance, had visited me at the hospital or even called to check on me. The exception was my roommate, Kerry Lynn. She had a good excuse, she was away for another of her weekend trysts with her boyfriend, Fernando. But as for the others, they had no excuse. Their neglect would only make it that much easier for me speak to them frankly, to tell them how much I despised what they had done.

Before I called them together, I told myself that I couldn't go too far in chiding them. After all, where would I go if they totally rejected me? I didn't want to go back to the residence club; I couldn't go back to George and Kay. I didn't want to be isolated again, on my own without some sense of family. But I was bound and determined to set up new guidelines regarding the use of my home, even if it meant being alone and lonely.

Chapter 20

ONLY A TINY NIGHTLIGHT SHONE in my room as I lay in bed with the entire apartment darkened. The neon lights from the hotel and restaurant across the street flickered through the living-room windows, sending sparks of green and yellow and red dancing across the double glass doors of my bedroom.

Wendy called and asked what time the group could visit me. Wally had called them and told them that he'd picked me up at the hospital. She said they wanted to see me and express their concern. I said I did not want them to visit me with their belated condolences and flowers. I announced that I needed time to heal and that I was too tired to speak to anyone.

I must have been lying there for almost an hour when the truth came crashing down on my head. What a far distance I had strayed off the path Mother Lois and Grandmother India wanted me to follow; how very far I must be from God's will for me. Once again, I was stretching myself to belong where I didn't fit in. I had wanted so desperately to be part of a family or some group that seemed like a family. But how far was I willing to go for membership? Wouldn't I ever find a group of my own people to connect with? I decided to figure out a plan. I needed to know where I had failed. Where were the people who would welcome me as the person I intended to be?

The more I tried to fit into the social circles of the black church I had chosen to visit for the purpose of establishing a community, the more I felt I did not belong. There were those marching for equal housing and such, but I no longer wanted to be at the cutting edge of civil rights. Members of the San Francisco chapter of the NAACP invited me to attend meetings and to speak. I felt reluctant because the last thing I wanted was to be cast in the role of a civil rights leader. But by virtue of that refusal, I cut myself off from many black folks I wanted and needed to know. Still, the thought of being in any "struggle" at that time frightened and depressed me.

Other members of the black community whom I'd met in California didn't seem to have the same focus as the black people I had left behind in Little Rock. They were relaxed and pursuing their own personal interests. They were comfortable and seemed to accept things the way they were. When I spoke up, they teased me about being from Little Rock. Some northern blacks felt superior to southern blacks because they didn't live under the rules of the segregated South; they saw southern blacks as ignorant and willing to be oppressed. They would sometimes tell me that I had a lot to learn about using my freedom, about being a Californian.

Now, lying in the dark alone, I felt a tear stream down my cheek. Could it be that I had not yet found my place—the place God had intended for me? It surely wasn't in this Nob Hill apartment where other black people were forbidden to live. If Grandmother India could come again and speak to me she would be so upset because my San Francisco situation was similar to my living situation in Santa Rosa. She would say that I was once again surrounded by white people in a white world; she would have wanted me in a more integrated setting. I could hear her voice telling me, "You always got to keep connected to your roots and who you really are." Besides, she would know that for more than a year her shawl had been somewhere in the Roaring Turtle, that place she would have called a honky tonk. Furthermore, with all the parties in my apartment, she would say I was living a honky tonk life.

What would she say about my latest episode—drunk and perched on top of a roof in my underwear? Would my tearful prayer whispered aloud summon her? I hoped it would. Maybe she could tell me how to find forgiveness. The soft whimpers of my crying echoed across the empty room. When a half hour passed and there was no sign of her, I turned on a light and took out the new blank book I had purchased in the hospital gift shop to use as a diary. I felt myself overflowing with words. I could write a letter to Grandmother, to God, to myself. I had to take charge and find my path once more. I was lost and lonely. In my diary I wrote:

> *Please forgive me Dear Lord for my sins and my not being conscious of You and Your will for me. I am lost in all the ticker tape fun of being on my own. I am lost in my own desire to be a part of something—not to be alone.*
>
> *But even though I sometimes struggle to belong—to be a part of this group that lives its life so unlike the way I've been taught, I know it is very wrong for me.*
>
> *Is there no place of welcome for me which requires no pretending, no taking on of bad habits, no stretching? Where do I belong? Please help me.*

I would have to learn once again that I must be lonely until the right situation appeared. I must have the patience of Job. After all, Mother Lois was pinching pennies at home in order to send me money. Her frugality and the money she sent made up the difference between my scholarship allowance and the actual cost of living and attendance at school. I owed her the respect of keeping a Christian home.

When Kerry Lynn returned late that Monday night, I told her she could either agree with my wishes not to have alcohol and constant partying in our apartment or I would move out. She agreed, explaining her own discontent with the partying, and so together we laid down the law to the others.

I was grateful for the fact that Kerry Lynn did at least half of the talking to our group. That way they wouldn't blame the change of rules totally on me and, as a result, exclude me from the group. Beyond all else, I was loath to admit that being left alone was my greatest fear. Now, I could still count on some acceptable social contact with them, like our Sunday brunches, without worrying about their rejection.

They didn't visit us at all for the first week after our talk, and we became lonely for girl talk over dessert or the pajama parties in front of the television. But after that they slowly drifted back. The good news was that they didn't take liberties by bringing in liquor or scheduling parties in our apartment. For the remainder of July and August, I devoted the evenings to my studies. I went to the library to work and to museums or church gatherings. I also spent a lot of time watching television news and reading newspapers. I was very lonely, but I used the extra time for Bible reading and steady churchgoing. I didn't know if I felt forgiven for my sin, but I felt free and more like the person I was meant to be.

At this time, I discovered Grace Cathedral. The magnificent Episcopalian building atop Nob Hill with its grand stone interior, vaulted ceilings and colorful stained-glass windows bespoke the presence of God at every Mass. I was filled with reverence at the services and they also offered an anonymous kind of experience because the crowds were so large and no one knew my name. Unlike the churches in Little Rock or in the Fillmore district of San Francisco or even the mostly white church near the college, people didn't rush up at the end of a service at Grace Cathedral demanding names and telephone numbers of newcomers so they could urge membership in the congregation.

Instead, the white-robed priests stood after the service at the enormous doors of the cathedral; they bowed and smiled at members of the congregation and extended a handshake, but they didn't pry. The ritual of the Episcopalian service appealed to me, and I felt compelled to learn more about it. I began to look forward to Sunday services and the enveloping music from the enormous organ that resonated through my body.

Hints of autumn interrupted October's balmy days. It was my second year at college. I was carrying a heavy load of classes this fall semester so I spent even more time doing homework, and Teddy's group said I was boring. Kerry Lynn started the teasing and the others continued to tease me because of my ladylike dressing habits. I would put on a girdle, stockings and a nice gabardine dress to go to the corner store on Saturday morning. When I donned more monochromatic outfits with gloves and a hat for church on Sunday, they giggled. "Church lady," they would say.

Everyone continued pondering how I could get a date. I was nineteen years old and everybody, including me, thought that I was probably destined to become an old maid. There wasn't anyone with whom I could discuss all my fears because my friends had beaus. They took risks I wasn't willing to take. I was looking for a male who would court me and wait until after marriage for serious lovemaking.

In any event, few if any of my friends seemed to care about what was happening in the world, but I did. On October 6, 1961, President Kennedy pledged nuclear fallout protection for every American because the Soviets were testing atomic bombs. I drew a deep sigh of relief. We were all now more conscious of needing shelters. Additionally, we had more to fear because of the split developing between the Chinese and the Soviets. On the 23rd, China's Chou En-Lai walked out of a Communist World Congress in Moscow. It wasn't so long ago that I was worrying about the KKK and hostile white folks. Now, I was worrying about the state of the world.

Keeping abreast of the news had served me well in my classes where the professors often based their discussions on current events. I continued to take sociology classes, which had become more and more appealing to me, along with astronomy and economics.

The holidays were coming and Mother had called, once again urging me to come home. I wrote in my diary:

> *I don't want to go home—not even for Thanksgiving. Mother Lois says I am becoming a person she doesn't recognize in my habits and desires.*

> *I hate Little Rock, and the thought of spending a holiday with people eating and talking about Little Rock oppression and how we keep in our place depresses me.*

Meanwhile, as the holidays drew near, Kerry Lynn was in our apartment less and less. I was even more alone since she had fallen madly in love. Her affair was a secret except to me. She talked of making love for the first time—of how sweet it had been with her boyfriend. As I listened to her, lovemaking didn't sound dirty and sinful like the conversations the other girls had about their sexual activities. Kerry Lynn's love for Fernando seemed pure and they hoped to be married soon. Although I knew it wasn't right to have an intimate physical relationship before marriage, I didn't condemn her because I felt somehow that her circumstances were different. I decided I had to pray for her adultery to keep her from going to hell.

The love of her life was trying desperately to get a divorce. Left behind in their native war-torn country, his wife was apparently unwilling to give him up. Kerry Lynn would chew over the details of this drama with me, expecting that I could help her solve the problems. I couldn't, but she was my best friend, so I listened. I appreciated her tact in not discussing all the sexual details of her love affair.

At Christmas I went up to Santa Rosa to stay with the McCabes, this time for a whole week. During our usual mealtime debates, George was discussing how the president was sending U.S. troops to a place called Vietnam. It was a topic on the mind of every thinking American. He explained the history of that country, and argued how far-fetched the premise of our involvement was.

I had studied so hard for my extra load of classes that semester that it felt good to get away. I slipped into the household routine easily, becoming a member of the family once more. We celebrated the holidays with typical enthusiasm and I delighted in being part of a home where current events were discussed on a daily basis. I also visited the Bronsons, the black family that had been so welcoming to me in Santa Rosa. Their warmth enveloped me.

Mother Lois was upset that I wasn't returning to Little Rock for the holidays, but I explained to her how hard it was for me to cope with the prospect of being afraid for my safety, of being oppressed. Carlotta and Jeff were back inside Central, which meant restlessness among the segregationists. At the same time, our tight budgets made the cost of an airline ticket a big issue, so we agreed to speak often on the telephone, exchange handmade gifts and pray simultaneously every day at noon for ten days.

When I went back to San Francisco in January, I had more time to relax but it was lonely. Kerry Lynn was still away most weekends, and I spent little time with Teddy's group. However, when the spring semester started I plunged back into my studies. On those rare occasions when Kerry Lynn did stay home, we spent time watching television together and speculating about what President Kennedy might do next about the Vietnam situation. I told her about school, where the issue of Vietnam occupied more and more campus debates.

Kerry Lynn and I were a rapt audience for Jackie Kennedy's television tour of the White House on February 14, 1962. We both swore that we would be ladies and dress as much like her on special occasions as our meager budgets would allow. Now, during school days, I mostly wore casual corduroy jumpers Mother made for me in my favorite blue, purple and rose colors, along with my trench coat and sneakers or saddle shoes. Only on weekends did I revert to the Sunday church look. I continued the habit of rolling my long hair each and every night in order to maintain the neat, controlled coif Mother Lois favored. Kerry Lynn and I were also determined to speak as much like the First Lady as we possibly could. We knew we were kidding ourselves, but what of it? It felt good to mimic such a fabulous person.

On a warm and rainy weekend in March, a sad cloud floated above our household as Kerry Lynn returned home from her date with Fernando with a red, tear-stained face. She sat in the middle of the bed eating voraciously, consuming peanut butter and crackers, cheese and noodle soup, pickles and Oreo cookies and drinking both milk and soda. She had a pencil-like figure and I'd never before seen her eat more than a bird. When I asked what was going on, she looked me squarely in the eye and said, "I'm pregnant and that's all I want to say."

Over the next few days I watched her bury herself in mountains of food and weep endless tears. In my diary I wrote:

Mother was right. No lovemaking before marriage, no matter what. Kerry Lynn is pregnant. It's so very sad. She and her boyfriend have decided on an abortion. But she must wait before it's done. They will travel to another place where it is legal. I couldn't listen to the details because abortion is such a huge, huge sin. But then maybe using those new birth control pills that prevent babies is even a bigger sin.

I am sorry to see her suffer and cry so much. She eats like it was her last supper. I know I can't allow a boy to make love to me because I am not ready to face all these serious questions about real love and sex without marriage and babies and whether or not to have an abortion. I'm so glad I'm the Vestal Virgin. Yea, Melba.

Kerry Lynn and Fernando went away to get the abortion and when she returned home, she was subdued and pale. The first night I sat and cried with her at the kitchen table, yet it was a relief to have the whole thing be over. As the days passed by it was obvious that Kerry Lynn and Fernando were not as much in love any more, because they seldom saw each other. Kerry Lynn was not the same person. Many times I saw her sitting alone with a sad expression on her face. We spent more time together once again, watching television as we ate the newly invented TV dinners and debated political issues.

Just after Defense Secretary McNamara announced American soldiers were exchanging fire with the Viet Cong, on a chilly Friday evening in late March, I returned to the apartment from the college library. I was preoccupied with my assignment as I entered the smoke-filled room to find Teddy, Mandy, Alison and Wendy along with several army soldiers in olive drab. They were eating pizza and the music was so loud it made my ears hurt. I was stunned to see that they had broken their agreement. The group had begun to spend more time with Kerry Lynn and me at the apartment, but now they were up to their old tricks. I was angry, but also momentarily amused, because I thought their guests seemed to be a cut above their usual dates. That night the men in the room were wearing the same uniforms as the solders of the 101st Airborne who had guarded me in Little Rock. Maybe their new dates might have that same military character that I had admired, unlike those unkempt swabbies from the Navy that the group usually dated.

Wendy said they had come to introduce one of the soldier boys to Kerry Lynn to cheer her up. His name was Matt. When Wendy and Kerry Lynn insisted on introducing him to me, I only looked at him because he wore the uniform of my former 101st Airborne guard at Central High School and he resembled Audie Murphy, a World War II war hero with a cute Texas accent, who was currently starring in a movie about his life. I hardly bothered making eye contact with him or saying anything more than "Hello" before I told my friends to turn the music down. I headed for my room, slammed the door behind me and turned on the radio news to block out the noise. Kerry Lynn knocked at my door to tell me that she and Fernando were leaving for the weekend. I didn't want to be heavy-handed with the group without her support. I was hoping this wasn't the start of more and more parties. Would I have to warn them again? Instead of telling them by myself that they could not stay, I put cotton in my ears and fell asleep.

At 7:00 the next morning, a Saturday, I was awakened by the ring of our doorbell. I didn't answer and after a moment there was a loud banging on the front door. Fearful that the landlady would have a fit, I got up, grabbing my yellow robe to cover my nightgown and raced to the door. The soldier from the night before, Matt, was standing at the door as though he'd been invited.

"Can I help you?" I asked.

"Do you remember me?" he smiled.

"Yeah, sure, you're the guy who came over for Kerry Lynn, but she's not here. She's gone to Carmel for the weekend. I'll tell her that you dropped by." I slammed the door, latched the chain and turned to walk away. He knocked loudly again. I unlocked the chain and stood in total silence with the door narrowly cracked open.

"I really came to see you," he said in a calm voice with a western drawl.

"Me?" I opened the door a little wider. His freckles seemed to be much more apparent because he was obviously nervous and looked almost ashen. His huge, pleading green eyes matched his drab olive uniform. As he looked down at me, his eyes held mine. His gaze was unrelenting as he said in a rush of words, as though he were compelled to say them quickly or not at all, "I'd like you to come to breakfast with me. I thought we would get an early start and then go to Golden Gate Park, but if you don't like that we could ride a cable car or do whatever you want. I just want to get to know you better."

"You're kidding."

"Nope. Not at all. I got on the six o'clock bus from Fort Barry army base over in Sausalito just to be here at seven so I'd catch you before you got other things going for the day."

"I already said it's Kerry Lynn you want and she's gone," I replied.

"It's you I came to see."

"Why me?

"Because I wanna be your friend—spend time getting to know you."

"I don't date white boys."

"Who said anything about a date? The girls tell me you're from Little Rock. I've never met anybody from the South before. You can tell me what it's like. I grew up in the southwest where I didn't get to know any colored people."

"Like I said, Kerry Lynn's gone and I'm going back to bed. She'll be back tomorrow." I slammed the door hard, latched the chain, went back to my room and pulled the covers over my head. This was my day to sleep in and nobody could take it away from me.

Chapter 21

LATER THAT SAME MORNING, I WAS awakened from my deep sleep by a loud, jarring sound. I sat straight up in bed and looked at the alarm clock. Why was it making that awful noise? I had set it for 10:00 but it was only 9:00 A.M. There it was again, that horrible banging sound. Was someone building something in the alleyway? The landlady hadn't left a note. No, it was someone banging loudly on my front door. I grabbed my yellow robe and moved as fast as my heart was pounding. Opening the door, I looked up once again into the freckled face of the Audie Murphy lookalike from the night before.

"Is that enough sleep?" Matt said to me with an innocent look of curiosity.

"I thought I told you to go away."

"No—I'm not leaving until you come with me to breakfast. I'm gonna keep pounding and pounding on the door and I might even march in the hallway and sing my Irish songs until I convince you to get dressed and share this morning with me."

"That's blackmail."

"Yep. But there seems to be no other way."

"I won't give in to blackmail. You were sent here to be Kerry Lynn's date. Leave me alone!" I shouted through the closing door as I slammed it shut and secured the chain.

"Okay, have it your way." He started pounding again—loud, obnoxious pounding that would surely irk the landlady.

Despite my adamant feelings against dating white men, I wasn't willing to lose my apartment. I had to do something. I could call the police but they might ignore my complaint or, worse yet, considering the incident on the roof a while back, they might arrest me. I was stuck.

"All right already," I said through the closed door. "Give me a bit to get dressed."

"No problem. I've been waiting two hours for you, what's a few minutes more?"

I was determined to be so rude and unpleasant that this Matt person would never, ever want to have another meal with me for any reason. I jumped out of the shower, not making any real effort to perfect my makeup, and put on a plain, casual school skirt and jacket. As I looked in the mirror, I noticed my weight had gone down somewhat, but I was certainly not to be considered thin. Maybe my ample body would turn him off. I was standing in the doorway twenty minutes later.

As we walked down Sutter Street in the morning sunlight, Matt continued his chatter, telling me about his work and the army base across the Golden Gate Bridge where he was stationed. He was a military policeman in a special group that trained and lived with patrol dogs that could perform security tasks. I said nothing. Instead, I took deep breaths and rolled my eyes at him. After a while my silence must have let him know that I wasn't pleased to be with him under duress. Nevertheless, he continued being pleasant.

Sitting at the window of a popular breakfast café drinking orange juice, I tried my best to remain silent or to speak only when I could think of something obnoxious and rude to say. I also stared outside at the sidewalk tourists and the passing traffic, ignoring him. Matt was utterly charming. He insisted that I look at a picture of his dog. He seemed so proud of himself, of his duties and his dog. He started asking me questions, questions that compelled me to speak.

"Now, see those people over there? They're staring at us. What do you think they're thinking?"

"That we shouldn't be together because you're white and I'm black."

"Well, maybe. They've sure been looking hard."

"Shall we leave? Suppose they come over here and say something embarrassing?" I suddenly felt threatened by their stares.

"Naw, don't worry about it. I'll take care of you."

He no longer seemed as nervous as when he first came to my door. Maybe he was feeling victorious because I had given in to him. *I should have said no; maybe I should leave now.*

With huge, seductive green eyes, reddish-brown hair and freckles and an erect, military bearing, he was a picture of self-confidence that I didn't feel entirely comfortable with but couldn't ignore. *Fine,* I thought to myself, *what harm could a little breakfast with this guy be?* Besides, I was hungry and this was so much better than spending another Saturday morning alone eating on that tattered wooden tray in front of the television.

By the end of our meal I was talking more than I had ever thought I would. Matt was such a good listener, never taking his eyes away from mine. At times the intensity of his focus seemed to bore deep into me, to some place that no one else had ever been. I felt as though he was closely examining all parts of me. No one had ever sat so utterly still and given me such absolutely undivided attention the way this man was doing.

After breakfast when he invited me to go for a walk, I surprised myself when I agreed. We walked through the heart of downtown San Francisco, past the Emporium on Market Street, and circled back to Powell and Market where we took a cable car over the hills and down to Fisherman's Wharf. We walked the waterfront and talked about everything and about nothing. I had seldom felt so comfortable with another person. It was as if I had known him forever.

In the late afternoon, we sat in wooden chairs eating cracked crab at a sidewalk café that overlooked the water. By then, his huge eyes with their intensity no longer frightened me. Instead, I gazed into them, welcoming his attention, which felt like a warm and cozy blanket. He made me feel as though what I had to say was more important to him than anything in the world. He listened to me so at-tentively and when my thoughts had spilled out, I found myself ea-gerly waiting for his response, which sometimes took a moment. He worded his replies as though he were taking great pains to select just the perfect thing to say—the thing that would comfort me and con-firm my own dignity and value.

After lunch, he asked if I wanted to take a taxi home or maybe we could walk by the water and then up to my apartment. I had to admit to myself that I chose the walk because that would mean I'd have more time with him. I felt so safe walking beside him. He always walked on the outside, careful to shelter me from traffic. When it was time to cross streets he took my arm, protecting me from any deci-sions about whether to halt or walk on. I could relax and he would take care of me. I would think about needing a drink of water and he would suggest we take a rest stop. I would feel a little tired from the heat and the sun and he would suggest we seek shade. It was a feel-ing I had never before experienced. It was like being wrapped in my mother's arms, knowing all would be well.

We walked all up and down San Francisco as the late afternoon sunlight shadowed the hills. I continued to pour out more words about myself, my past, my future and my current life. I felt embar-rassed that I was talking too much, but I couldn't stop. It was as if something in him insisted on knowing everything about me so our connection could be forged with speed. He just listened and often paused and turned toward me to ask a question, confirm my opinion or just to say, "Yes," and agree with a feeling or an action I'd taken.

When we arrived back at the apartment building, it was eight o'clock. He stood as I turned my key in the lock and then insisted on walking me up the stairs to my front door.

"Well," I said, feeling embarrassed, "I guess I've talked your ear off."

"No, I've enjoyed hearing what you had to say," he replied.

"Thank you, I've had a wonderful Saturday. I'll tell Kerry Lynn that you'll call her," I said.

"No," he said, emphatically, his eyes holding mine. "Don't say anything to Kerry Lynn. It's too late for that. I'll call you tomorrow."

Astonished by his presumption, I didn't say anything. I just stood there in the doorway and watched him walk down the stairs. Once inside I slumped down into the green velvet chair that reminded me so much of the one Grandmother India had in our living room when I was growing up. I sat there motionless for the next hour, going over and over the details of our day together in my mind. I found myself smiling and cherishing the comfortable warmth I'd felt with him.

Early Sunday morning the phone rang. It was Matt. He said he'd go to church with me or meet me afterward, whatever pleased me. That was the beginning of a chain of visits from Matt that I couldn't find the strength to say no to. After each visit I swore to myself that I would not see him again, but found myself unable to keep my promises. Apprehensive about his white skin, I was at the same time drawn to his kind manner, his strong silence and willingness to listen. For hours on end that spring and early summer, we walked and talked in Golden Gate Park. Mostly, I talked and he listened. I was surprised and annoyed at myself that I felt compelled to tell him intimate details about my experiences at Central High School in Little Rock.

"I wish I could make all this up to you," he said. "I'll do my best."

His responses always let me know how much he cared about what I was saying, from the way his eyes brimmed with tears when I explained how some people treated me at Central High, to the way he squeezed my hand or touched my arm when I was recounting how sad I had been. There was no doubt in me that he was listening with his heart and soul. His undivided attention was as seductive as his soft-spoken western drawl. I was hypnotized by his personality, so comfortable, so self-confident and yet so relaxed. He spoke few words and yet always they seemed to be the words I needed to hear.

I felt I could only talk to Kerry Lynn about Matt. I trusted her to be caring and sympathetic and I told her what a dilemma he posed for me. She wouldn't listen to my repeated vows that I would never see him again. Instead, she pointed out that if I really believed all that Bible stuff about everybody being God's child, what was wrong with being with Matt since we were both God's children?

After the very first day I spent with Matt, I began losing weight. I no longer craved junk food to fill the empty spot inside my soul. To my astonishment, the emptiness had been filled by thoughts of Matt, daydreams of Matt and the constant anticipation of being together again and wondering what would happen next. I completed my homework faster and disciplined every other aspect of my life in order to be available and at my best when Matt phoned.

Waves of consternation poured over me every time I thought about having Matt in the same room with Teddy or my other friends. They were beautiful white girls and I was not. The thought that they would take him away, that I would never get to spend time with him, always threatened me. I became nervous and manipulative, altering our meeting times, seeing Matt away from my apartment and doing whatever it took to keep him away from their unexpected visits.

It wasn't that I didn't think myself pretty or smart. After all, there had been that headline in a Cincinnati newspaper that said, "The Fox Is in Town" as a tagline beneath my picture at age sixteen when I had toured with the Little Rock Nine. Several periodicals made mention of my Jayne Mansfield–like figure and my pretty, dimpled face. But the girls in Teddy's group were so forward and so sexy, so seductive and adult, and I was not. They knew how to treat men and how to make men like them. I felt so naive in contrast to them.

Even after all the dates we'd had, and all my insecurity about losing him, I still did not admit that he was anything other than a friend. Whenever he said things like, "What should we do for our Saturday night date?" I'd say, "We're not dating, remember? You promised."

"Oops! You're right. This is not dating. We're just working out race relations," he'd reply.

I had begun to feel something for Matt that I could not describe or discuss. I didn't even share it with Kerry Lynn or Kay McCabe. I was afraid to tell a white person, even a close friend, that I might be in love with Matt. I was afraid that they might be opposed because of our racial differences. And I couldn't confide in my mother. She would be horrified. I could hear her asking me how I could get myself in such a predicament after all the prejudice, all the harshness I had endured from white people. I wondered the same thing. How was it possible to care for a white person the way I knew I cared for Matt?

How I longed to have someone close enough with whom I could discuss my feelings. How I needed someone whom I could question and who could help me begin to understand what had overtaken me. I was smitten, in a trance, in Shangri-La—I didn't know what. But, for certain, I was not myself. I had become obsessed with wanting to touch Matt, hug Matt and feel his arms around me as I kissed him. It was something I thought about day and night. I had to pray myself conscious—pray myself back to the path God had chosen for me.

At the same time I was frightened that he *would* try to kiss me or hug me or be romantic. Four months had passed and he continued to be a perfect gentleman. He never once said or did anything inappropriate. He never even tried to hold my hand in a romantic way, only reaching out for me in order to guide me across the street or to assist me up hills or stairs.

May had come and gone and I had passed my finals, not because I was focused on study but because I had studied as fast and as hard as I could every single day so I could have my nights with Matt. During classes I had begun unconsciously scribbling his name over and over again, doodling at the edge of my papers. Now, whenever he had guard duty and was forced to remain on base for the weekend or had guard duty for two nights in a row, I took to my bed with a sick heart and stayed there waiting for his phone call. My greatest fear was that he would go away and the incredible warm glow he had installed in my heart would vanish with him. When I was with him I felt as though I had swallowed the sun with all of its bright light. Joy was not a big enough word to describe what I felt when I heard his voice on the telephone or his knock at the door.

Every activity I undertook, other than those relating to Matt, was done on automatic pilot. Not only did I continue to study more efficiently, but I completed tasks faster, kept a clean house, was fastidious with my hair and wardrobe, exercised and most of all I never, never had the slightest urge to overeat. Without effort, I slimmed down by some twenty pounds.

When I wasn't with Matt, I longed to be with him. I fretted over my increasingly undeniable desire to spend time with him and my increasingly undeniable consternation about dating a white man. How could I care about him, want him, desire him in a way I had never

ever experienced before, after all those white men in Little Rock and at Central High had treated me so badly?

How could I be such a bad daughter? A bad Christian? I would fret. Still, after all the inner conflict, I would wait on pins and needles for his phone call, vowing to say no when he asked me to go out. But then when I heard his voice I would melt inside, saying, "Yes, yes, yes."

Excitement would fill every vein in my body in the hours I spent waiting for his arrival. My all-consuming concern was to be dressed in the right outfit with the right makeup, standing in the right place.

I felt protected and enveloped by his kindness, his caring manner and macho, muscular presence. I was most comforted by his casual dominance over things that frightened me. When people stared at us together, he would say, "Let's give them something to talk about." He would put his arm around my shoulders and draw me close, but he would release me immediately after they turned away.

When I was alarmed over upsetting the landlady he would say, "So what? I'll get you another apartment." No matter what my worry he would quiet it with a solution. On one of our outings to the beach for a Saturday picnic, I vowed to spend the day searching for reasons to hate Matt. Despite my dislike of picnicking outside, Matt coaxed me down a sheer rock cliff to a deserted beach. To my surprise he was able to make me comfortable, and I had such a pleasant time that I forgot my vow.

Every moment of every day Matt was on my mind. I began to have little control over my feelings. Whenever the negative voice of my mother or grandmother entered my head, bombarding me with their criticisms, I found myself talking aloud or huddled on my bed, crying.

I felt catapulted into an unfamiliar place by my feelings for a white man which were so totally out of control. How could I imagine holding and even kissing him? My God! I felt tortured. Once again, I had begun praying hard to have him taken off my mind. I asked for forgiveness and asked God to take Matt away, knowing that I would be devastated if that came to pass.

By August, we were seeing each other at least five times a week.

Increasingly, I was feeling wanted and loved by him and yet he was not making any physical advances toward me. I had distanced myself from Teddy and the other girls, rarely seeing them, and I reveled in the times when Kerry Lynn would go away for the weekend. Then Matt would come over Friday, Saturday and Sunday and we would play chess, make tuna sandwiches, watch television and take our familiar walks over every foot of Nob Hill.

One Saturday evening in late summer, Teddy and the girls arrived with several other men without any notice, saying they had been wondering about me. Matt was at the apartment with me, but I didn't want to be impolite and so I allowed them to push their way in. Offering them a soda was like a signal giving them permission to crank up the stereo, which they didn't hesitate to do. Mandy was digging in the kitchen cupboards for chips and one of the guys headed out the door to the corner store to buy more food. Matt said I should relax, that it might be fun to have a social evening, but I was nervous about the girls. Not all of them had dates.

Midway through the evening, as I came out of the kitchen carrying a tray of glasses filled with soda, I turned the corner into the living room to see Wendy nestling close to Matt. He seemed to enjoy her advances, snuggling with her and murmuring to her in a low voice. I set the tray down hard on the coffee table in front of them and went to my room. Choking back tears, I felt as if my heart were crumbling into a thousand pieces. After ten minutes or so, Matt came into my room and put his hand on my shoulder.

"Something wrong?"

"No. What could be wrong?"

"You look like you're upset."

"No. Not me."

"Then you don't care if I date Wendy?"

"No, of course not, she's white and a very pretty girl."

"Liar."

"I'm not." I couldn't hold back the tears. They were streaming down my cheeks as he stood me up and turned me toward him.

"Sooooo . . . you were saying you don't care if I date," he paused and then went on, "but you're lying. Your secret's out. You feel the same way about me as I do about you."

"I do not!" I protested as he pulled me into his arms and just held me for what seemed like forever. He dried the tears on my face with his hand and then held me there, looking deep into my eyes, deeper than anyone had ever gone.

"Don't you know? Don't you realize? I'm gonna marry you," he said, smiling, chucking me under the chin with his fingers.

Chapter 22

"MARRY YOU?" I WHISPERED THROUGH my tears. I was stunned to think that he would honor me with his name. It meant he must feel the same way about me as I did about him. Nestled in Matt's arms I was so confused. Hearing his comforting words and the promise of marriage made me want to cling to him forever and ever.

But, if I were going to be committed to all the things Mother Lois had taught me—finish college before marriage, marry within your race, always be honest with your parents about your intentions—then I should be running in the opposite direction. Also, Mother Lois preached often about how I should marry a professional man, a doctor, lawyer or teacher. But being held by Matt was everything I had waited for: to feel his heart beating next to mine, to feel the strength of his muscular chest and arms enfolding me.

Nevertheless, I reasoned that feeling the way I did about him, my confusion and weakness, must be the work of the devil. I had to enjoy his arms right now and then be willing to put him out of my life.

How could someone like me, who had been in the headlines as a civil rights heroine, someone who had been physically beaten and whose spirit had been bruised by whites, now turn the other cheek and make a white man her husband?

"Don't talk that way, Matt." I broke away from him. "Look, you'd better leave now, please." I steeled myself against the pleasure of his touch and smile. He had to be the enemy. I thought back to those mobs of Little Rock white people who shared his skin color, their faces contorted, their voices shouting "nigger" as they made ready to hang me and my mother. They'd been ready to kill me if I went to their high school.

Suddenly, the faces of George and Kay flooded into my mind. They were white people whom I loved. Yes, indeed, they had been so loving, so kind to me. That was proof positive that it was all right, that I could love somebody like Matt. But I couldn't have a white husband—I had to resist this devil thought. It felt like different parts of me were battling to take control.

"I mean what I said. I'm gonna marry you."

"We can't! What would people say? What would they do to us?"

"Don't worry about that. I'll protect you."

"Don't be crazy."

"Crazy would be staying apart just because of what people might say or do."

"Please, Matt, go now. We'll talk about this later."

"I don't want to leave you like this, but I have to go. I'm on duty tonight."

"No, it's fine. Please, please."

"All right, I'll go. I'll call you tomorrow and we'll get this straight."

When the door slammed behind him I felt a pain cut across the middle of my body as though lightning had cut me in half. I doubled over in tears, trying to stifle my sobs so that the girls in the living room would not hear. Putting out the light, I climbed into bed with all my clothes on. They would get the hint. They knew very well when either Kerry Lynn and I left the room and turned out our bedroom lights, visible from the living room, that it signaled an official "See you later, alligator."

Even though I knew my decision never to see Matt again was firm, I cried most of the night. I slept briefly and fitfully and when I awakened the next morning, I must have looked terrible because Kerry Lynn insisted that I phone the doctor. Protesting that I would be just fine, I drank soda water in an attempt to settle my stomach. I felt as if nothing would make me feel whole again and I doubted if anything would ever be right with me. It felt as though someone had cut my heart out. Somehow I had allowed Matt to become my pulse, the passion that gave me reason to do and be. I couldn't be with him, but the idea of life without him was almost more painful than I could bear.

When Matt's first phone call came, I made Kerry Lynn say I had gone away. I had been forced to tell Kerry Lynn the truth because she could clearly see that I was extremely upset. However, I felt that no one else should know. Matt insisted that she tell him where I was. She merely said I had gone away to think—that I had gone up to Kay and George's house in Santa Rosa. The truth was that I couldn't tell them or anybody what was happening to me. How could I say what I knew now to be true? I loved Matt with all my heart.

By five o'clock in the afternoon he had called three times. Then he began calling every hour on the hour, telling Kerry Lynn that he had pulled guard duty for the remainder of the weekend through Tuesday evening and that I must telephone him as soon as possible. *What a relief,* I thought. *At least I don't have to deal with him face to face for the next few days.* He was on duty and I would bury myself and my heartache in my school schedule.

On Wednesday morning at 8:00 A.M., Kerry Lynn reported that Matt was camping on my doorstep. I was in back in summer school and I'd expected him to come over to my apartment to try to talk to me after he got off guard duty. In order to avoid him, I'd left the night before and slept at Teddy's place so I could be free to leave for my classes. Since he had never been to Teddy's apartment, Matt had no way of knowing that I was only two blocks away. He hounded Kerry Lynn, following her to work and back home again, threatening to hound her further if she didn't tell him where I was.

I will always remember that week of my life as a living hell. I was certain I was burning in fire and brimstone. While Matt continued to camp out on my doorstep, I camped out in my girlfriends' apartment two blocks away, eating junk food, watching television, listening to their loud music and their constant chatter. They'd figured out that something was wrong in my life but they couldn't tell exactly what and I didn't take them into my confidence. They took turns making up stories, and giving me advice based on their scenarios. I was growing increasingly irritated and falling behind in my homework.

By the following Sunday, one week after I had parted with him, I had cut a few days of classes to sit around their house in my bathrobe, munching on candy bars and corn chips. Not only was I heartsick, feeling that old, familiar emptiness again somewhere deep inside, but I finally made myself physically sick from eating junk food. I was depressed over my food binge, and my slipping commitment to school.

One week later, convinced that Matt was by now resigned to the fact that we wouldn't be seeing each other, I packed my things and headed up the block for home. I wasn't inside the apartment five minutes before the doorbell rang. At the front door stood Matt, sparkling eyes and smile, and spit-polish clean with a fresh haircut and a sad face in spite of the smile. I looked into those eyes that always appeared like liquid emeralds and I wanted to drop through the floor. What was I going to do about the terrible gnawing inside, the feeling that urged me to reach out and welcome him to me?

"You can run but you can't hide, Melba. I'm in this for the long haul. I have all the patience in the world."

"No, Matt, we can't."

"Can't what, be friends? I'll do whatever you want. Just let me in and we can talk about it."

"We can't get married."

"Fine, I'll never mention marriage again."

"What good will that do? I know now what you're thinking."

"And I know what you're thinking. But all I want is to be with you."

"I can't."

"You have no choice. I'm not going away, not ever. I'll camp out here in the hallway, I'll pound on the door. I might have to leave when I draw guard duty, but on my days off I'll be back."

Taking a deep breath and giving myself over to the voices inside urging me to surrender, I gave in to him and in to my heart's desire.

"You win. But remember, we're just friends."

"Call it whatever you want. But don't leave me."

I turned away so he couldn't see how awful I looked or the tears flooding down my face. I'd been grief-stricken for two weeks, my eyes were puffy and the junk food I'd consumed was beginning to show in my complexion and at my waistline.

Matt had brought a duck and other groceries with him for our dinner. I couldn't tell him I had never cooked a duck, but I was determined to do it all by myself. Besides, I wanted to keep away from him until I could master my almost uncontrollable urge to embrace him. I sent him into the living room to watch television while I cooked.

I tried hard to figure out the instructions for cooking duck. When I couldn't, I phoned Mother Lois. She sounded lonely and was very curious about why I was cooking dinner for the girls. I had lied, but I couldn't tell her that I was cooking for Matt. She didn't even know about him. I'd never revealed to my mother that I was seeing a white man.

With dinner in the oven, I was proud of myself. I had followed Mother's instructions to the letter and everything looked good. The rice wasn't sticking, I was certain the string beans would not be overcooked, the canned biscuits were rising and the duck was roasting.

"I think we ought to check the duck," Matt said, rushing suddenly into the kitchen. "I'm getting a strange smell."

Lifting the lid of the roasting pan, we were startled to see soapsuds bubbling up all around the duck. Soapsuds rose up and dripped over the sides of the pan and fell sizzling onto the hot surfaces of the oven door, the oven rack and the bottom of the oven. The suds were mixed with a combination of pan juices and grease from the duck. All of a sudden small flames shot up from the pan.

I was momentarily paralyzed by astonishment, but Matt was quick to grab for a pot with a handle as he shouted to me to get some baking soda, all the baking soda that I could get my hands on. He doused the flames with baking soda and then, using the pot, he poured water over everything. We stood side by side watching as grayish suds dripped onto the floor.

"Do you want to tell me about the suds, Mel?" he said in a calm, sweet voice with a sympathetic expression.

"Well, Mom said to wash the duck. So I did. I gave it a good going over."

"Wash the duck? How?"

"I put it in some Tide and did what she said." I was mortified at the outcome of my meal. I wanted so badly for Matt to think me a good cook, and now I was so embarrassed that I couldn't even look at him.

"Tide?"

"Well, she said wash it thoroughly."

"Oh, Mel," and he burst into laughter.

"Maybe she didn't mean that I should use Tide?" I asked and finally I began to giggle uncontrollably.

That broke the ice with us. We cleaned up the mess and went out for hamburgers. Our strange friendship was rejuvenated and that elixir that filled up the emptiness inside me was replenished. I stopped eating junk food immediately, no longer cried myself to sleep, started studying again and told myself that, for now, I had no choice: Matt had to be in my life. He was as necessary to me as breathing. I made vows to pray about it and wean myself off him slowly. I was like a baby giving up the bottle it depended on for its very life.

Eight months after our friendship began, on October 1, 1962, a black man, James Meredith, was battling to enroll in the segregationist stronghold, the University of Mississippi. The University of California's Sproul Plaza was ablaze with free speech rallies and student activists were recruiting all around me on the San Francisco State College campus. I felt I was betraying my race and my commitment to civil liberty by dating a white man. This was a time of rising support among my people for strength and pride in perpetuating our race. According to the dictums of the Black Panther movement in Oakland and the Black Separatists, to date a white was to detract from the movement and dilute our strength.

With my abiding devotion to Matt, I had no time to even think about equal rights, black pride, the NAACP or any of the struggles for civil liberties. Not even the crisis in our country over the discovery of Russian missiles in Cuba seemed to make an impact on me.

I could no longer deny we were dating. I couldn't stop myself yearning for, praying for and waiting for those times we spent together. I decided that we both were suffering from some kind of alien invasion that attacked people and took total control of their minds and bodies.

On some dates, Matt would pick me up and we would go a tiny restaurant two blocks away. We would sit and simply stare into each other's eyes over the table. Never taking his eyes away from mine, Matt would order all my favorite foods without looking at the waiter. The food would come, and we wouldn't touch a bite for the first hour. We sat and stared across the table at one another, instead.

Caught up in gazing at one another, Matt would chuckle sometimes when the waiter asked us for the third time if we did not like what we'd ordered. Matt would eat a bite, put down his fork, reach for my hand, and stare across the table into my eyes once more. I felt so silly, but so good. Just sitting across from each other was enough to satisfy us. We preferred to spend time alone, seldom socializing with other couples.

His friends were always on base or living in army housing across town. I had wondered if he would be embarrassed to introduce me to his friends. Then, one Saturday, he arrived with a fellow military policeman named Joaquin and his wife, Marta. The four of us had a wonderful time on Fisherman's Wharf. We drove all over in their car, and when Matt got out of the car to get movie tickets, Joaquin said that Matt talked about me all the time.

On those rare occasions when we were trapped in the apartment with members of Teddy's group who wanted to share an evening, we noticed that, recently, some of the girls were getting quite serious in their romances. Teddy had begun dating Cliff steadily and now they announced the date for their marriage. Mandy and Elvin were inviting us all to come to Reno with them to get married. John and Wendy had exchanged rings and decided to move to their own apartment and live in sin for a year before wedlock.

I waited for one of them to comment about my being with Matt, but since we always declared that our friendship was platonic, they didn't talk about coupling. Sometimes when the girls came over and we got together without any men around, both Teddy and Wendy would comment that Matt and I appeared to be deeply in love. Why did we deny what was so evident in our expressions, they asked. I told them that it wasn't possible for us to become romantically involved because of the difference in our races. The girls giggled, teasing me with their rhyme, "Liar, liar, pants on fire." I chose to ignore their teasing.

One Sunday morning in late November, just as I was about to get ready for church, the doorbell rang. Matt stood in the doorway holding two bags of groceries. "I thought we'd spend the day together, just enjoying each other's company and this duck I bought. Only this time, I'll cook."

He winked and smiled at me and I didn't care that he was early. I pushed away the twinge of guilt about missing church. We had planned to get together after church, but I was even willing to abandon church in order to be with Matt. I would surely go to hell, nevertheless I welcomed him into the kitchen and helped him put the groceries away. I was grateful that Kerry Lynn was once again away with Fernando, trying to work out their problems. "For better or for worse," she had said as she picked up her overnight bag for their trip to Carmel.

While I showered and dressed, I could hear Matt puttering in the kitchen. When I emerged wearing the yellow dress Mother Lois had made for me, he stood very still staring at me for a long moment. I stood in front of him, feeling the warmth of his admiration and approval radiate through me. "You're the prettiest little colored girl I've ever seen," he said. "No, I take that back, you're the prettiest girl of any color I've ever seen."

Awkwardly, I took a seat at the breakfast table where he had set it up with the best breakfast I'd ever seen. I started to pick up my fork to dig into the omelet he'd put before me, but I felt the sunlight of his admiring eyes still focused on me. I looked up to meet his gaze and he held my eyes. I had no urge to look away, no urge to eat the omelet, and I knew that the only place I wanted to be was sitting right there across from him. He leaned across the table and kissed me. I let him.

My mind said push him away, resist, turn away from him and run away from him, but my heart beat so softly, and I felt such a sweetness in the touch of his lips as he pressed them against my cheek and my forehead. He dropped his napkin and fork so quickly and rose to come around to my side of the table so suddenly that my initial resistance seemed to have drifted off to some detached and distant corner of myself. I felt dizzy as he pulled me up into his arms and covered my face and neck with tiny gentle kisses. He pressed against me, holding me tight. I felt only a warm joyfulness surging through every cell of my being as he held me closer and closer. With an increasing urgency that I felt rising deep inside my body, I was compelled to put my arms around his neck. It was a feeling I had never had before and I didn't want him to ever release me. *Finally,* I thought, *here is the one place I am certain I belong on Earth—in Matt's arms.*

Chapter 23

"HOW CAN YOU MARRY A WHITE MAN after all the pain white folks have caused you?" It was the day after Christmas, my wedding day, and those were Mother Lois's first words when Matt and I phoned from Reno, Nevada, to tell her we were man and wife. She asked me lots of pointed questions about Matt and then she said, "It's not just the difference in your races, it's the difference in your cultural up-bringing. His people are ranchers—country people. We're profes-sional people—educators. Is he going to finish college? Does he know that you must finish college?"

"Yes, ma'am." Mother's condemning questions were coming fast and furious. I cringed as I felt tears brim my eyes. Matt put his arms around me and pulled me close to comfort me.

"I suppose he wants you to quit school now and have babies, and such?"

"No, ma'am, I'll graduate, I promise." There was no joy in her response to our exciting news. Matt and I were so thrilled, so proud of ourselves. Now her attitude made me very sad, and she hadn't yet finished raining on our parade.

"If he's a macho man who wants the perfect housewife, it won't work for the two of you, Melba. We Peyton women don't kowtow to men. We are here on earth with a mission to educate ourselves and to achieve, to contribute."

"Yes, ma'am." I couldn't think of what to say back to her—how to stop her.

"You've disappointed me, Melba. I had so many plans for your future and now you've ruined them all. I'd wanted you to marry one of our teachers or lawyers. At least if you're going to marry a white boy, marry one from a good family. Marry one who is highly educated."

"But Mom, Matt's a corporal. He's a military policeman." Mom was so angry that I couldn't get a word in.

"Trash, that's what you've gone and done. You've married trash. You've ruined all the hard work that I invested in you. Married." She took a deep breath and said the word once more as if it were something dirty. Tears were streaming down my cheeks.

"Mother, he has three years of college," I interjected. She went right on past my statement. By now I was shivering in that zero-degree Reno weather. Matt was hovering nearby with a red nose.

"You'd better take precautions. The very last thing you need right now is to get pregnant. You've got to finish your education and be somebody. Anybody can get married and have babies. You were meant to be a professional, contributing to humanity."

"Yes, ma'am." I just wanted this conversation to end. I had hoped she could share a small portion of our joy. As it was, she was ruining our beautiful day.

"And Melba, there are things I have never spoken to you about. Some white men want to do strange sexual things. Things we Christian women don't do and don't put up with."

Oh gosh, I thought, *what was she talking about now?* I was already apprehensive about making love with Matt. I had read things and listened to Kerry Lynn's advice. But Mother had never really had any sex education discussions with me until here, now, on the phone, and she was frightening me with her advice. I didn't want to cut her off and hurt her feelings, so I stood at that telephone patiently listening with snow up to my ankles in the zero degree weather.

Finally my grim telephone conversation with Mother Lois ended and I stepped out of the phone booth, took a deep breath, wiped my tears away and took my new husband's arm. In the cold, winter twilight he guided me along the slush and snow-covered sidewalks toward our hotel, Christmas lights twinkling in the windows we passed.

Matt had called for reservations two days before, requesting a special room suitable for a honeymooning couple. When we'd arrived earlier that day, the desk clerk had glared at us across the lobby hung with holiday lights and garlands of pungent evergreens. There was no doubt that he chose to ignore us and when we demanded service, he was rude. We'd gone up to our room to look it over. I was shy about being alone in a hotel room with Matt, and besides, it was bad luck for the groom to see the bride's dress. I had quickly designed and sewn a creamy-beige–colored taffeta dress with a velvet jacket and I wanted to surprise him. Abiding by my wishes, he had gone downstairs while I got dressed, agreeing to meet me at the chapel where we were to be married.

Now, we were walking down the street to our hotel in the winter twilight, holding on to each other, amazed at how quickly and how easily we had become a married couple. It didn't matter what Mother Lois said. It didn't matter what anybody said. I was Matt's wife and I felt a magical glow inside, in spite of the snow and the deepening gray skies.

Once upstairs, Matt told me to get dressed in something fancy. I wore a royal blue velvet suit that Mother Lois had hand-sewn and sent to me for Christmas, with a pink taffeta blouse. He took me to a wonderful restaurant, a truly romantic place with candlelight and a pianist playing sentimental tunes. We lingered over dinner and when it was done, I could no longer hear Mother's words swirling in my head. I was feeling so content, so joyful. I could only think of the weeks, months and years that I would share with Matt. They would be the best days of my life, because I wouldn't be lonely or left out. Now, I belonged with Matt.

I couldn't help holding my wedding ring up to the candlelight.

Matt had been so matter-of-fact two days before, when he'd insisted that I take a look at the wedding rings he'd purchased for both of us. After that moment, I knew for certain that he was serious about marrying me. Still, I had been apprehensive about telling Mother Lois and the McCabes about our plans, fearing their reaction. What if they could do something to stop us? I decided to wait until after we were married to tell all of them, even though it meant talking to them on Christmas Day as if nothing unusual were going on. My omission of such earthshaking news had made me feel guilty.

Holding the box that contained the gold bands with a diagonal brush of diamonds across the center—my ring wide, his narrow—I had become suddenly very frightened. I had looked at Matt and said, "What are we doing?"

"It's either get married or live in sin. You're driving me crazy, girl. I can't continue living at the edge of my manhood wanting something I can't have. I love you and I want us to make a life together." He had made the hotel reservations that night for our stay in Reno. We were nearly the same age; I was barely twenty but he seemed so much older and wiser in the ways of the world at twenty-two.

On our wedding night after that wonderful dinner, we lay together in the huge, luscious, round bed in our hotel room while Matt read his Army karate manual titled *Kill or be Killed*, aloud. At first, I was shy about lying down beside him in bed, but he reassured me by saying he'd read to me. Indeed, the book was fascinating. And by gently demonstrating the karate holds on my body, he slowly made me comfortable as he touched every part of me. After a while, my apprehension melted into desire and we were gazing into each other's eyes, as he stroked my cheek. Being with him that way was something I had dreamed about, but none of my dreams could have matched his tenderness. All the reasons for parting with Matt that had tortured me in the past, reasons that seemed so valid and so important to me once, dissolved in our lovemaking that night. In my diary I wrote:

Now that you are here, the half of me that cried out is whole. The part of me that wailed with incompleteness is silent. The immeasurable pain that festered inside is healed by the sweet nectar of

your loving. I am heard, I am seen, I am cherished by you—and
oh, how grand it feels.

When we arrived home from Reno we telephoned George and
Kay to say that we were married. They greeted my news in the way I
wished Mother Lois had received it.

Kay said, "Well, dear, this must be a very special person if
you've chosen to marry him. We look forward to meeting him." Then
George added, "You're a smart girl, Melba. You'll figure what it takes
to make life work. Think about continuing in school. I know it's not a
priority right now, but in the long run your education will be. You'll
be a better wife and mother if you fill yourself with knowledge."

A better mother, I thought. *Hmm, not yet. I'm not ready to share my
Matthew with any other human being.* We had talked it over and he had
made an appointment for me to see the Presidio Army Base doctor. I
would get birth control pills and continue school until I graduated.
Meanwhile, he would complete his Army time and then I would work
while he finished his last year of college.

Six weeks after our wedding we shopped for dinner in the store
across from our apartment we now shared with Kerry Lynn. I spied
some cans of pork and beans on the shelves. I was drawn to them as
if a giant magnet had taken me over. I absolutely had to have them.
Immediately! I was furiously tossing cans of pork and beans into the
shopping basket while Matt stared at me as if I were losing my mind.

"What's gotten into you?" he asked.

"I don't know. I just gotta have these."

"You hate pork and beans."

"Not anymore."

When we arrived home, I opened a can of the beans to eat cold
while Matt heated up the second can. I was gobbling beans straight
from the can as though it were my last supper. Matt stood stock-still
with his back to the cook stove staring at me, his eyes growing bigger
with each spoonful I gulped. His expression was filled with astonishment.

"You're pregnant, Melba," he shouted. "That's it!"

"I am not!" I protested.

The doctor confirmed Matt's suspicions a few days later. It had happened even before I could get to the physician for the birth control pills. Upon hearing the news, I felt very strange, as though some alien being had taken up residence in my body. The first night, I lay in Matt's arms, crying. I didn't want to believe I was pregnant. And when the truth finally sank in, I lamented the fact that soon I would have to share my husband with another human being. Not only that, but being a mother seemed to be a big job—something people did when they grew up, and I wasn't a grown-up.

When I told Mother that I was pregnant, she said she would contribute to my education but not to my self-destructive act of becoming an uneducated mother. She withdrew her contribution toward my rent and food. We had never stopped to figure out the finances or the practical aspects of housekeeping. We had very few kitchen utensils or bed linens, and absolutely no furniture except my stereo. I would have to quit college and find a job. We were now compelled to find a less expensive apartment by ourselves. This was fine with Kerry Lynn, who was ready to return to her home to go to college. Her relationship with Fernando had wounded her spirit and caused her to reconsider the fun life in the big city.

My job search was successful. In just a few days I found work as a secretary for the federal government. Despite my elation at having my first real full-time job, the day I withdrew from San Francisco State College I was sad. I felt I was putting aside my dream of becoming a teacher.

Memories of hatred and segregation when I lived in Little Rock were rekindled in my mind when we went apartment hunting. I had not anticipated the horrendous task of finding an apartment as a racially mixed couple, even in San Francisco. I couldn't believe the managers who invited us into their offices or homes. They questioned us about our experiences as an interracially married couple, lectured us on the evils of race mixing and then refused to rent to us for that reason. After several days of knocking on doors and getting my feelings hurt by some very rude racists, Matt demanded that I stay home.

Ultimately, Matt found an apartment for us in the Haight-Ashbury district of San Francisco, where street life was just beginning to unfold with the takeover of the flower children. He had found a place off the main thoroughfare on a side street that crossed Haight. It was a quiet, family neighborhood. During my third month of pregnancy, we moved into the sunny second-floor, one-bedroom apartment that was clean, freshly painted and furnished. Our combined salaries afforded us only a little extra to add decorating touches, but we both delighted in our first real home together.

At work, my consuming task was to keep from throwing up on my desk. How could a woman explain to a man the queasy feeling one gets in the early stages of pregnancy? I couldn't hold down food and so doctors prescribed various medications, but nothing worked. Finally a doctor told me that I must eat and try to keep down whatever food I could, if only for a few minutes. That didn't work either. The very aroma of some foods cooking or packed in lunch pails sent me running for the restroom. My co-workers soon knew about the baby. Two of the women told me how worried they would be if they were having a racially mixed baby.

I agonized all day over their comments and raced home in anguish to Matt, wondering if we had committed an injustice by bringing a baby of mixed parentage into the world. "How's it gonna grow up?" I cried.

"Towards the sky, like everybody else," he answered. "He'll be born of our love and that's all he needs to know. He won't be the first or the last mixed kid around."

His answer was so simple that it quelled all my fears. I focused on who this tiny soul kicking in my tummy like a football team at practice might turn out to be. As the weeks turned into months, I became more and more uncomfortable, but I also became more and more enamored of the idea of becoming a mother.

Matt worried as I lost weight rapidly and spent much of the time after work lying in bed green-faced or rushing to the bathroom to throw up. Every day that he could get off from his duty as a military policeman he was home. He always cooked wonderful meals. Most of the time, I would go to the table, smell the food and throw up right there. He would embrace me, clean up the mess and say kind words to soothe my fears.

On those rare occasions when I could eat, I craved pistachio malts with dill pickles. I wanted okra on everything, including my cornflakes, and I had to have chocolate syrup. Many a midnight Matt trotted out to procure the odd foods that I craved. He was the most wonderful human being I had ever encountered. He took care of me, making all the decisions. I was finally beginning to get the long rest I felt I'd needed but never had following my Central High School experience and the subsequent move to California with all the major adjustments that had required. I didn't have to do anything but exist and follow Matt's instructions. Sometimes I felt like I was living with a benevolent father. He waited on me hand and foot and labored tirelessly to satisfy my every whim.

By the sixth month of my pregnancy I had regained my appetite and stopped throwing up. The baby inside me had become the focus of my life. It was all I thought about and planned for. What's more, now I could talk to Mother about our expected little stranger. She even began looking forward to the birth. It was wonderful to be a young married couple in San Francisco. I felt as though I had found paradise. I could perform the duties of a secretary without even the slightest exertion of my brain power. With the challenge of my studies put aside for the moment, I concentrated on learning more about cooking Matt's favorite foods, keeping a good house and being the best wife I possibly could.

Since Matt had grown up on a farm with a father, mother and older sister, he was great at all kinds of chores, whether indoors or out. And he enjoyed good food and liked to cook. Under his tutelage, I learned the art of gourmet cooking, rather than the southern ways I had been trained in. He insisted we spend long hours reading cookbooks and preparing delicious meals. And he gave me tips on plain cooking: how to spoon oil over the eggs to keep the yolk standing, just as Grandmother had taught me earlier. I learned to cook beef steaks at the exact temperature that permitted just enough red to remain in the center; to mash potatoes with garlic; to make vegetables al dente; and to fold laundry so it pleased my husband.

His German-Irish mother had been a neat freak, he said. A place for everything and everything in its place. I learned to organize my household just the way he desired. He wanted his underwear and socks folded and neatly placed in separate drawers just so. It wasn't so different from Grandma India's teachings. Whatever we were doing together was a joy and I found that I could lose myself in even the simplest tasks, as long as he approved of and delighted in what I was doing.

Whenever I watched the television news or listened to the radio I became a guilty spectator of all the civil rights activities which were flourishing by March of 1963. Major civil rights groups were coordinating Mississippi's voter registration drive. Dr. Martin Luther King was spearheading a massive campaign to halt Birmingham, Alabama, segregation. *What should I be doing,* I would ask myself. But then Matt would sit me down and say, "Relax, don't watch it, don't think about it for now. You've done your share already, pretty lady. What you do is rest now and let me love you." He would turn off the news in favor of comedy or cowboy shows.

One Friday night in June, as Matt and I drove away from a grocery store near the Fillmore district, we noticed we were being trailed by a flashing red light. I was panic stricken. Police chasing me down in their official cars at nighttime were one of my worst nightmares. In Little Rock, if you were black, the police seldom meant real help. Often they were the predators. They frightened me out of my wits even here in California.

Matt pulled over to the side of the street and stopped the car. "Remember, honey, you've got our baby in the oven, so stay calm. When I show them my M.P. badge, it's all gonna be all right." He tried to reassure me, but my heart was thumping a mile a minute in my chest. The policeman walked up to the car and insisted that we get out.

"Where'd you pick up this nigger whore?" the tall, thin officer asked, as he pushed his horn-rimmed glasses up off his nose and shined a giant flashlight in my face. "Get out of the car, now, both of you."

"Officer, this is my wife you're talking to. Please have some respect," Matt said, as I struggled to stand with the added weight of my baby-full tummy.

"Respect?" the officer said, laughing aloud as he suddenly grabbed me by one arm and shoved me forward so that my bulging belly struck the side of the car.

"Spread your legs and put your free hand up above your head on the top of the car," he ordered, twisting my other arm behind me. I started crying, pleading for him to release my arm and ease the pressure on my stomach as he pressed me harder against the car. Besides, I had been told repeatedly by doctors not to stretch my arms high above my head. He wouldn't listen, but kept shoving me harder against the car with his elbow while he kept my feet jammed far apart with his own stance.

"My wife is six months pregnant," Matt said in a deep, calm, low voice but with anger grinding in his tone.

"What do you care, boy? Why don't you drive on off and we'll relieve you of your problem."

"I love my wife and my baby!" Matt said, and he lunged toward the officer who was holding me.

At that point his partner, a stocky man, grabbed Matt's arms and made him assume a spread-eagle position up against our car beside me. I turned my head to look for help, but the streets were dark and the few bright headlights passing by blurred my vision. I didn't see a soul. My Lord, this was California. Were we going to die right here and now? I knew not to say anything. Instead, I prayed for our lives. *Please God, save our baby.*

I could see my husband's face turn red, his jaws tighten, his shoulder muscles tense. He had never been treated this way before and he was about to do something stupid, something heroic that would put us both at even greater risk. I winked at him and smiled as I lowered my chin, using it to direct his sight toward my stomach.

"Officer, if you'll just allow me to reach in my pocket, I'll show you my badge. I'm a military policeman stationed at Fort Berry over in Sausalito," Matt said.

"You're a cop and you're popping this nigger bitch? You ought to be ashamed of yourself, son. What do your folks think?"

Once again, I saw Matt's jaws tighten. Suddenly, a pain shot through my stomach and down through my pelvic area. Pulling my hand down from the roof of the car, I grabbed my stomach and let out a grunt involuntarily. The next pain followed quickly. I cried aloud.

"Please," Matt said. "If she loses my baby over this, we're gonna have a party, you and I," he spoke with anger and tears in his voice.

"You're not threatening me, are you, son?"

"No sir, I'm promising you war—if you hurt my wife or my baby. I'm gonna do the same thing to you that you'd do to me if the situation was reversed. That's just a fact." Matt's voice was low and even, and he burned a glare toward the man. Something in my husband's tone and face must have affected the officer. He shined his huge flashlight again in Matt's face and allowed him to show his military badge. Finally, they let us go. I was crying out in agony by this time. Matt drove me directly to the hospital.

I cringed and whimpered, struggling not to scream out in pain as doctors examined me with rapid force. Each time a new specialist joined the team, he poked and prodded a new spot. No part of my anatomy was left unexplored.

I felt their gloved hands and cold steel instruments boring up inside me, invading my very core. Then, one of the doctors stepped to the head of the examining table and addressed Matt. The placenta may have separated from my baby. I was bleeding and the baby and I were both at grave risk.

Chapter 24

MATT AND I CLUNG TO EACH OTHER, trying to make sense of what the doctors were saying: "separating placenta," "grave risk." Did that mean both our baby and I could die? Neither Matt nor I dared to say the words.

Once settled in the white quiet of the hospital, the tiny person inside my tummy was no longer content, at first thrashing about as though he or she wanted out. After a while, I only felt a slight movement or kick every now and then, but there was a new feeling of downward pressure. For the first two weeks, I was not allowed to get out of bed for any reason, not even to go to the bathroom. After that I was compelled to spend most of my day in bed.

I thought I would go stir crazy in that military hospital ward along with other mothers-to-be who were having difficult pregnancies. One of the expectant mothers was also a black woman married to a white soldier. Lonnie and I became pals. Our husbands became friends and that helped to pass the time.

Visits from my old friends from the Inn, Teddy and Alison, and Renee, a newcomer to the group, and their husbands were wonderful. Matt came every day, most often twice a day, to have breakfast and dinner with me. Oh, how I missed being at home with Matt — missed our cuddling, our cooking together, his private kisses. At home with him I had felt so special when he hovered over me, fulfilling my every wish, treating me as though I were his princess. Now, I was out in the world once more.

Mother Lois had long since become an exhilarated, expectant grandmother, with the caution that she never be called "granny." She phoned daily and offered to come out to be with me. She and Matt decided it would be better if she saved her visit until sometime after the baby was born.

Although the hospital was filled with people of all races and creeds, I saw evidence of prejudice, of separate but unequal treatment. I noticed a difference in the respect accorded to black females. Doctors addressed us differently, calling us by our first names right away, whereas they asked the white pregnant women for permission to use their first names. They also asked the white women for permission to use them as teaching examples. In contrast, they showed off my bottom to as many as ten residents at a time, never once asking my permission beforehand. This observation made me want to stand up and march and bespeak this subtle but painful injustice. But I knew I was down for a long count.

While I was trapped in the hospital, I felt like the world was passing me by. In San Francisco, there were picketers demanding fair employment for blacks, and marching on businesses like the *Oakland Tribune*, a local newspaper, or the Sheraton Palace Hotel or Mel's Diner, a popular local eatery. In Berkeley, the Free Speech Movement was flourishing. And I just lay there — captured and disabled by a fetus I hadn't met. At times I resented being left out of the events taking place all around the Bay Area. At other times, I was grateful for an excuse not to have to be involved.

I was in pain from frequent examinations. I spent a lot of time worrying because I was ignorant about even the most basic information of the birth process. I wasn't even certain where the baby was going to exit my body. I couldn't imagine a baby could emerge from the narrow orifices the doctors probed. Mother Lois had never talked to me about female anatomy and there were no sex education courses in the schools I had attended. I couldn't even ask the doctor for fear I would be deemed stupid. When I asked Matt, he grinned and said that I would find out soon enough. I spent so much time fantasizing and worrying about the actual birthing process that my conclusions became laughable, even to me.

The only pleasurable thing about my confinement was that I could watch television endlessly. I lay in bed gazing at the tube until I was bored beyond words. Too much *Queen for a Day* and quiz shows. It was getting to me. I waited breathlessly for the evening news.

When the commentator announced Medgar Evers's murder on June 12, I was once again reminded of how much my civil rights hung in the balance because segregationists would kill to keep what they thought was theirs. Evers had become a martyr, giving up his life to the shooter who would punish him for claiming his civil rights.

For hours after the announcement of Evers's death I just lay quiet, listening to radio music and wondering what would become of me—of my people. Would my baby suffer the prejudice I had endured? How could I prevent this child from having my experience of racism? All those questions made my head hurt, and the doctors had told me that I had to relax because my high blood pressure could affect my unborn baby. Maybe, as in Peter, Paul and Mary's popular new song, "Blowin' in the Wind," the answers I sought were not available to me. In my diary I wrote:

> *Maybe I have to wait to see what God has in store for me. My hopes and aspirations wear thin as I watch Mr. Evers's attackers reign victorious. Will they ever be caught and punished? By some miracle, will my baby be free? Will he or she suffer the indignities that I did?*

On the second of August I went into premature labor. The doctors tried desperately to stop the labor pains but they weren't successful. I was in labor for thirty-six hours. The increasing intensity of each pain was measured by the elevated decibels of my cries for help. From the beginning, I couldn't stop screaming. At one point, during one of my loud screaming sessions, a nurse ordered that my husband be brought from the waiting room to quiet me down.

The nurse's aide must have gone out and summoned the first black man she saw. The poor guy entered the door of the small birthing room with my nude bottom exposed to him. He stared at my face through the angle of my spread legs as the nurse shoved him forward.

"This is definitely not my wife," he protested.

I screamed, "Get out of here! You're not my husband! Get out!"

When finally they located Matt, he came into the room grinning, saying a buddy of his had just had a very unconventional introduction to me. He apologized for the mistake.

"I love you and it's all gonna work out. You'll see." He began talking to me in that calm voice, reassuring me and telling me stories of what we would do when the baby was born. Clutching his hand, I quieted down and between pains I even dozed off.

Our cinnamon-colored baby girl, Kellie, was born with huge, doe-like green eyes and black hair shining like satin. The nurses teased that she sported a hairstyle that resembled the one worn by the famous singer Keely Smith—straight wisps of bangs lay on an even path across her forehead with slight curls about her ears and neck. Since Kellie was premature, her low birth weight dictated that she be placed in an incubator. It would be a few days before I held her, but when her warm, squirming body finally nestled in my arms it was like holding a chunk of heaven. As I looked into her eyes, I vowed that she would never, ever experience the same prejudice and hatred that I had felt at Central High School. Her life would be different. From the outset she would live and breathe her own freedom. She would see and be seen as an equal!

All the pain of the actual delivery and everything unpleasant in my life was erased by this tiny creature who so resembled her father. Matt and I were so in love with her that we would sit for hours just watching her sleep. In her we felt the strength of our connection and it was a wonderful, new experience for both of us.

It was only when Matt phoned to tell his parents of the birth that I learned he had not told them we were married.

"I thought I'd save all the good news for one phone call," he said, winking nervously.

"And?"

"Well, they're not overjoyed. They have questions. But I told them either they accept you or lose me." Like always, he had expressed his feelings in a straightforward manner and I respected him for it. But I was concerned that he not alienate his parents. "Give them a chance to get used to the idea," I urged him.

My mother was gleeful when I announced she was a grandmother. She immediately asked what baby clothes we needed. Her only requirement was that we not allow Kellie to ever call her "Grandma." We had to teach her to call her by a cutesie-poo name like "Zidie" or "Nan" or "Nonie."

"Fine," I said, as my brother Conrad took the phone, "she can call her 'Nana Lois.' " He was eager to spread the news that he was an uncle and he planned to hand out cigars. *Cigars,* I thought. *How could my little brother Conrad be giving out cigars?* It reminded me that he was now eighteen years old and that at twenty-one I was a full-fledged grown-up.

George and Kay were so happy about Kellie's arrival that I felt renewed joy. They visited us and delighted in her every feature and movement, and Matt cooked a meal for them. It was a sweet evening to be recorded in our family history.

On August 28, holding my baby daughter, I sat riveted to the television screen as Dr. Martin Luther King delivered his "I have a dream speech" at the Lincoln Memorial rally that was the climax of the March on Washington. Mother Lois phoned to observe that I must be sad that I couldn't participate. *I should have been there,* I thought to myself. *I should have been there, but here feels better and maybe I deserve to feel okay for a while.*

We had been allowed to bring Kellie home the week before. She was so tiny that there was difficulty keeping her body temperature up, so for the first several weeks she slept on Matt's bare chest at night. In addition, because of her diminutive size, we could not find any baby clothes to fit her. One day Matt took our grocery money and bought an expensive collector's doll dress for Kellie. He held her up dressed in her new finery and announced, "Now, we really have a baby girl."

During that September I mourned the four little black girls killed in the Birmingham church bombing. I could feel something going terribly wrong with my dreams. I had hoped that integration would happen with dispatch, or at least in my lifetime. If segregationists were willing to kill four little girls to keep things their way, it meant that it was going to take forever for me to be seen as an equal. Would my Kellie suffer the oppression of prejudice? I was distraught even thinking about that possibility. Would she ever be the victim of a church bombing?

By early November I began working once more as a secretary for the federal government in an overseas aid program that sent American goods to foreign countries needing help. Matt's military pay would not cover our expenses; we desperately needed the income that a second job brought in. Each morning we drove little Kellie to her babysitter, my friend Renee. I cried when I had to leave her behind. I hated leaving our baby with someone else, but we could not survive without a second salary. In addition, I'd had a taste of staying at home day in and day out with an infant and I suspected that the life of a full-time housewife was not for me, much as I loved my little girl and husband.

When President John F. Kennedy was assassinated just before Thanksgiving, I was devastated. His sudden death took the spark of light from my dreams and I wondered when, if ever, it would be rekindled. His presence had made me believe that the nation, for the first time, was headed by a man who was totally conscious of my existence and my needs. Former presidents had virtually ignored the existence of my people. How could somebody just shoot Kennedy, our president? The awful cloud that crept over the nation was very heavy over our house. Matt and I sat in tears watching the television coverage of the president's funeral, wondering what we could or should do.

The shadow of President Kennedy's death hung suspended above us, darkening the Christmas holidays. We had to force ourselves to perk up our spirits for celebration. We weren't looking forward to much fun, because there was no extra money in our budget for gift exchange or celebration. Although I was working, the baby was expensive and we had fallen behind during my months confined to the hospital. I was embarrassed when I heard Matt mention our predicament to his parents during a phone conversation.

Four days before Christmas a huge box arrived. His dear mother and father had sent an entire Christmas: an artificial tree, candles, decorations, a canned ham, a fruitcake, personal gifts like socks and jewelry, story books, records, teddy bears, clothes for the baby and absolutely everything we needed to have a special holiday. On that same day, Mother Lois's generous check arrived. It was my most wonderful Christmas ever. I had Matt and Kellie and both Mother Lois and Matt's parents seemed to be growing accustomed to our marriage. We were a family.

The new year, 1964, began, and President Johnson declared his War on Poverty, 101 Americans had died in Vietnam and the Beatles had taken America by storm. Matt and I had fallen into a routine of work and domesticity, and we continued to be absolutely enthralled by our baby daughter and by our own love for each other. My husband still brought me flowers once a week, a practice he'd begun right after our marriage. No matter what our financial situation, somehow he managed to find money for a bouquet. And twice a month we went out on a date. We arranged a babysitter for Kellie, and Matt and I would go to a bargain movie, take a tour of Chinatown or ride the cable cars. I was not at all athletic, but Matt loved to climb the rocks and negotiate the rugged terrain above Ocean Beach. He had begun going on these climbing expeditions alone. At first he invited me, even though I inevitably turned him down, and finally he insisted that I accompany him. It frightened me to look down hundreds of feet and know I would have to climb down and then back up. Matt said it built character. Sometimes we went there on a family outing and Matt carried the baby in a pack on his back. I protested all the way up and all the way down.

In July of 1964, I celebrated when President Johnson signed the first broad-based civil rights bill, the Civil Rights Act of 1964, which banned discrimination in public facilities and created other opportunities denied to blacks for so long. At the same time Lester Maddox, a staunch southern segregationist, urged people to use axe handles against blacks who tried to eat in his restaurant. These two occurrences, so completely opposite in their declarations, painted an accurate picture of the civil rights movement as far as I was concerned. The president's signature on the Civil Rights Act and his obvious pride in it was an incredibly positive stroke for change, even though we did have a long, long way to go. Johnson had coerced, cajoled, enticed, threatened and reasoned with the members of Congress to get the bill passed. Our national leaders were beginning to admit that we black folks were in America to stay.

On the fourth of August, the day after we celebrated Kellie's first birthday, the bodies of three men, two white and one black, who had been organizing voter registration of Mississippi blacks were found buried. It reminded me once again that white segregationists would kill even their own people to keep us in our place.

Despite all the tragedies, I continued to experience an almost tangible feeling that the country was moving forward, that freedom for all was possible. The civil rights movement continued gaining momentum.

Berkeley students were demanding freedom of speech in the face of the university's clampdown on soliciting for, donating to, enrolling in activist groups like the Congress of Racial Equality. Thousands had stood up to protest the arrest of Jack Weinberg, who manned the CORE table near the campus in Berkeley. His arrest set off an explosion that would rock the University of California campus and the American psyche. When it was all over, the regents voted overwhelmingly to permit free speech. For me, that was evidence that we could not be held captive by those who would take away our right to express an opinion in opposition to the powers that be. It gave me a sense that the struggle for total freedom was expanding and each time there was a win, all of us, no matter what our issues, won a little bit.

Life in the Haight-Ashbury in those early days of the sixties, with its emphasis on free love, eclectic dress and freedom of speech epitomized the general feeling of hope and progress.

I will never be happier, I thought, as Matt and I pushed our daughter in her stroller down Haight Street on weekends. We would stop at a coffee shop every now and then and join the flower children's debates on free speech, free love or the Vietnam situation. Holding hands, we would walk for hours, pushing the stroller and drinking our fruit ice, enjoying the warm sun and odd sights. What could go wrong with my life? I prayed it would go on that way forever. It felt so good not to have clouds of doom and oppression hanging over my head. Nobody treated us as though we were oddities or shunned us because we were an interracial couple. We saw many other mixed couples and sometimes we couldn't identify their races. Partners were sometimes so diverse in their physical appearance that I was beginning to feel that, although Kellie would resemble a combination of

Matt and me—half black and half white—there would be a place for her in the new world. We were ecstatic with love for our little daughter and for each other. We spent hours just staring at Kellie or playing with her on the floor pad. She was a delight, growing each day and recognizing us as her parents. When I entered a room and Matt was holding her, her face would light up at the sight of me. She had the same response when Matt came into view.

Saturdays were our favorite family time. On one Saturday, one week after Kellie's first birthday, however, I had the opportunity to make extra money by working overtime. At 4:00 P.M. when I returned home, I opened the front door of our Haight apartment. It was empty, totally empty of all of our things. None of our furniture, not curtains, not even the garbage remained. What could have happened? Had Matt and the baby been kidnapped? Why would they take the furniture? My heart pounded in my ears. I sat on the floor, crying, and the phone rang. It was Matt.

"Surprise!" he laughed aloud. "You don't know where you live, do you?" I couldn't say a word.

"Well, I got some of the guys from the base and we moved, lock stock and barrel. Wait till you see the new place!"

I was so angry that I was shaking. What could I say that would make Matt understand how much he had frightened me? We had talked about wanting a bigger place, but nothing was definite. Besides, I liked living in the Haight.

"You'll love it! Great neighborhood, more space. Come on over," he said, as though this was some great joke.

When I arrived at the new apartment, I told Matt that I thought the neighborhood was dry and sterile, even lifeless. He said he thought the Haight was getting cluttered.

Amid eight of his buddies, all guzzling beer, celebrating their triumphant move and the hoax they'd carried off with me, I felt there was little that I could say. I suppose Matt expected me to be grateful that we now had a bedroom for Kellie, more furniture, which he had selected, and the addition of a piano. I'd expressed the desire for a piano, but I would have liked the opportunity of choosing it myself, as well as having a say in the furniture.

I remained silent over dinner, over breakfast the next morning and for the better part of a week before Matt noticed.

"You're not happy here? I did it all for you," he said angrily.

I knew that nothing I could say would make Matt see that I wanted to be his equal partner in these kinds of decisions. He had treated me as if I were a child.

One week after we had moved, Mother Lois announced she and Conrad were visiting. It would be the first time since the baby was born. We rushed to put everything in order, frantically settling into our house, sprucing up with decorative items from Penney's department store and setting our church routine straight.

When Mother held my daughter, it was obvious how much they resembled each other. Kellie had Mother's coloring, hair texture and facial expressions. I felt such a connection between the generations and an even closer connection between Kellie and me. Although she didn't resemble me, she looked like my mother.

Conrad and Matt enjoyed each other's company and Mother seemed to accept my husband. We were a joyful, loving family as we toured San Francisco, showing my mother and brother the sights. They were typical tourists, falling in love with the cable cars and being delighted with the Golden Gate Bridge, although my brother was disappointed, just as I had been, that the bridge wasn't gold but orange. We ate at Fisherman's Wharf and walked along the docks looking at the fishing boats.

Naturally, the flower children on Haight Street were particularly intriguing for out-of-towners. Mother Lois demanded that we drive back and forth through the Haight so she could get a close look at what she had read about.

"Precious Lord, children, this is Sodom and Gomorrah!" she exclaimed, and then insisted we return over and over again so she could get a closer look at "sin" in the daylight. She was fascinated with the sights and sounds in the district, but balked at parking the car and walking. She feared that someone would harm us, because the people seemed so free, without a moral code or any rules for dress. But her fears did not keep her from requesting that the Haight be a daily part of our sightseeing.

The Castro district was just beginning to be a showcase for alternative living. Men held hands with men as they sauntered up the sidewalk. Mother was absolutely flabbergasted. "Sodom and Gomorrah for certain," she repeated. "Hell can't be too far away."

We went to the Japanese tea garden in Golden Gate Park, visited the aquarium and then the Cliff House and watched the waves of the Pacific breaking on the beach below while we ate dinner. We shopped in department stores, explored Chinatown and sat at a coffee house in North Beach watching the people go by. We had a wonderful time.

At first, Conrad's sole preoccupation at age twenty was seeing Broadway. He wanted to check if "topless" really meant without tops. He and Matt were disappointed after their boys' night out because, in Conrad's words, "The women have to be topless, because their faces could stop a clock." Not only did he think the women's faces were strange, he wasn't very impressed with the quality of bare bosoms he saw. "They hang down like those little, skinny, beaded evening purses that girls carry," he said. He grimaced after he noted that Mother was right, "Some things are better left unseen."

I had wanted my mother and brother to have a taste of the comparative freedom in the North, in the hope that they might decide to move to California. I took them to all the places they could never enjoy in Little Rock. We went to restaurants, shopping centers, and, of course, the Haight-Ashbury district, where all races mingled in harmony.

After a week, Mother Lois said she felt calmer and could now really enjoy museums and recreational activities. She was unaccustomed to planning play and leisure activities, because opportunities for blacks to participate in Little Rock were so limited. She also said that she noticed how free she felt, unfettered by the constant constraints of the segregated South. It was like being cut loose from the tether, she said. She wasn't burdened with remembering and following the rules and civilities for dealing with whites.

After two weeks, they left San Francisco for the return trip to Little Rock. I was sad to see them go, but a little hopeful, because they were full of enthusiastic talk about moving to California and getting jobs here.

Matt, Kellie and I celebrated our second Christmas together and by February, 1965, Matt had completed his service in the Army. The baby's arrival had forced us to delay our plans to continue our education. Matt began work immediately as a part-time policeman and a full-time armored car driver. It was around this time that we had the first major argument of our marriage. He insisted that I become a housewife once again.

"Kellie is going to be two years old soon. It's time she had a little sister or brother. That will give you something to do. I won't have a wife of mine working now. My salary will support us. A woman's place is really in the home. My mom never worked," he said, as if that should settle the issue once and for all. But I wasn't ready to give in.

"No," I argued. "What about our plans to accumulate enough money to go to college?" My heart was broken when he declared that he really never had any intention of finishing college or allowing me to complete my education. He told me it was something we didn't need. He said that he and his parents had talked about it and that we would soon be moving to their Arizona ranch.

I was shocked at his response. He had never said anything about our becoming ranchers. He had made his decision alone, without so much as a minute's consultation with me. I was livid. Anger flooded my body and my temples pounded. I had to hold my tongue for fear I would say things that I would regret.

Slowly, tenaciously, according to my well-thought-out plan of discussing our future in calm, pleasant moments, I continued presenting my case. I had dissected the future and separated the issues. I needed to keep working, I told Matt, because no matter where we lived I needed more college and would have to earn the money to pay for it.

Matt said that was impossible. He told me that the ranch was isolated and it would be difficult to travel to classes.

That's when I began discussing the possibility of remaining in San Francisco. I told him how much better I thought it would be for Kellie, a racially mixed child, to grow up in the city. If I kept working, I said, we could stay on the West Coast. Matt was not interested in my reasoning.

I resisted, but by the end of February I found myself a housewife once again. When I had resigned myself to the notion that I had to obey Matt, I decided to make the best of my situation and give it my all. I sent away for correspondence courses and completed one course in pre-law and one in philosophy. I began to submit stories to magazines and the rejection slips from *Family Circle* magazine and others only encouraged me to try again. I also sought friendships with other church women who had similar interests.

During that time, the country was reeling from the assassination of Malcolm X, the Black Panthers, lunch counter sit-ins and free speech movements, as the Reverend King focused on Selma, Alabama, and voting rights for black Americans. I joined the group in my church supporting the latter effort. They not only held discussions, but collected money to support the drive for voting rights for blacks. Having completed President Kennedy's term of office, President Johnson had been inaugurated for his first elected term the month before and he ordered the first sustained bombings of North Vietnam. Wherever I went, everybody wondered if bombing innocent people could solve anything.

I was home being a full-time wife and mother. No matter how hard I tried to adjust to this life, I had to admit that the tranquility, housekeeping and soap operas that at first had been a comfort to my battered spirit were by now becoming a decided bore. My wounds from being a civil rights warrior had partially healed, and I felt as though I ought to be out in the world accomplishing something. Mother had a saying which now meant more to me than ever: "If you make a bed, wash clothes or cook a meal, somebody is bound to sleep in the bed, wear the clothes and eat the meal. But read a book or earn a degree and they are yours forever."

My life seemed to be floundering, marked only by the time I spent making lunches, feeding the baby, reading to the baby, washing clothes and vacuuming, and then doing it all over again the next day. I felt as though I were stuck on a merry-go-round in hell.

Matt continued to bring me flowers each week and the little gifts with which he liked to surprise me. And he doted on Kellie more than ever. While I valued my family and our love, I needed more — to feel that I was learning, growing and making a contribution. I continued keeping up with current news. It was sometimes the only activity that seemed to belong to me and me alone. I was anxious to hear the progress of the Freedom March, the walk from Selma to Montgomery, Alabama, by three thousand Americans of all colors, supporting the drive for voter's rights for blacks.

I watched the news in August, 1965, when President Johnson

signed the Voting Rights Act, outlawing literacy tests and other requirements for voter registration that had been used to keep blacks
from the polls. And then, less than one week later, rioting broke out
in Watts in the city of Los Angeles. I was glued to the regular television news and the news analysts shows. Matt complained, flipping to
the senseless comedy shows, family nonsense or westerns and sus-
pense that he loved so much.

I started a campaign to return to work, but Matt was still
adamantly against it. Nevertheless, I persisted in my request, pressing him with reasons why I shouldn't stay at home. I tried to make
him see that I could not be happy and fulfilled as a housewife. I
pleaded with him to see things from my point of view. I had been a
national figure in the civil rights movement, and now I was not making a real contribution to that movement, or to any of the other of the
magnificent revolutions whirling about me. I felt like a bystander.
Working would enable me to have the money to connect with the
movement and even make an occasional trip to join marches or
demonstrations.

Caring for Kellie was a full-time job that I sometimes resented.
While I was undeniably crazy about her, I resented all the time and
energy a toddler could take from one's life. I wanted one day a week
off just to be Melba again, to do all my favorite things like reading
and playing the piano. I was gratified, though, that Kellie had begun
to exhibit some of my physical features, although her hair color
turned from satiny black to brown. She had looked so much like
Matt during the first part of her infancy, but now her green eyes had
turned brown. She had my eyes and nose, and her smile resembled
mine. She was toddling about and talking now, becoming a real person with demands and claims.

Matt persisted in wanting to have a son. I couldn't give up my
dream of claiming my personhood, but nevertheless, I was determined not to disappoint my husband. Maybe if we had a son he
would compromise and go to college or allow me to complete my education. I loved Matt with all my heart and I wanted him to stop fretting and, instead, to be pleased with me. I gradually gave in to the
notion of another baby, and finally, in October, 1965, I discovered
that I was pregnant once more. Christopher would be his name if the
baby was a boy and Kelsey was our chosen name for another girl. I

felt that warm movement deep inside and I was certain that I was carrying a son. It must be a boy. That would satisfy Matt and allow me to get back to college. "Please, God," I prayed, "let it be a boy."

Matt was just as excited and caring during my second pregnancy as he had been during my first. I was relaxed and more content about being at home. Time seemed to be passing with more ease and joy as I delighted in my homemaking. I wrote in my diary:

> *Thank you God. I am learning to be a good housewife and we are a real family. I have to put my studies off, but it will be worth all the delay to hold Christopher in my arms. Then I will have charge of two of your angels. Thank you for Matt and for my family.*

It was June of 1966 and once again I was eight months pregnant, but this time I was home instead of in a hospital, my belly extended and Kellie perched on the edge of my lap as I watched the news on television. All over the airwaves the news people reported the United States' bombing raids over North Vietnam. News broadcasts continued to set a pace for my life. It was the way I marked time, and felt a small moment of being Melba. Watching them was something I enjoyed, and it was my choice — not Matt's. I felt powerful and unique.

On the Friday afternoon when I went to see Dr. Davies for my regular checkup, I was feeling a little sluggish and wondering why my baby had stopped kicking as much the last few nights. Maybe this person respects my need for a little rest, I reasoned. When the nurse put the chilly metal apparatus on my belly to check for the baby's heartbeat, I thought nothing of it. But when she went out for the second nurse, followed by the arrival of a third nurse, all trying unsuccessfully to monitor the heartbeat, I was nervous and anxious. When the doctor entered the room with a pained expression, I was filled with a growing panic.

"Where's Matt, Melba? I'm gonna need to call him. Is he walking a beat today or in a patrol car?"

"I don't know, why?"

"I'll get some numbers from you and we'll make the calls. Why don't you go to the lounging room, climb into bed and take a nap."

"A nap? I'm going shopping," I said. I'd left Kellie with my friend Renee and was going to take advantage of my rare free time by getting my friend some errands done. I was looking forward to shopping for the new baby.

"No, dear, not now. You take it easy and I'll be right back."

How I hated it when this male doctor wouldn't talk to me about what was going on in my body. I knew there was no point in protesting. He was a male chauvinist. He would wait for my husband as though I was inept, unable to handle whatever it was. Something must be wrong with the baby. Was he frightened that maybe my baby was ill? Maybe he wanted to do a blood test, or take a picture of the baby inside me. *Okay,* I thought, as I sat on the lush mattress and touched the pillow, *whatever it is, I will cooperate fully and he'll fix it. Why would I want to take a nap?* Yawning, I snuggled beneath the lush, sky-blue blanket, and stared at the ornate tiles on the ceiling. That's when I discovered how weary and bone-tired I was feeling. Sure enough, I was grateful to be lying down and sinking into a deep sleep. But as I drifted off I couldn't stop asking myself why the doctor had made me wait there for Matt.

Chapter 25

"HELLO MY SWEETHEART." I awakened to the sound of Matt's voice. It took me a moment to remember that I wasn't at home in our bed, but rather at my obstetrician's office in the sleeping room, await-ing my husband's arrival so the doctor could tell us what was hap-pening with our baby.

"How do you feel, honey? You had a nice, long nap."

"I guess." I didn't know what to say in response to the pitiful tone of Matt's voice. Besides, I was alarmed by the tears brimming from his emerald eyes. He was pale white, his freckles much more ap-parent than usual.

"Honey, we need to talk."

"About what?" The doctor stood directly behind Matt but he was silent. There was an expression on Matt's face that spoke a sad tale. My husband turned to look the somber-faced doctor in the eye as though they shared some secret, some conspiracy.

Taking my hand in his and looking me in the eye, Matt said,

"Our baby seems to be having a hard time. It's not kicking or moving very much."

"So? What does that mean?" I sounded hostile. I was angry. They shouldn't have talked things out without me. I could handle the fact that our baby might be deformed or ill or . . .

"So, the doctor thinks it's best if you deliver right away."

"No, that's not right. I mean, doctor, don't we take a risk, inducing labor at this stage? The baby's only eight months. All the books say the longer it stays inside the womb, the greater chance for a long and healthy life." My words came in a rush.

"Well, yes, yes," the doctor stuttered, as though he knew much more than he was telling me. He hesitated, then looked at Matt in that knowing way. Their expressions were so serious.

"Tell me the truth. What's wrong with our baby?"

When neither of them answered, I said, "No, you can't take my baby right now."

"I'm afraid you have no choice, honey. There's a risk to your health as well as the baby's," Matt said, as he reached out to stroke my cheek.

Choking back tears, I sat upright on the bed.

"My health?"

"Yes, Melba, I'm really sorry, but we're gonna go right now and get this over with. I can't risk losing you!" Matt's expression told me he was terrified. Something was really wrong. I felt my whole body shaking as tears poured out of me.

I heard myself begin to scream hysterically. And then I felt the prick in my right arm. Matt was holding me so I couldn't wrench away from the doctor's needle. "Kelsey, Christopher, Kelsey, Christopher." I whispered over and over the names we had chosen for our boy or girl. I struggled to remain conscious so that I could protect my baby.

I remained awake long enough to feel them strapping me onto the gurney but I couldn't speak. I was aware of being wheeled down the hallway and into an ambulance, and I tried desperately to gather the strength to release myself. Matt just brushed my forehead with his hand and gently kissed me. I wanted to ask him how he could do this? How could he side with the doctor against our baby? But I wasn't able to form the words. There was nothing I could do but lie there and watch the dark shadow hover over me and then draw me into its center.

When I awakened, there was no mistaking my whereabouts. I was in a hospital room. The gravel-voiced nurse bid me good evening. She seemed so chatty that I figured she would answer my questions honestly.

"Where's my baby?"

"Oh, honey, they took it away." She didn't look into my eyes, instead focusing on the water pitcher she was filling.

"Is it a boy or a girl?"

"It was a little baby boy," she said with sympathy in her voice.

"Was? You mean my baby's not in the nursery?"

"Oh no, uh, it's in the uh, mor . . . uh. We're so sorry about that, I mean, you're gonna be just fine." She was nervous, dropping a glass and cutting off her own words as though she were afraid of revealing some kind of secret. In silence, she hurriedly scraped up the broken glass.

"But my baby, may I see him?"

"Oh, no," she said, her voice sounding shrill all of a sudden.

"Where is he?" I persisted. I feared asking the question but I was terrified of not knowing.

"They'll keep it in the hospital cooler over the weekend and then complete the autopsy on Monday."

"Autopsy?" A cold chill rooted at the very top of my head and cascaded like ice water downward through my body. I felt as if I were paralyzed, frozen absolutely still like some statue. After staring at me in silence, realizing that she had perhaps revealed something to me that she wasn't supposed to, the nurse took a deep breath.

Unable to believe what I was hearing, I swung my legs over the side of the bed and stood up, feeling the tug from the intravenous tubing connected to my arms. I said to the nurse in a loud voice, "I have to see my baby! You can't keep him from me. I have to see him. Now!"

"You can't, ma'am. Let me get the doctor."

"No! I want to know where my baby is, right now!"

"In the morgue. He's deceased."

Deceased? Dead? My baby couldn't be dead! A strange calm settled over me. My body felt as though it was in the eye of a storm. *My Lord, dead? He died and I never got to hold him, even in his last moments?*

Sitting back down on the bed, I felt suddenly as though all the life had been drained from my body. I turned my face toward the wall and said, "Could you please get my husband for me?" The moment she left the room, I stood up and pulled the intravenous needles out of my veins. Disconnecting some sort of monitor that was strapped to my chest, I got my coat and purse from the closet and walked through the hallway and out the front door of the hospital. How could I remain in that hospital unable to see or touch or hold my Christopher, my dead son?

Climbing out of the taxi in front of our home, I could barely stand up long enough to dig the money out of my purse to pay the fare. Once inside the front door, it was all I could do to climb the stairs and get into bed. Matt and Kellie were nowhere to be seen.

"Melba! Melba!" A while later, I heard Matt's voice shout my name from the bottom of the stairs. "Are you here?" Then there was the *clunk clunk* of his footsteps taking two stairs at a time until he stood over me with a strained and puzzled expression.

"Why did you leave the hospital? I was talking to the doctor in the waiting room."

"I had to get out of that place."

"Honey, you scared me to death! The doctors are looking all over for you."

"I can't stay in that place," I said emphatically.

"We need to get you back there so you can feel better," Matt said.

"Matthew, why did our boy die?"

"Let's not talk about that."

He was treating me like a child again, refusing to talk to me about Christopher's death. Instead, he smothered me with kisses and hugs and left the bedroom to make warm soup. He was behaving as if I were recovering from the flu or something, not like our baby had just died.

I hadn't stopped crying by Sunday morning when the doctor came to the house. Once again I felt the prick of a needle in my arm that sent me into a haze lasting for the next few days. When I was totally conscious of myself and my surroundings, I realized that it was Wednesday. I was so angry at Matt for allowing the doctor to take away my consciousness, but I was still tired and drifted back to sleep. When I awoke the next time, Matt was sitting across the room in our big, overstuffed rocking chair, reading the paper.

"Your little girl is anxious to see her mommy," he said. "I'll get her."

"No, I want to talk to you. Alone." I had to say what I was feeling.

Matt ignored my request, leaving the room to get our daughter. Kellie climbed onto the bed to give me a hug and that's when I felt the loss of our Christopher even more intensely. She stayed on my bed playing with her dolls and teddys, while Matt fixed our dinner. Although I tried to remain calm and appear normal, I felt a desperate cry inside of me.

Three days later Matt went back to work, leaving me alone with Kellie. I found that I couldn't get up, couldn't fix breakfast for my daughter, couldn't dress her, couldn't think. I could only cry and picture my son lying somewhere cold and still.

Matt came home at noon to check on me and found Kellie at the foot of our bed eating dry Cheerios and still in her pajamas. "You haven't moved an inch since I left," he said, picking our daughter up in his arms.

"I can't," I cried. "I can't. I want to talk to you." He took Kellie into her bedroom and when he returned, I could see impatience written across his face.

"I think I'm losing my mind," my words blurted out before I was really ready. I was talking too loud, fear raising my voice. "Everything is so confusing and now my baby is dead!"

"You just need some rest, honey." He sat on the edge of the bed and looked into my eyes. That's when he explained in a matter-of-fact way that if I had a breakdown now, I would be sent to the state mental institution. He described that as a dreary place where indigent crazy folks played with clay when they weren't in straitjackets. "I don't think you'll be very happy there. Maybe you should wait a while," he said with a serious face and a calm voice.

"Wait?"

"Yes, if you can wait until we have more money, I can put you in one of those fancy funny farms where you won't be embarrassed to invite your friends, you know, the ones where they have individual rooms, visiting shrinks and you get to play with paper dolls and water colors, as well as clay. And you can wear your own clothing."

My God! By the look on his face, he was serious. He meant every single word. His facial expression and manner compelled me to think about the practicality of what he was saying. I didn't want to invite Kay and George or any of my friends to the state asylum. And there was Mother Lois. She would tell me that God is my mind, so how could I lose it? She would be really upset. What would Grandma India say if she were able to speak to me?

Matt's logic jarred me and hastened my efforts to recover physically and mentally. Over the next few weeks I lived in a fog, but I pretended all was well. Physically, I felt fine, but I became obsessed with being the best mother and housewife I could be. I cleaned for hours. I read endless stories to Kellie. I bathed her too many times a day. I was frantic when one thing in the house was out of place. I couldn't shake the feeling that my world was upside down, and when I was alone, I couldn't stop crying about our baby's death. Still Matt would not talk to me about the cause of our baby's death or share his feelings with me.

On the news I saw that there was a great furor in San Francisco because the Beatles were about to play their concert on August 29. I desperately wanted to go, because it would signal to me that we were resuming our life as a couple. We'd have a fun date together. But Matt wouldn't hear of it.

"When will you grow up?" he chided. "We're married. Grown-ups. We need to devote that time and money to our child. You need to get a good night's rest so you can heal your body and mind and deliver us another son."

By late September of 1966, my mental obsessions, my endless dreams about our dead son and my struggle to cope with ordinary tasks made me realize that I was spiraling down a deep shaft. I felt like I was cracking up. I had constant stomachaches. I had to do something, I had to get out of the house and get into the structured routine of a job. I thought that might bring me some relief. I pleaded with Matt to let me go back to work. He was adamant, insisting that I stay home, rest up and get pregnant again as soon as possible.

Day after day we argued. I was feeling smothered by him, trapped in the clutches of his absolute control. Like a mad dictator, he wanted to control my every move, my every thought, even down to the television shows I chose to watch. "Not too much news," he said to me one evening after dinner. "When you watch what's going on in the world, you tend to get restless, sweetheart."

What had been caring decision-making on his part now felt to me like oppression. He behaved at all times as though he knew what was best for me, no matter what the issue in question. On one particular day, he came home to tell me he had purchased a new house. The modest, two-story home in an Italian neighborhood might have been what I would have chosen, but I wanted the privilege of sharing the decision. With a pouting mouth and wilted spirit, I prepared to move in and decorate. But even as I hung our pictures on the walls and pressed the doilies to place on the end tables, I was thinking about going back to work or going any place that would allow me some personal freedom to find myself.

My feelings about Matt were changing so rapidly that I couldn't discern whether or not I loved him too much, not enough, or not at all. I sometimes felt like he was the enemy, especially when he denied me what I so desperately wanted, to work or study, and insisted that I be the wife of the year. According to his schedule for me I should have been cleaning, baking, cooking, ironing and mothering Kellie all day. When off duty, I should have been devoting my time to learning how to do these tasks in a better way. He expected that upon his arrival each evening I serve the perfect meal, comprised of his favorites, of course, afterward do dishes while he watched TV, read stories to Kellie, bed her down and then become the "sex kitten." His amorousness arose just at the time I wanted to relax, to watch the news or write a poem.

I was terrified of making love by that time, fearful of getting pregnant again. I couldn't live through the painful experience of having another baby die. There were times when I wanted a second child, especially if that child could be just like our precious little Kellie. But, I needed time to heal myself mentally and physically and time to be Melba.

I figured the answer was to have the doctor give me birth control pills. That would allow me to satisfy Matt's sexual advances, to keep our romance alive, while avoiding another pregnancy. I was deceiving him but I felt that he gave me no choice. I knew he would never approve of practicing birth control until we'd had the son he wanted. He turned a deaf ear to my pleas that we weren't ready to have another child. In my diary I wrote:

> *Dear God, I know I am a good mother but I am no longer certain I am a good Melba. The marriage to Matt, motherhood, housekeeping, all this is not the all that I am to become. I feel that Mother Lois is right, I have a mission and I am not fulfilling it. Please help me. Please answer my prayer: help Matt to back off and let me have some say about my own life and my body.*

I began to feel as though we were one of those families on the television programs we watched religiously each evening. Matt would come home, we would have dinner, play with Kellie and put her to bed. Then promptly we sat ourselves down in front of the tube. After an hour or so, he would kiss me on the cheek and then urge me to hurry the cleanup while he hinted about bedroom frolicking. I yearned to go to lectures, to a museum, a play, to get a sitter and attend at least one political event, a march, a rally, something where the air was electric with the social changes that engulfed the country.

Matt's most fervent wish seemed to be that all evening television shows be televised in color by the end of 1966, as the network predicted. He had purchased five television sets, including one for the bathroom. By November, when a massive power outage hit the East Coast, I was wishing that I could be one of the 30 million people in that blackout. Maybe it would give Matt and me a chance to talk to each other again.

Just before Christmas of 1966, Matt's parents invited us to spend the holidays with them on their ranch in Arizona. Driving all those hours gave me time to triple the amount of the anxiety I felt about meeting them for the first time. I would be staying on an isolated ranch just outside an all-white town in the Southwest. I knew Phoenix was a city without a history of intense racial problems, but the situation still frightened me.

Upon our arrival, Matt's dad greeted us at the car by saying that all the relatives had gathered to meet Kellie and me. Their home was a beautiful, white shingled ranch house bordered by winter-blooming perennials with cattle and horses grazing in the fields beyond. Truly, it was a picture-postcard setting that resembled the set of a big-budget cowboy movie. Inside, the decor was much like Grandma India and Mother Lois might have created if they'd had a bit more money to spend. It was cozy and colorful, lush with antiques, white ruffles and doilies. There were all the special touches in which a caring and meticulous homemaker takes such pride and pleasure.

Being thrust into the living room amid a group of twelve white folks, all hugging Matt and looking at me with curiosity, was a gut-wrenching experience. The women reminded me of Mrs. Cleaver on the popular television series *Leave It to Beaver*, and the men were rough, John Wayne cowboy types with muscular bodies, glazed eyes and huge, rough hands. They wore jeans, cowboy hats and all the western fixings, just like in the movies.

Getting through that first introduction with apprehension and a grand stomachache, I was delighted a few days later to conclude that they were generally a bunch of very nice people. Matt's mother was the only one who took every opportunity to emphasize my racial difference.

June looked like an angelic elf—petite, very attractive and with a liquid voice and perfectly coiffed hair. It was obvious that Matt had inherited his mother's green eyes. She would smile sweetly, offer me chocolates or dispense offers of southern welcome whenever Matt or anyone else was in the room with us, but the first time I was alone with her I couldn't believe my ears.

"Matt married you in order to help the Negro people, you know."

"Excuse me?" I said in astonishment. "What did you say?"

"You heard me. My son can't really love you. He married you to help your people," she said, smugly.

"I don't quite see how our marriage helps my people," I said, trying not to lose my temper.

"Well, never mind. If you looked more like Lena Horne then he could be proud of the way you are." She was eyeing me from across the room like I was a piece of furniture.

"He thinks I'm pretty," I said, tears stinging my eyes. I was stunned. I couldn't believe what she was saying. At that moment

Matt returned to the room. I said nothing, hoping it was a one-time thing.

Over the next few days, every time we were alone together, she would change her voice and face to sour lemons and repeat her hurtful words.

"You ought to lose some weight. Most of your people are fat. You don't wanna be that way." Or she'd say, "Nobody knows you're Kellie's mother. I mean, you don't look like her. She's so light."

I began to defend myself and I asked her why she didn't save her comments until Matt was present and could hear them.

When Matt surprised us, coming into the room unannounced and saw me standing up for myself, he questioned me. I tried to explain what his mother was saying but he cut me off. He didn't want to listen. I could tell he felt torn apart. It was clear that he had no intention of confronting his mother about the hurtful things she said to me. My solution was to remain quiet and try to avoid her as much as possible.

One afternoon Matt's dad, Rocky, was walking down the hallway past the bedroom. He was the spitting image of Matt, only sunwrinkled and much bigger. This rugged, gentle soft-spoken man had been mostly silent, looking on quietly when we were in the same room. That day I sat with Kellie in our bedroom folding her freshly laundered clothes. Without even saying "Hello," he came into the room, sat on the other side of the bed and began folding clothes along with me. Pretty soon, Kellie approached him and he picked her up and sat her on his lap.

"This is our baby," he said. "These are my hands, my forehead, she has our hair, our skin tone and our features. There's no denying, she's one of ours and we love her." He continued talking, but switched the subject. "Give mama some time," he said. "She'll settle down, don't you know." He winked at me. From that moment on, I felt closer to him. Each day he would help me with a chore, whether it was folding Kellie's clothes or taking her in his arms when she cried in order to give me some relief. He even played games with her. I became more and more relaxed with Rocky. He never said a harsh word and sometimes even smiled and winked at me if he chanced to hear Matt's mother raking me over the coals.

Country living on a ranch was not my style. I hated the mud, the odor, the endless care needed for the cattle, and I loathed trying to ride horseback, seated on the saddle behind Matt. Being there made me feel inadequate, as though I were an alien in a different world. I couldn't join in their conversation about making fresh bread, cottage cheese or buttermilk, or raising sheep or cows. The only glimpse of farm life I'd had was watching the McCabes doing all these tasks so foreign to me.

I also found that the womenfolk displayed an attitude that was very unlike the attitude I had learned from Mother Lois and hoped to nurture in Kellie. Their macho husbands reigned absolute. They dictated when, where, how and what took place, no matter what the task or event might be. The choices of a sightseeing trip, the dinner menu, the time to go shopping, how long we would stay, what movies to see, or when we would gather for Christmas dinner and our attire for the occasion, these things were all decided by the men.

I felt lonely during that Christmas, wanting someone with whom I could share mutual ideas of life and express my point of view. I was so happy when Mother Lois phoned to check on me. "Call again, every day," I pleaded.

When at last we left, I was pleased to have met Matt's family but ecstatic to be heading back to California where I would see other black people, sleep in my own bed and have a discussion on current affairs to wake up my brain. I would have to call George and Kay and go up for a visit. They were up on current events. I would be overjoyed to hear someone talk about foreign policy, politics, or civil rights. Besides, I needed to feel their love and acceptance.

By the beginning of 1967, I was determined to become a rebel. I had fought hard to come to California to be free, but I was feeling as I had when I lived in Little Rock. I wasn't free. How had I so gleefully exchanged my personal freedom for the prospect of being totally cared for? I wanted to be loved and I loved Matt, but I certainly didn't like being manipulated. I pondered what I could do to quell his constant badgering about my not being pregnant. He kept asking me if I was pregnant; when I said "no," he scowled, and pouted and demanded that I go see a doctor.

On New Year's Eve, I decided I had to stand up for myself. The next week I registered at City College of San Francisco and began taking night classes in law and sociology. When Matt balked, I declared that I would attend classes two evenings a week. Matt hit the roof. He accused me of not being a good wife and mother, expecting him and Kellie to fend for themselves, especially at dinnertime when he deserved to rest. "I work hard all day. A man deserves to be served a proper meal." His mother had done it for his father for thirty-five years, his sister was doing it for her husband. What was wrong with me?

I had never seen him so angry as the first night of class when I grabbed my blue wool coat and headed for the door. I refused to get into any deep argument; I was determined to be on time for my first class. Furious with my "disobedience," he left our marital bed to sleep on the living-room couch. When two weeks had passed and I continued going to class and did not plead with him to come back to our bed, he returned to the bedroom, saying that I had his permission to finish the current semester but could not enroll again.

Two months after the spring semester had ended, in August of 1968, I was preparing for Kellie's fifth birthday. As I placed the candles on the cake, I suddenly collapsed and buried my face in my hands. How unhappy my life had become. I had a constant gnawing stomachache. In the last six months, Matt and I had been virtual strangers living under the same roof. We pretended to be amicable for Kellie's sake. I feigned smiles and even pretended that I enjoyed myself when we made love. The truth was that we were walking through our lives together like two robots, never discussing our real feelings.

His hostility about my school attendance had only increased as I refused to quit. On one particular night after class, I drove up to see a police car parked at the curb in front of our house. Rushing up to the front door, I could only think that either Matt or Kellie had been injured in some way, and forgetting that I had a key, I banged on the door like a maniac. In the eternity that passed before someone answered, I thought my knees would buckle. A police officer finally opened the door with a pleasant smile and it was obvious that at least no one was hurt. He told me that neighbors had telephoned because they heard gunshots in our basement. Matt and two of his part-time police buddies had set up target practice in the basement, shooting at the concrete walls with Kellie standing right beside them. As I walked into the room, another officer was explaining to Matt that it was lucky that none of the bullets had ricocheted and hit his daughter. Matt responded by saying, "Oh, I didn't think about that. I'm so used to practicing in the wilds."

Anger rose in me that rivaled any volcano that ever erupted on this planet. He had risked my daughter's life to have a bit of fun with his pals. He could have killed her! Having handled guns all his life, how could he not know the danger of what he was doing? Did he think that if I came home to this disaster, I would see it as reason to quit school? The words that leaped out of my mouth were unlike anything he'd ever heard from me before. The police hadn't even pulled away from the curb when I gave him a piece of my mind.

As I spoke I could see an expression of horror come over Matt's face. "You don't want to talk back to me this way in front of my friends," he said. "Wives don't insult their husbands this way." But nothing he said stopped me. On and on I went, out of control. I pointed my finger in his face. His two friends headed for the front door red-faced with expressions of astonishment that matched Matt's. I was certain the entire neighborhood heard the extent of our wrath that night.

I remember Grandmother India saying one could not "unring" a bell. She warned that a body must never speak harsh words in the hopes they will go away. They don't disappear. Words can be weapons that wound. That's what Matt and I did to each other that night. We wounded each other and from my perspective, the wounds would not soon heal. The bottom line for my husband was that he did not see wives as human beings with rights and thoughts and feelings to express. Women were to be cared for and controlled.

Weeks passed before we exchanged a decent word over the dinner table. And even that occasion was a pretense for Kellie's sake. She now sensed there was something terribly wrong. It would be two months before we even tried to make love. Each day I was spending more time concentrating on my studies. I was hearing Mother's admonishments loud and clear about getting my degree, because that was something she'd said no one could take away. I wanted a professional career. I wanted to be respected. And most of all, I didn't want to be left out of the civil rights movement, whether I became an active participant marching and protesting or prepared myself to take a significant post that served and empowered.

When I spoke to Matt about future plans, his were different

than mine. He never planned to return to school. His family owned a ranch, he reminded me. He said he didn't have to worry about making something of himself. He was destined to become a rancher. "I'm not out to prove anything, just to live comfortably," he would say. "You ought to take a page from my book and settle down. What's your rush to conquer the world? Take a load off, relax."

Relaxing was something I had never learned to do, especially when Bobby Kennedy was dead, Martin Luther King was dead and the news was reporting that the U.S. had dropped more bombs during the war in Vietnam than in all of World War II.

Our war of words continued beneath the roof of the home that he had chosen and I had only come to tolerate. As time passed, I noticed that Kellie was stuttering. When the doctor said she appeared obviously nervous and inquired about disharmony in our household, I took stock. I must stop the shouting matches with Matt. I vowed to settle our differences in private or not at all.

On a Tuesday morning in early December, 1968, I awakened at 7:00 A.M. as usual to start breakfast. Matt and I lay for a moment cuddling and talking about Christmas plans. We laughed and chatted in the old way and I thought to myself, *Maybe we can mend our differences.*

As Matt made his way to the shower, his attention was drawn to my pink case of birth control pills that lay on the dresser. I had forgotten to put them in their usual place. I winced, recalling that I had been tired and obviously careless the night before.

"What's this?" he asked, with an agitated tone.

"It's nothing, honey. That's my medication. You'd better hurry or you'll be late." I reached for the case but he wouldn't let go. My efforts to distract him failed. He picked up the case and read the inscription.

"Birth control pills? You mean all this time I've been thinking we're trying for a baby, you've been deceiving me?"

Matt was livid. He refused to hear my pleas to quiet down and not disturb Kellie or the neighbors. After a while, Kellie awakened and came into the room as he stood there nude, preaching to me, shouting at me. We would never get past the wounds of the words we exchanged that morning. And what's more, now we were wounding Kellie. Her tear-stained face, her stutter, reflected our wrath. Gathering her into my arms, I went to the kitchen, leaving my husband to scream at the walls of our bedroom.

Reassuring Kellie that Mommy and Daddy loved her and each other, I began making breakfast as though everything were normal. Kellie was shaking and her little face told me how frightened she was and how much her heart ached. When Matt came down, finally, he saw her face and traded his pouting expression for a smiling face but he did not speak to me.

"Will you be home on time for dinner?" I asked through the wall of silence, as breakfast ended and he stood to snap on his holster and gun to leave.

"Like always," he said. "You're the night owl that likes going out to classes. I prefer my family after dark." With that, he got in his car and drove away.

That evening when Matt wasn't home by six o'clock I began to worry. When he hadn't called by eight o'clock I was truly frightened. By ten o'clock that night, I was frantic. I phoned his workplace, the armored-car company, to ask about his whereabouts. They told me that Matt had made his last delivery, parked the truck and left in his car, as usual. By eleven o'clock that night, after calling everyone I knew, I called the police to report Matt as a missing person.

Chapter 26

THE POLICE TOLD ME that I needed to wait for twenty-four hours before they would interview me and file a missing persons report, unless I had clear evidence of a harmful act or kidnapping or a crime being committed. I would always remember those twenty-four hours without Matt as absolute hell.

By five o'clock the next morning I was dressed and bathed. Every time the phone rang I ran for it, hoping to hear that familiar voice that had once made my heart sing.

By noon that day, I was grateful for the time and effort it took me to care for Kellie. She was now a five-year-old child with her own agenda, clear demands and constant chatter. In some way, it was my determination to be a good mother that was keeping me sane. I couldn't tell her that I was on hold because her father wasn't around. After all, it was only a few weeks until Christmas. She was very focused on Santa's arrival. And no matter how big the crisis, my daughter had to have breakfast, be bathed and dressed and allowed time to play with her dollies. I had to read her a morning story, and then get her to her preschool. On that first day I completed all my tasks like a robot, existing in a fog.

I told myself I could function, I could get along by myself, because Matt would surely be returning today. Going out the front door was the first time it hit me that I didn't have our car. He had taken the car. Was I going to have to do all our errands, get the groceries, and ferry Kellie back and forth to school every day on the bus?

Allowing the two white policemen to come into my house that night frightened me out of my wits. But the possibility of living without Matt's love and protection frightened me even more. Now, twenty-four hours after his disappearance, I would give anything to have him boss me around—to ask me once more if I were pregnant. Even as I beckoned the policemen to take a seat in the living room, warm tears flooded down my cheeks. There was nothing I could do to stop the flow.

The tall, lanky officer with gray at his temples took out his notebook and pen. The stocky policeman paced about, looking at the array of family pictures before he took a seat across from me. "Are you sure this is the first time?" sneered the short officer. "He's probably out having a breather, out with his own kind."

"Excuse me?" I said, glaring at him. "What do you mean?" I hoped I hadn't heard him correctly, so I gave him a second chance.

"Maybe he was tired of chocolate and wanted a little variety."

I stared at him with disgust. Obviously these men weren't going to be of any help to me, but I had to get them to fill out the paper to put the process in motion.

Clutching the collar of my corduroy jacket at my throat, I sat in the high-backed brown leather chair that was Matt's favorite and tried to answer the policemen's questions. No, Matt did not stay out this late. Yes, he would always call if he were going to be even fifteen minutes late. Yes, we were accustomed to having dinner together with our daughter every night. No, we had not had a major argument about any issue.

I figured I'd only add fuel to their racist fire if I described the awful argument we'd had over the birth control pills. The policemen persisted in telling me once again, that Matt was probably out on the town—their implication that he was out catting around was clear. If they knew about our argument I was afraid they'd dismiss my fears and not bother looking for him. The way they looked at one another, their poorly disguised snickers when I said certain things or teared up, made me feel as though I was being interviewed by two good ol' boys.

Besides, I wanted to keep some aspects of our marital relationship private. Surely our disagreement wasn't cause for my husband to run away. It wasn't like him to refuse a confrontation to get what he wanted. Matt would have sulked for several weeks and then taken the birth control pills away from me and insisted that we have yet another try at having a baby.

It was the older man with gray sprinkled at his temples and a flaming red mustache who asked me, "And I understand that you and Matt are an interracial couple. Do you mind showing us your marriage license?"

Something inside me wanted to ask whether they required such documents when a white spouse filed a missing persons report but it was a fleeting thought. I was so distraught that I only had time and energy to focus on finding Matt.

Suddenly, a sharp pain, like a flash of lightning struck me. What if Matt had been kidnapped, carried off to be punished because he married a black woman? What if they killed him because he was liberal enough to marry me? *That's nonsense,* I told myself, as I found the license and handed it to the officer. I noticed then that my hands were trembling.

With sheepish grins that made my stomach curdle, the officers left, saying it was unlikely that I would hear anything right away.

By bedtime, I was exhausted. I turned on the news to watch all the furor over Dr. S. I. Hayakawa's use of police to end the strike on the campus of San Francisco State College. Matt would never have allowed me to watch the news on television in the bedroom at that time of night. Tonight, sitting in front of the TV like a zombie distracted me from my awful dilemma for just a little while. Then, suddenly, at the thought that Matt might come in and catch me, I clicked off the television. I didn't have a right to feel okay about going against his wishes. He might be suffering or held captive somewhere or dead. I missed Matt. I felt so helpless. There was nothing I could do about the situation, absolutely nothing.

I lay awake for a while, listing all the things I had done during the day. I wanted to make certain I had done them as he would have. There were so many tasks Matt had taken care of, like seeing to it that the doors and windows were locked, getting meat for the next meal from the freezer in the basement, carrying the wash from the back porch, walking Kellie about the house on his shoulders before bedtime. I had done it all by myself today and now I was still alone that night, in the bed we had shared for almost six years. The sheets and pillowcases still held the scent of his body. Clutching his pillow to my chest, I whimpered into it, trying to muffle the sounds so Kellie would not know how sad I was. "Where are you, Matt? Please come home," I whispered.

Surely, Matt was a decent enough man that he wouldn't just disappear. He was too strong, too traditional, too caring for such an act. No, I was certain he was being held somewhere against his will. "That's it!" I said aloud as I turned out the lights and lay there in the dark. And then I started to sob.

If Matt had been kidnapped, was he all right? Was he alive? Was he warm? Why was someone holding him hostage? Over and over again, I ran the events of the last days through my mind. Was there a clue to Matt's disappearance? Did he really make up his mind to leave us, or was he forced to do so by some stranger? Was his anger over the birth control pills enough to make him take off in order to punish me?

"Maybe Daddy is visiting Grandma," Kellie said the second morning of Matt's disappearance when her father was not at breakfast. My sad-faced little moppet was such a beautiful child with her olive-complected cherub face sprinkled with her father's freckles. Her long, light brown curly hair reached to her waist. When she was sad, those huge, liquid brown eyes were haunting, much like her father's. "He's coming home soon, Mommy, so you don't have to cry any more."

The days drifted one into the other and became a large painful blur. I moved through the endless hours and did my chores, accompanied by heartache and by thoughts that were like a strand of same-colored beads, a repetitive theme circling round and round in my head: missing Matt, wanting Matt. As the days passed, I wondered if

I would ever see him again. The physical ache I felt for him in my heart began to feel a like a familiar part of me.

I became adept at making excuses to explain Matt's absence to our minister, to our friends, to Matt's folks when they phoned, to Mother Lois. But on December 15, late in the afternoon, my friend Renee dropped by. Matt and Renee's husband had developed a friendship, we shared common interests, and the two families had become quite close. She arrived with her three-year-old Alex and her five-year-old twins, carrying a plate of Christmas cookies. She walked up the steps just as the police were walking down and toward their patrol car. They had been reporting to me that they still had no information to give me about Matt's whereabouts.

"Tree's not up yet. You're slow this year." She put baby Alex down on the couch. "You'd better get in gear. Only ten more days, you know." Anxious not to reveal my secret, I mumbled some excuse about not having my decorations up. She continued chatting, obviously avoiding the question she must surely be thinking—why were the police there? Tears began pouring down my cheeks. She escorted our children into the next room, and when she came back the words escaped from my mouth like a rushing waterfall. I felt so embarrassed because she was so white, so well turned out, so happily married, so perfect. But I couldn't stop the rush of words. I needed to tell somebody about the horror I'd been living through.

Renee urged me to telephone my mother and Matt's parents and to get in touch with Kay and George. She said I had to prepare a Christmas somehow for Kellie; I had to keep going. She asked me to keep her children while she ran a very important errand. An hour later she returned with some special decorations for our Christmas tree, a few toys hidden in bags to be saved for Kellie's Santa to deliver and green velvet fabric so that I could sew a Christmas dress for myself.

Together we unboxed the plastic tree that Matt's parents had sent the first year of our marriage. We had used it every year since then. Now, I was looking at its twisted branches, unfurling them without Matt's instruction. At first I thought my insides would explode with a combination of sadness and anger and pain, but having Renee there helped me to keep going.

When the Christmas lights were flickering on and off, the angel topped the tree and the candle Santas and elf figures given to us by Matt's folks were neatly in place, I was pleased with myself. I even felt a flutter of pride in the way I finished decorating the house and started a routine of my own—the same as I had when Grandmother India had died. There was an undefinable emptiness, but I had to find a way of doing the necessary things to live. And there was a feeling of guilt for moving on, even in this small way, but life keeps moving on despite our problems and makes its demands and I had to respond. All the while, little Kellie kept prodding me with her questions, the sadness written on her beautiful little face.

I hadn't imagined that Kellie and I could have Christmas without Matt. I guess I thought someone would make a national declaration postponing Christmas until his return. But there were carols on the airwaves and crisp red and green holiday colors were to be found on television, on every street corner, and displayed in the stores where Kellie and I strolled as if we had money to buy. It was good to get out and walk where there was noise and people and bustle.

Over turkey dinner at Renee's house with her family and friends, I had to get up from the table and go to the bathroom to hide my tears three separate times. She must have told everybody that Matt had disappeared or that we were having trouble, because no one asked about him. Kellie told the other children that her father had to stay in Arizona and have Christmas with his mother.

The day after New Year's, January 2, 1969, I awakened and for the first time since Matt's disappearance, I wasn't crying. Something deep inside me felt gray and stone-like. I looked into my eyes, reflected in the bathroom mirror, and I saw determination staring back at me. I had to live, to be strong for my daughter, to stop feeling sorry for myself. Most of all, I had to be a responsible adult for my daughter. Even before I could ponder my actions, I took the scissors and cut my long hair off. First the long braids and then up over my ears, up off my face.

I would wear a natural, as a sign of my defiance. Matt would never have allowed me to wear short hair. Even when I hinted at it, he bristled.

Now things were different. He wasn't there. One tear streamed down my right cheek as I looked down at the floor covered with the hair I had combed, set and meticulously styled for years. All my life Mother Lois had said that wearing long hair was my reflection of our family's Indian heritage—the pride of our rainbow mixture. Indeed, it had been my crowning glory. It had been the sign of suburban privilege. But I was no longer wifey. I had neither the time nor the money to keep it pristine. I had to use my time to make a new life for Kellie and me. If wearing a natural meant being radical, I had to be radical to survive.

Back in bed, Kellie climbed in with me that morning and said, "Mom, you've got 'daddy hair.' What happened? Too short, Mom."

I said aloud the words that I needed to hear, "Daddy's not coming home right away, my darling. I'm certain he's missing you and loving you very much, but he just can't come home right now."

"I miss my daddy," Kellie said, and began to cry.

I held her close and we cried together for a long moment, and then I said, "Daddy would want us to get things going. We've got to start our day."

After that morning, I vowed never to let Kellie see me that way again. I was determined that if she wasn't going to have a father, at least she was going to have a fully functioning mother. Grandmother India and Mother Lois had done it before me—they had successfully parented their children after losing their husbands.

As more and more time passed and Matt didn't return, Kellie became more and more insecure, believing that I would disappear as well. Each day I tried to reassure her that I would never, ever leave her. Though she hugged me tight and seemed to trust my assurances, I knew deep in my heart that she wasn't certain. Every time I dropped her off at school or at the babysitter's house, she questioned me endlessly about where I was going and exactly what time I would be back to pick her up. It saddened me to see her so nervous and worried, even though I did my very best to make her feel safe and secure.

One morning she looked at me and said, "He's visiting Grandma for sure and when he gets an envelope and a stamp, he'll write to us." I didn't try to correct her. I had to let her down easy, to give her time and space to learn to do without the daddy she adored. If he should come home in the next few days, I wanted her to welcome him wholeheartedly.

"Go back to school. Don't think now, think forever. Whatever it takes to get a degree—do it." George McCabe's words nearly echoed Mother Lois's advice. Neither of them offered money to support my schooling, but they argued vehemently that I should not go back to work. "You're gonna have to give up something—sacrifice," Mother said, "but it will be well worthwhile."

The next day I registered for courses at San Francisco State College. The counselor told me that as a single mother I might be able to get welfare. "Welfare?" I was embarrassed to let the word come out of my mouth. But I knew I had to take hold, to consider my options, whether they were humiliating to me or not. What else was I going to do? How could I work and go to school? Besides, my salary as a secretary would not support the two of us.

I had looked into the mortgage payments and other bills a few weeks after Matt's disappearance. Was there money in our bank account? I couldn't find the checkbook at first. When I located it, I discovered there was hardly any money. We had no savings and a huge mortgage payment. I knew I was fast running out of food and money, and I had to do something.

I decided after talking to the counselor at school that I would have to go on welfare. When I reported Matt's sudden disappearance and the ensuing hardship to the welfare department social worker, I was able to get food stamps and a small amount of money that same day. It would sustain us until I could figure what to do.

With great consternation, and after several nights of grinding my teeth during nightmares and crying buckets of tears, I realized that I would have to let go of our current lifestyle completely. I would have to give up our house. I didn't have any idea how a person went about giving up a home. Was I supposed to sell it or what? That would be so complex, I concluded.

I telephoned the previous owner and told him he could have his house back, that my husband was gone and I couldn't afford it. Replacing the receiver in its cradle, I just stood there in silence, looking all around me. It was a three-bedroom, two-bath home with a living room and separate dining room. I had decorated and come to love our home. What would the new place be like? Not only would I need welfare but I decided to apply for public housing.

I found a moving company, and took only the things I needed to get by; I left seventy percent of our household goods behind, including some of our most beautiful possessions. The former owner had allowed us to remain there for two months for nothing, and I wanted him to be able to sell whatever he could and apply the proceeds toward the money I owed on back payments.

On the day we moved, Kellie was distraught and in tears. She figured if we moved without her dad that he would not be able to find us. I sat down with her and she wrote a letter to her father in care of his mother. She told him where we were moving and asked him to get a pencil and write to us as soon as possible.

I looked out the front door to see that the few possessions I chose to take were loaded on the small moving van. The movers were almost ready to leave. Kellie seemed content for the moment with the letter to Matt. Walking with her through the house, I said a last good-bye to the treasured possessions that Matt and I had accumulated during our years of marriage. Although I had told Kellie that we were not coming back to our home, it was clear from her comments as we went from room to room that she thought it was going to be a temporary move.

I stood for a long moment in the front hallway, my mind flooded with memories of all the happy times we had spent in our home as a family. I shook myself back into reality, knowing that I might collapse in a pool of tears if I continued reminiscing.

I took Kellie's hand and slammed the front door hard behind us.

Chapter 27

SUNNYDALE HOUSING PROJECT ON THE OUTSKIRTS of San Francisco was a place I wouldn't have even driven through before I moved there. In fact, I had not known it existed until the welfare department gave me a list of low-income housing. When I told friends where I might live, they said, "Oh, my God, you can do better. Surely you don't have to go there!"

Our tiny, two-bedroom apartment was all concrete with only the most basic amenities. A narrow, four-burner gas cook stove, a one-basin sink and a very small refrigerator filled the ten-by-ten-foot kitchen. The living room was the same size as the kitchen and up a narrow flight of stairs were two tiny bedrooms and a small bath. The whole apartment was shaped like a square box. A trip to Woolworth's netted me cheerful curtains, a few pillows and candles.

I had stopped only a few times to ponder Matt's reaction should he discover that I had given up the house he purchased and loved so much. There hadn't been time to grieve too much and, also, I had to keep moving or I was sure that I would fall down in a heap of sorrow, pining for what might have been.

I was now an official college student, and it felt like I was climbing Mt. Everest each morning as I took Kellie to school and went to my classes. I had to take four buses in the morning to get us to our destinations and four buses in the late afternoon to return home.

The single most irritating aspect of living in Sunnydale was the sound of conga drums being played day and night. Stationed at the nearby bus stop were a group of black guys dressed in clean, creased work-a-day clothes who played the drums. They seemed to have an endless supply of players. All day, every day, and many nights, they thumped away, and the constant pattern of rhythmic thuds almost drove me nuts. I decided that they'd discovered some new, mind-altering method of torture as I listened to the continuous, never-ending rhythm of the drums.

Kellie and I now lived in what some people described as a dangerous ghetto. I discovered as much when one Saturday night at 10:00 P.M. I heard gunshots and looked out to see the bleeding, ravaged body of a man collapsed on our sidewalk less than six feet from our front door. I didn't recognize the man. I had never met him, I told the police as they questioned me while a crowd of about two hundred people gathered outside. Our yards were full of people after the police left—restless, whispering, angry people who frightened me. Even at midnight the crowd still lingered, refusing to move on. Their behavior reminded me of the rioters, the segregationists, who confronted us as we attempted to integrate Little Rock Central High School. By 11:00 P.M. I was so frightened that I called Mother Lois. We prayed together. She told me to be strong, to know I was protected.

When the knocks came on my door, they awakened Kellie. I ignored them, keeping the light out and sitting quietly in the living room in the dark with Kellie on my lap. The next morning several neighbors questioned me about the dead man. I only hoped that I convinced them that I didn't know him or his business.

Every moment after that day I feared someone would come after us, threaten us or injure Kellie. Late one night, as I lay in my bed reading a textbook, I heard a *click click* just outside my bedroom window. Peeking out Kellie's window, I could just see the arm of a man chiseling the paint at the bottom of my bedroom window that had been painted shut. He was coming in. Was he a burglar, or just out to kill us? My heart was thumping so loud it almost drowned out the beat of the conga drums. What should I do? Everybody knew the police didn't come fast to our area, if they came at all. By the time they arrived, I could be dead.

I raced about the house looking for something with which to defend myself. Who could I call? Mother Lois? No. What good would that do? There! The nightstick that Matt had used as a policeman. I had kept it as a sort of souvenir to remind me of him. I grabbed it and raced down the stairs and out the back door, until I was standing directly beneath the robber.

He was hanging precariously by his fingertips, clutching at the outside window sill. That's when I saw the metal garbage cans. Suddenly, I knew exactly what to do. I started to pound on the metal cans as hard as I could, screaming, "Help! Help! Help!"

"Shhhhhhhhhh!" the burglar said, peering down at me. "Look, baby, you gonna wake up the neighborhood." He looked around, checking adjacent doorways and windows and then looked back down at me and said, "All I need is a little cash. This ain't a big thing."

"Please get down and go away. I don't have any money."

"You got to give Mack a little cash, that's just the way it is."

My tactics weren't working at all. In a heartbeat, I decided to mimic the rough talk I'd heard the other ladies in my neighborhood use. Deepening my voice and shouting as loud as I could I said, "Cash my ass! I ain't got no cash for you, mister! Get your butt down from there right now!"

I was glad Mother Lois was in Little Rock and couldn't hear the words that jumped out of my mouth. But after all, in only a short time I had learned that life in Sunnydale required unique survival skills. You had to be willing to do whatever it took.

"Ohhhhhh lady, you're somethin' else," he was mumbling as he slowly started to climb down. "Are you sure you ain't got no money?"

"I've called the police. They'll be here right now, because my boyfriend is a cop!"

That did it. The burglar started to climb down fast. I scampered into the back door and locked the latch. That's when I realized I had been out in the cold night air wearing only my nightgown for all to see. Peering out the window, I saw the burglar hit the ground running. I grabbed my robe, checked on Kellie and ran next door to ask for help.

The woman just across the way, Annie, was a part-time nurse's aide who lived with her two children, ages ten and thirteen. She came right back home with me and insisted that we have a cup of tea together so I could get things straight. She said she would take me under her wing and teach me the ropes, otherwise I wouldn't survive.

Tall, slender with copper skin and long, dark brown hair, Annie's extraordinary beauty reminded me of Mother Lois, except her manner was much different than Mother's. She had a lot of self-confidence and a way of flaunting her beauty, like movie stars did on screen when they were trying to make men really like them.

"You gotta get a grip on things," she said, inhaling deeply on her cigarette and looking around for an ashtray as she crossed her legs beneath her blue see-through robe and leaned back, making herself comfortable.

"Grip?" I handed her a newly washed tinfoil plate from the frozen dinner we had eaten for dinner earlier to use as an ashtray.

"Never again do you bang on your can when a burglar's at your door. Grab your child and come over to my house. Let him see you got nothing so's he'll tell the others and they'll leave you alone. Otherwise, they'll think you got something to protect and they'll be back again and again."

Great, I thought to myself as she continued listing rules of survival for Sunnydale. Her conversation reminded me of a discussion with Grandmother India about how to survive with the white people on your neck. On and on Annie went, saying that if the Black Panthers knocked on my door during one of their marches, I had to open it, extend my hand, tell them how proud I was and compliment them over and over again. If I didn't do that, then they would make it hard for me.

Life in that housing project was to grow me up faster than any other experience. It was do or die. Gunfire rang out on many a Saturday night. One day, the small grocery store less than two blocks away, which I counted on for last-minute necessities, was trashed and burned. The owner threw up his hands and closed his doors.

In the coming months I would be compelled to lean on Annie

and her family for counseling on the ways of life in Sunnydale. In an effort to do Annie a small favor in exchange for her constant caring advice and at least one meal served to Kellie and me each week, I started talking to her about how she might go back to school. She was a bright woman and seemed so suited to being a teacher or a business executive.

"I don't think about those possibilities any more," she said. "I can make as much money as I want to, any time I want to. I'm saving to buy a house."

"On a nurse's aide's salary?" I wondered how she could do it, but I didn't ask. Meanwhile, I found myself clinging to her and her mother as if they had adopted me. Sunnydale was a world that frightened me because the rules were so different and there was that same oppressive feeling of having someone else in charge, just as there was in Little Rock.

Venturing out my door one Saturday morning to greet the man who drove the vegetable wagon, I held on tight to Kellie's hand. I didn't socialize with the other ladies and few gentlemen who had gathered there. When I got closer, I wondered why they weren't reaching out, touching or gathering and bagging the fruits and vegetables. Cucumbers, oranges, lemons, apples, everything a body needed for good cooking. And the prices seemed reasonable, I thought, as I reached out for a tomato.

"Lady, watch it. You'll break my vegetables." The driver of the vegetable van was dressed rather oddly, I thought, as I quickly withdrew my hand. He was wearing something that resembled a shiny tuxedo. His skin color was the same shiny, steel blue-black as the suit. His hair was slicked back very straight and he wore a green, rhinestone-covered bow tie. I wondered what he meant by "break" his vegetables?

"I'd like three tomatoes," I said, in a calm voice. The other ladies snickered. That's when he lifted up a section of what had appeared to be a wooden vegetable cases filled with tomatoes. Hidden underneath was a radio. All the vegetables were fake, painted wax replicas glued to the surface to fool somebody—the police, I guessed.

"Look, lady, I ain't got no time for your nonsense."

"She's new," Annie said, walking up behind me and grabbing my arm.

"Oh. Look 'a here, honey, you want somethin', a radio, records, a record player, cigarette lighter or whatever, just let me know and I'll provide it. An' if it ain't here, just tell me where it is—Macy's, Emporium, be clear now . . . say which rack and which floor and I'll have it here in twenty-four hours. Can I take your orders now? Time's a-wastin'."

Annie grabbed my arm and started dragging me back toward my front door. "See you, Mr. Parsons. Have a good one," she shouted back at him. She wouldn't let go, rushing me away and I was tugging just as hard at Kellie's hand, trying to keep up.

"Listen up, Melba, don't you do anything else here 'lessen you ask me first."

From that moment I didn't make a move without Annie's advice. I tried to be outside in Sunnydale only when I walked between my front door and my car. Rarely, unless Annie was at my side, did I walk onto the lawn or even up the block.

By April of 1969, the Vietnam combat toll exceeded that of the Korean war. The anti-war protests were an everpresent part of American life now. The streets of San Francisco were filled with protesters. A whole lot of people who wouldn't ordinarily take to the streets were now a part of widespread movement. Vietnam and the cancellation of the Smothers Brothers network television show due to continuous censorship battles were the topics on everybody's lips.

Every morning and every night I watched television news, fascinated by the reporters and their stories. I was taking a news writing class and the teacher had urged me to join the staff of the student newspaper. He said I had real talent as a writer, that all I needed to do was to let the words out, to say things my way and let my own feelings loose on the paper. His kind words had made me very happy.

I thought about all the news reporters that had come to Little Rock and how their presence had saved my life. I thought about their freedom, the take-charge way they approached things. I remembered then that I had dreamed of becoming one of them. Somehow my dream of being a news reporter had been buried in the clutter of Santa Rosa and the residence club, and I had totally let it go when I married Matt.

The next few months sped by in a hodgepodge of frustrations and pleasures, all centered around my driving struggle to survive. I thought about Matt constantly, but not with the same intensity that had haunted me in those first days of his absence. I had brought his blue toothbrush with me and placed it in the bathroom holder beside mine. I had hung a few of his clothes in the closet. On occasion, I cried for what might have been, and that made me all the more determined to be somebody. Whether he was dead or kidnapped or had made the decision to leave, I was going to earn my degree and become self-sufficient.

School was a delight. It took up time and space in my head, so there was that much less energy to worry about Matt's safety and whereabouts. I loved the campus and I was beginning to make real friends. I met a Rastafarian man named Eddy in my sociology class. A black man with long braids who stood six feet, six inches tall and had a deep voice and a howling laugh, I found him to be one of the greatest minds I had encountered. I was invigorated by debates with him. He had a read a lot about the Little Rock integration in 1957 and was intrigued by me. Both Eddy and his wife, a white instructor on campus, would become dear friends in a short time. We would share lots of good times debating and eating and laughing together.

Eddy's take on his interracial marriage relieved a pain in my heart. He was a radical in his black consciousness and in his fight for civil rights, but he said, "The person I choose to love and bed down with is the one who gives me passion to be a radical. The color of love is whatever color makes your heart race, whatever makes you feel alive."

Commuting on eight buses a day, keeping up with the rigors of classes and studying, plus mothering Kellie, took everything I had to give. It was all I could do to change into my pajamas and crawl into bed most nights. My weekend pleasure consisted of an occasional dinner with Renee. I shunned my other friends and even stopped seeing George and Kay. I felt ashamed of Matt's disappearance. I had taken the huge risk of marrying a white man—the source of much consternation in my life—and what had it gotten me? Kellie was always the answer I got back in my head. Without Matt there would be no Kellie and I loved my daughter more than life itself.

Still, I didn't know how to behave around people, not even those that I was certain felt sorry for me and loved us. I was fearful of long tearful explanations and hearing "I told you so." Increasingly, my time socializing was spent with Eddy and his wife Shirley, with Renee and her kids, or with Carmen, a new black woman friend I had met who also had children. She was married to a Japanese musician and they had such a delightful and passionate relationship. Carmen and I would take the kids to the park or the zoo and all the time we were together I found myself learning from her. She had grown up in California without the strict segregation restrictions imposed on blacks in the South. She seemed fearless and I was eager to learn what made her tick.

Carmen was a brilliant student and showed me the ropes at San Francisco State College. She inspired me to look for on-campus opportunities to connect with faculty so I could get a part-time job. She explained how the student loan department worked and showed me how to apply.

My daughter was by now so accelerated in school that teachers pleaded that she be taken out and put into a school for advanced children. She was a first-grader, matriculating in second- and third-grade classes, causing some havoc in the public school she attended. She would finish her homework and then saunter around the room doing the other children's homework. She attended the third-grade classes regularly and the children resented this first-grader's superior reading ability.

Mother had advised that I find a school where her accelerated capacity would be nurtured, a place where she wouldn't stand out like a sore thumb because of her advanced abilities, so Kellie and I set about exploring places where she might fit in. I decided on a private school called Presidio Hill Open Air School. There we found a haven, a group of people who would become like family, accepting and loving.

On Sundays, there was church and the highlight of our entertainment for the week if we didn't go out with friends. We'd share one burger with fries and one orange soda at a fast food restaurant called Doggie Dinner. Then, we'd board the first of four buses and go back home again to the place where I was becoming increasingly afraid of living.

I had read about the Black Panthers, seen them on the television, wondered about them, and Annie had instructed me to treat them with kid gloves. Now, day after day, I saw the precise lines of black men wearing black berets and black jackets, marching across the lawns near my home. Their anger showed in their facial expressions and they carried guns and clubs. Several times they called out to the neighborhood, asking people to join them in one of the center yards for their rally. When they came knocking on my door at night, asking for my support, I followed Annie's advice. I unhooked the night latch and whispered through the crack in the door that I admired them enormously, but I was a woman alone with a baby to support. Then I dimmed the front lights, retreated to my bedroom and cracked open my books, studying for the double load of courses I was carrying.

Nothing, not civil rights, not the Panthers, nothing could delay or destroy my graduation. I was wavering between Mother's advice to be a teacher, a notion that made her ecstatic, or following my own dream and my instructors' advice to consider a career in journalism. Whatever field I chose, I wanted a respectable way to earn a living for Kellie and me.

In May, Renee's husband allowed me to buy his rebuilt 1957 Chevy coupe with no money down and small monthly payments. Mother agreed to buy the car for Kellie and me. Kellie and I thought we had been scooped up and transported to heaven. I drove her all over the city and our Sundays became a blast. To the park, to the zoo, to the beach—we went all over. We had little money in our pocket but we had a lot of gratitude because we could eat our peanut-butter sandwiches and drink our powdered milk as we picnicked at all the wonderful spots San Francisco offered.

I also offered to help Annie and her mother, Josie, do grocery shopping since I had transportation. Josie would often make gumbo on Saturday nights and several women in the neighborhood would gather for dinner and talk. I learned a lot about the lives of the people who lived in Sunnydale at those Saturday night gatherings. They were an inspiration to keep studying and graduate, so I wouldn't end up with a mundane job and mundane life. Most of those women encouraged me, but a couple of them reminded me of the Little Rock hopelessness. They said I was wasting my time, "'cause the white folks ain't gonna give you no job no matter what you study."

Josie, an olive-skinned, big-boned woman who looked like pictures of American Indians I'd seen in books, bustled around the kitchen energetically during those gatherings. She was southern and she always said she understood me better than her northern-raised daughter ever could. We shared a common upbringing. But all along she'd say that Kellie and I were "just camping out."

"You don't belong here, you're not one of us," she'd say. And she was always urging me to get out because I didn't know what I was doing.

One day I was taken aback when Annie explained that the drummers who drove me nuts with their rhythm day and night were young men who had no place to go. Each morning they got dressed and played their drums because they had dropped out of school and given up hoping for a decent job. They didn't want to get involved in criminal activity, so they devoted themselves to their music instead. It was their vocation and education.

It was many months before I found out that Annie was not only a nurse's aide but that she also had a second profession. At night she spruced up considerably, magically becoming a sultry, wildly dressed creature whom I hardly recognized. As she strutted to the bus stop one Friday evening, I leaned my head out the door.

"Got a hot date?" I said, kidding her.

"You got a lot to learn about life, honey. I got a day job and a night job. It takes both to make ends meet."

I stood there stunned. I couldn't believe that my neighbor was a hooker. She had such nice children whom she was obviously devoted to, and her house was so neat and clean and I liked Josie, her mother, so much. I wondered what Grandmother India would say about my associating with them. They had become my protectors, people I trusted and counted on for my own safety.

A YEAR PASSED AND I was astonished to see that my love for Matt had changed. I sat staring out the front window one day, wishing with all my heart that he was there sitting beside me, and I realized that my love was fading like the subtle scent of a very expensive perfume. Each morning, when I touched his clothing or the blue toothbrush I kept as a memento in the bathroom, it was like opening the bottle of fragrance. Only at those times when I dared to let the fragrance escape its bottle did it fill me and the whole room, bringing with it his image and memories of good times.

But when I allowed myself to think about the possibility that he might have planned his disappearance, might have wanted to get away from us and had done so, there was a part of me that now hated him for what he had done to our daughter. Now, a year after his disappearance, she still waited at the front door for the mailman to bring a letter from him.

It was Kellie's obsession with the daily mail delivery that would eventually compel me to leave Sunnydale. One Saturday morning, as she stood peeking through the mail slot, something suddenly made me pull her away and demand that she sit in the kitchen with me and color. A chill danced up my spine as we heard a gunshot ring out moments later. I grabbed my baby and my purse and headed out the back door and then circled wide through the yard to the car.

As I cranked the engine, I saw that once again there was a circus of violence that was becoming more frequent. I had to do something, I could no longer risk losing my daughter.

In journalism class I wrote a story about the violence at Sunnydale and my news writing teacher insisted that I join the staff of the student newspaper. My first assignment was to write a story about the Black Studies controversy. A Black Studies department was being established at San Francisco State College that would set a precedent for colleges across the country.

Lynn Ludlow, the instructor in charge of the student newspaper and also a working reporter for the *San Francisco Examiner,* gave me rave reviews on my story. He said I would get regular assignments and asked whether I had ever thought of becoming a journalist. I was so delighted with this rediscovered part of myself that I couldn't stop smiling. It seemed so right for me, as though it was meant to be. I felt like I had found some long-lost home.

That post on the school paper would lead me to interview a man who directed on-campus married students' housing. I told him about my dilemma at Sunnydale and within two months, Kellie and I were moving, relocating to a small on-campus apartment. We were safe at last, and in no time we were very much involved in neighborhood activities. How wonderful it was to allow Kellie to play outside with other children her own age and to walk hand in hand with her at sunset. I could allow her outside on a Saturday morning without fear of a shooting. But the most wonderful thing about it was the quiet. No more conga drums.

I would miss Annie and Josie. I went back to visit them twice, but the violence was increasing. It was too hazardous and I decided not to go back. I issued them an open invitation to visit me. They took me up on it a few times, but then I suppose we all began to realize that we had very different interests and goals and we didn't keep in touch.

Meanwhile, I had studied so hard and taken so many courses each semester that in January of 1971, I fainted while taking my economics final. The paramedic told me I had to get some sleep. I had been up studying thirty-six straight hours to pass my exam.

After resting up and getting a healthy start on the new semester, I decided on a Friday afternoon after school in February that we should celebrate the fact that mother and daughter had made it on our own for a year and two months. Our chosen celebration was walking through the Emporium and then going to a movie.

Laughing, we were holding hands as we returned home skipping down the sidewalk toward the front door of our apartment. Kellie and I considered ourselves pretty lucky on that day. I wondered just what the leather-jacketed motorcyclist was doing in front of our place. Who could he be and what could he want? He frightened me. He stood quietly and calmly, leaning against his shiny, huge Harley motorcycle, which Matt had taught me was called a "dressed hog." As we drew near he glared at us.

"Are you Melba?" he asked in a cold, detached voice as his expression turned blank.

"Yes," I said. "Who are you?"

"Then this is for you."

He handed me an order summoning me to court. Matt had filed for divorce and for custody of Kellie.

Chapter 28

MY LORD, MATT'S ALIVE, I THOUGHT to myself. *Thank God, he's alive, but where is he? Why didn't he phone us?* Shuffling through the sheaf of papers in my hand, I couldn't believe my eyes. *Do the papers say where he is? Where has he been?* Maybe the summons was for someone else. But there was my name, plain and clear, and there was my baby's name. Ignoring my daughter's pleas to tell her what was going on, I pointed out the birds nearby, diverting her attention while I finished reading.

Divorce? I can't believe it. Why does he want to take my daughter away from me? I can't believe he would want to do that. Maybe if I could talk to him we could straighten all this out.

Riveted to the concrete, I read the paragraph in which Matt said that Kellie was more white than black, that he and his family were financially more stable, and he could provide the best setting for Kellie. To me, the paper read as though I were an unfit mother be-cause I was black. Matt would never say these things. He was not a racist. It must be June, his mother. The document also said that I didn't have any resources. Terrific. He leaves for a whole year without sending money and then accuses me of being without resources? Crumpling the papers in my hand, I looked down at my daughter, at her smiling dimples, huge brown eyes and missing front teeth. I'd take her and go to the ends of the earth before I'd give her up.

I grabbed Kellie's hand and ran for the front door of our apartment. Who could I call? What should I do? I had no money. I couldn't hire an attorney. I telephoned my social worker immediately and reported the matter to her. She told me there were attorneys who provided free legal aid for people who were without funds. She gave me a telephone number.

From that moment on, I felt as though I were in a race, only someone had fired the starting gun long before I knew about it and I had to catch up. I ran everywhere and did everything faster and faster. I was nervous and agitated. I had to catch up to Matt. His family had money and influence. They were white. They could take my daughter. How I hated him for putting us through that year of hell, leaving both Kellie and me to wait and worry about him. And now he wanted to drag me into court for a big fight. To add to my upset, every now and then the part of me that still loved him, still longed to hold him, would rise to the surface. "Wimp! Wimp!" I said aloud to myself. *I have to be a warrior again. If ever there was a time to fight, this is it. I can't spend even one moment loving Matt.*

The legal aid attorney was tubby, sweaty and breathed very loudly. He sat perfectly still in his old-fashioned, wooden swivel chair behind an ancient, huge mahogany desk. He peered at me through Coke-bottle lenses and continuously wiped his forehead with a graying handkerchief. His folding, paste-white cheeks cascaded into his neck which was fitted onto wide, round shoulders. His shirt was open at the collar and black hairs were sticking out above a white undershirt. "This is my savior?" I said to myself.

His office was in a dumpy building south of Mission Street in a district I would not walk through at night. It was piled with dust and papers and tattered law books. Looking around gave me little hope of victory. I was certain Matt's family would use all their money to hire the best attorneys.

But Peter Griffin, Esq., was a no-nonsense man. After our preliminary conversation he said to me, "You're a smart young lady. Crack the law books. I'll tell you how to work your case and you get busy. We don't have the time we need to devote to your case, but you can do it on your own — if you are willing." He peered over his glasses at me.

"Willing? Oh, yes. I'm not going to lose my daughter." I was willing to do whatever it took to keep her, including becoming a fugitive and leaving the country. I had been doing research, looking for countries that were not bound by law to return a fugitive.

"That's a good start." He tore off a page from his yellow legal pad and handed it to me. It was filled with law book citations and notes referring to my case. The next day, instead of studying for my sociology class, I hit the law library.

At first it all looked like mishmash to me. But I started to recall the law classes I had taken at night before Matt left. Methodically, I plodded through law books, page after page, and began to understand that Matt's desertion without warning and without providing support for Kellie and me was going to help my case.

Collecting the information, I reported back to the attorney. He began work to file a brief for me. It was only after those five or so days, totally devoted to keeping my daughter through my own work and research, that I could turn my attention to the other tasks of my life.

The local CBS affiliate had invited me to be a news writer in the television news department. They had discovered me through the journalism department where I had recently won four awards for the stories I wrote for the college paper. Now, in February, only four months from my graduation, they offered me a full-time job in the news room.

"It's perhaps an answer for now," Mother said in one of our now daily phone conversations. "But child, it's not permanent. The only permanent thing is to hold onto your baby with all your might with one hand and with the other, reach out, take that diploma. Get that degree!"

Mother Lois and I had grown closer and closer since Matt's disappearance. She was a formidable ally in my struggle to make my way and she was becoming a good friend. She had sent us what money she could spare to help us survive.

So I turned down a solid job offer, a coveted opportunity to be in the newsroom of a major network affiliate, for the prospect of getting my sheepskin. But I accepted an offer from the Sunday section of the *San Francisco Examiner,* which was interested in printing a story I had researched and written for them.

It felt to me as though I were seesawing between agony and ecstasy. I had faced the horror of losing my husband and now, I might lose my child. At the same time my professional career was soaring.

The pain of what Matt was doing to me cut into my soul. How could I have loved this man who now wanted to take away my baby? He must have known what that would do to me.

Was someone persuading him to take Kellie from me, talking negatively to him about me? I suspected that was the case, and I imagined it was his mother doing the talking. Had she known where he was all the time? Was she pressuring him to do this horrible thing to me? Matt had always said I was a good mother.

Meanwhile on campus, Eddy, the Rastafarian, was coaching me about appearing in court. While he worked on his graduate degree at State, he attended law school at night. He was reading my documents and advising me about my approach. He told me to get letters from my professors, from the church I attended regularly, from friends who observed me, from Mother Lois and from anybody who would vouch for my being a law-abiding, moral, upright citizen and good mother.

I dove into the junk food with all my might. I was not sleeping at night. Instead, I stayed awake and plotted my escape, in case I had to flee with Kellie. Should I wait? I felt crazed. I was preparing to go to court where I could lose my beloved daughter. At the same time that I made my legal preparations, I was torn, wondering if I should I take the risk of a court battle. *Maybe I should just take Kellie and run away, now.*

The consternation I felt, the brewing acid in my stomach and the pain in my heart as I tried to study and listen to my professors during class were indescribable. I was haunted by that legal document informing me that I was an unfit mother. Why was he saying that? It was only because I was black and poor that he said his daughter would be better off with his family. They had the resources to care for her, the document said, while I didn't.

My hands shook all the time. My left arm went numb. The doctor said it was nerves and that I had to find some way to calm myself. He told me that my blood pressure was abnormally high and my heartbeat was arrhythmic. I still couldn't sleep at night and when daylight came, I launched into my quest to be the absolutely perfect mother, a wonderful student, and all-around good person.

I kept the pretend-all-is-well smile on my face as Kellie continued to inquire daily about her daddy. I began to plug into the stories she made up to explain why he never wrote or called. "He doesn't have a stamp," she said, or, "There aren't any envelopes." And I would agree, with a smile and a caress, hoping she wouldn't get to know that maybe Matt was prevented from writing, or worse, chose not to.

On the day of my court appearance I was desperate to make a good impression for the judge, but I could not figure out what to wear. I tried on everything I owned, until clothes were strewn all over the apartment. I didn't own anything decent. Navy blue casual had to be okay and besides, I was late. Rushing through traffic to the courthouse, I was so nervous that I almost rear-ended another car. Hands shaking and tears streaming down my face, I strode breathless through the enormous hallways of the courthouse, the sound of my heels echoing on the marble floors.

Inside the courtroom, I felt lost in the cold, cavernous space with its shining wood surfaces. The room held rows of benches and wood railings that separated the spectators from the attorneys. I felt as though it would swallow me up. My knees were shaking so badly that my legs could hardly hold me up. I looked all around to see if Matt had arrived yet. At the table where I was told he would sit was a host of attorneys in movie-star–looking suits. Matt wasn't in the room.

The echoes of voices surrounding me only made the moment seem more eerie. My legal aid attorney, Peter, arrived with consoling words.

The judge was a huge man with a round, warm face and large brown eyes. Six feet six inches tall, he must have weighed 350 pounds and he loomed large, peering down at the courtroom from the bench above.

I sat with my attorney at a desk facing the bench and listened to

Matt's attorneys talk about me personally, about my mothering abilities and my relationship to Kellie. They offered live witnesses. I felt as if I was not being defended because my testimonies had been submitted in writing. Most offensive was their notion that I had nothing to offer my daughter. If they were to be believed, Kellie would be better off with her father because he and his parents offered her so much more opportunity.

At first my attorney asked me a long series of questions about things I preferred not to discuss in that open courtroom with all those strangers listening. When had Matt left and had he tried to get in touch with me? Had he told me he was leaving beforehand? Did he make financial provisions for Kellie and me prior to his leaving? Did we ever discuss anything about his going away? I blinked back tears and gripped the arms of my chair until my fingers cramped.

In turn, Matt's attorneys asked me several questions that embarrassed me and made me feel sad, but as they forged through the insulting list, I felt angry—very angry.

"How long before Matt asked you to marry him had you decided to be his wife?" one attorney asked.

He continued, "By the way, was it Matt who asked you to marry, or was it the other way around? Did you and your husband plan to become parents so soon after your marriage? Did you force him to marry you by getting pregnant?"

My lawyer objected, beckoning me to stop answering. After the attorneys' wrangling back and forth, the judge said, "Gentlemen, please approach the bench."

With their backs to me and their chests pressed against the tall bench, they spoke in low murmurs with the judge. When my lawyer returned to the table his expression was noncommittal. Matt's lawyer was poker-faced as he walked back and took his seat. I wondered what was going on. My hands were shaking so badly that I put them in my lap so no one would see how upset I was. There was complete quiet in the room.

Then the voice of the judge, smooth, caring and deeply melodic, broke the stillness.

"Race is not the measure of a woman's ability to mother, neither are financial resources the sole criteria of that ability."

His words echoed in my head. What could I do but leap up, run out, get my baby and run, run for the border. I couldn't give Kellie up to Matt. And then I heard words that awakened me.

"The custody of this child is awarded to the mother. The father has reasonable visitation rights," the judge declared, and pounded his gavel. Court was adjourned. I sat frozen in my chair, unable to move. My heart was pounding and I was still hearing his voice even though he'd stopped speaking. It seemed to be coming at me from the other end of a long tunnel. I could hear the words but oh, my Lord, what did they mean?

"What does it mean? What does it mean?" I was shouting and tugging frantically at the sleeve of my lawyer as everybody else stood while the judge left the room.

"The child is yours, Melba. You have sole custody. Your husband has visiting privileges. You'll get alimony and child support. However, let me warn you that the case can be reopened or appealed with the slightest provocation on your part."

Kellie was mine. "Thank you, Lord," I whispered. I sat down on the bench, remaining there long after the room had emptied.

At home that evening I held Kellie close to me and sobbed, shaking uncontrollably. "Mommy's happy, sweetheart. Mommy's so happy," I said. I hadn't told her about the court battle, and I didn't then. I was so grateful that she would be mine. When the phone rang I couldn't let go of her.

"You win," Matt said. "I want to see my daughter before I go away." He wouldn't tell me where he was going.

I began dressing the moment I put the phone down. In spite of all the horror, some small part of me believed that if I could look pretty enough, things would be like they were. Maybe we could be a family again after all this. The burning lump in my chest said, "No, no, no, no. How can you think of such a thing?"

Then I looked at the tiny girl sitting on the couch with Matt's forehead, his smile, his hands, and I thought it would be worth compromising all my dreams if we could be a family again, for Kellie's sake.

I was so embarrassed at the thought that he would be coming to our tatty little apartment. He would see it as proof positive that his allegations about my resources were real. However, there was nothing I could do about it except race around the apartment making myself crazy, putting things in order. I felt a twinge in my heart as I dressed Kellie in her green jumper and white blouse and brushed her hair, which fell to her waist. Her resemblance to her father was remarkable. She had grown so much in the time that he had been gone. What a shame that he had missed those days and moments of her growth and development.

OU'VE CUT YOUR hair. You look so different. Uh, you look good—yes, good," Matt said, as he stood in the doorway with the late afternoon sun at his back.

It was a windy but warm day in April. Matt was dressed in khaki pants and shirt with a dark brown sweater thrown over his shoulders. He was immaculate, his green eyes liquid as he looked into my eyes for only a moment. Then he looked past me at Kellie sitting on the couch and holding her doll. He was obviously nervous and uncomfortable in our unfamiliar surroundings. My heart felt as though it was exploding in my chest. I blinked back tears.

"Come in, have a seat." My voice was tight. I could feel the tears, feel them welling up inside of me. But I couldn't let them out. Awkwardly, he brushed past me.

Sitting on the couch beside Kellie, Matt reached out to her but she was too shy to take his hand. They smiled a similar smile at each other, which receded from each face the same way, leaving a slight frown in the middle of their large foreheads which looked so like each other. When they finally embraced, my heart stood still. For just an instant, I longed to have Matt hug me too. I would have given anything to have the three of us hug.

"Daddy, why didn't you write me?" she asked. "Didn't Grandma have a stamp?" Kellie sat in Matt's lap, looking into his eyes with her probing questions.

Matt broke down and began to cry uncontrollably. He held his daughter, weeping intermittently and asking her questions about her school and her dolly for the next half hour. I stood frozen at the bottom of the stairs, holding on to the bannister, unable to speak, to sit down, to move at all. It was as though something had pumped liquid iron into all of my veins. I was paralyzed by my thoughts, my fears,

my pain, by my memories of our wedding night and the day Kellie
was born. I remembered Christmases together and cuddling in bed
with popcorn on Saturday evenings.

Hearing his voice once more brought back all the times he had
said to me, "I'm so full of love for you that I think I'm gonna burst."

Then suddenly, like an earth-shaking shift deep inside of me as
I stood there staring at him, I just wanted to be rid of Matt. I looked
at those muscular shoulders I used to stroke during our lovemaking,
glimpsed the chest I used to rest my head on, marveled at the muscu-
lature of his magnificent body, erect, strong and so masculine. It
could not be mine anymore. I didn't want to look into his eyes. I
couldn't live through that again. I had to keep my love for him sealed
up, the fragrance inside the bottle. I just wanted him to leave, get up
from the couch, say goodbye to Kellie and go. We needed to get back
to our new life, the one to which we were accustomed, the life I had
carved out for us. Being with him this way was like opening up old
wounds and rubbing salt in them for both Kellie and me. It was too
hurtful.

He asked only a few questions of me: Was our house gone?
Would we remain here for now? Is Kellie doing okay in school? All I
could say was, "Uh huh," and nod my head. When he walked toward
the front door Kellie clung to him and taking his hand she said,
"Come on, Mommy. Daddy's going to take us back home."

I reached for her and squeezed out the words, "Not now,
honey."

He walked down the sidewalk with his back toward us, turning
only once to wave. I took a deep breath and let the tears out. I didn't
make a sound. I just felt the river of tears coursing down my face and
drenching my hurt soul, washing away my confusion.

I realized with a rush of sadness that whatever we had been to
each other in the past could never be again. The wounds were too
deep. Parts of me yearned for him, needed him, hoped for him,
wished for him, prayed for him. But if he would allow his mother to
take away my baby, to berate me in court documents in the way he
had, then I would have to get over him. He was weak. I could never
trust him again. The next morning, with shaking hands and a soft sob
I threw his blue toothbrush into the trash, boxed the clothing which
he had left behind and mailed it to his parents.

. . .

*I*N MAY OF 1971, less than a month before graduation, Lynn Ludlow, my San Francisco State journalism teacher, summoned me to his office.

"I think you ought to consider going to Columbia to their journalism summer program," he said.

"Columbia?"

"When you're finished they'll have a job for you in the mainstream media. It's a program funded by the Ford Foundation and Columbia University to infuse more minorities into media. They choose thirty-two folks from across the nation and it's highly competitive. But I think you can make it."

Lynn gave me a series of forms to fill out and told me to write an essay. I had never heard of the program and the more he described its elite graduates, the more I doubted I would be accepted. But I followed his instructions, staying up all night to write the best essay I could. I submitted it to him right away and he mailed it immediately on a Thursday. By the following Monday afternoon he had a call from the program officials. They had posted a ticket for me at the San Francisco airport. I was going to New York for an interview.

Kellie stayed with Renee and I left almost immediately for my interview in New York. The last time I had been to New York was on tour with the Little Rock Nine. For an instant, I thought how nice it would be if one of them were going with me now. And then like an arrow shooting through my heart, I wondered about Matt. What would it be like if Matt were with me?

As I lay in my bed, alone in my fancy hotel room, I was struck by the truth. Matt would never have allowed me to finish college. Had we remained together, I would never have realized that I could write or be a journalist, hence, I wouldn't have even gotten to New York. There never would have been an interview at Columbia.

The next morning, as I prepared to go to Columbia, I looked in the mirror to see my determined eyes. My hair was pulled tight on top and close at the sides of my head with a few curls at the nape of my neck. As per Mother Lois's instruction, I wore a monochromatic outfit in hues of blue. I had learned to compromise my style of dress;

it was a blend of my former prim color combination and the hip look of California cool in 1971. I smiled at myself. I was proud of the way I looked. I would have loved to have been thinner, but for the most part, I looked like a well-pulled-together adult.

Outside the room I prayed for at least an hour awaiting my turn. Once inside, I was stunned and embarrassed at the way the two men complimented my writing. I answered their questions and as I left one of the instructors said, "I don't know, Miss Pattillo, if you can be a television news journalist because you are so immersed in the written word. You're such an incredible print writer. You will have to learn a new language, learn to write in the shorthand of story-telling." His compliments both frightened and thrilled me. I wanted more than anything to be selected.

"I can do that," I said.

The interviewer at Columbia said that if I were chosen, I would earn a graduate degree in broadcast journalism and film as well as an opportunity for a job in television or radio. It was an elite program, taught by the respected masters in the field. Mr. Ludlow had honored me by even suggesting that I might be accepted.

On the day before my graduation from San Francisco State, I received an express letter congratulating me. I had been chosen as one of the thirty-two candidates from throughout the nation for admittance to Columbia's journalism program. I sat down in the chair beside the front door, looking at Kellie. Now I would have the resources and power to insure that we stayed together. Now I would have some control over our lives. "Thank you, Lord," I whispered and hugged my little girl.

During the graduation ceremony in the vast auditorium of San Francisco State College, I found myself sitting in my cap and gown with my little Kellie seated beside me. It was a moment I knew I would never forget, but I now wished I was surrounded by family. Mother did not have the money to come and neither did brother Conrad. I hadn't asked George and Kay to my graduation because I figured they had to sit through the four graduations of their own children. Later on they would chastise me and say I had hurt them deeply by not inviting them.

As each person stepped up to the podium to receive their degree there was a roaring applause by supporters. When I stepped up to receive my degree there was a lull in the applause of the huge audience. That's when my friend, Eddy, stood his tall lanky body up and shouted at the top of his lungs. "You-all better put your hands together and clap for mama, 'cause she done come all the way from Little Rock, Arkansas, to get this diploma and it's a long, long, long way from Little Rock Central High School to San Francisco State College."

My heart fluttered as the roaring sound of applause drowned out my sobs and I stumbled back to my seat next to Kellie clutching my diploma.

A few days later, Kellie and I closed up the apartment and took a plane to Little Rock. Kellie was going to live with Mother Lois while I was at Columbia. I hugged Mother for all the support and love and money she had given me to aid my quest for my degree. Without her faith in my ability, without her prodding and support and caring advice, I knew I could not have made it.

IT WAS A tough task to earn my graduate degree from Columbia. I never worked so hard in my life. But it was also exhilarating because it felt as though it was meant to be. I had received my personal calling. To answer it was pure pleasure. I enjoyed reading the six to ten newspapers per day, reveled in listening to all the notables in broadcasting, really liked going around the city covering stories. I was fascinated by the process of putting together the pictures and words that told a balanced and interesting news story. I marveled at the way they trained me to speak in the lower registers of my voice to sound authoritative. The professors saturated me in news and the art of understanding and debating issues.

I began my career with the public broadcasting station in San Francisco on the air, reporting with a cutting-edge television show called *News Room!* A year later, I was hired as an NBC newscaster with KRON television in San Francisco. On my first day at work, I was greeted by a handsome man with gray sprinkled at his temples and a youthful face behind black wire-rimmed glasses. When he spoke to me his voice sent chills dancing the length of my spine. That deep, warm voice was so familiar to me, ringing in my head like a pleasant chime from my past. As I returned his sweet smile, he repeated his name, "Hello, I'm Frank Johnstone, are you gonna be with us?"

He was the man whose voice I had heard twelve years before on that first lonely, desolate night when I arrived in San Francisco and was taken to a stranger's home. It was his voice that followed the clanging of cable car bells and the a capella choir singing the call letters K-S-F-O in San Francisco. Now I was thirty years old and had come a lifetime from being that frightened young girl, newly arrived from Little Rock and hunting safe refuge from the mobs and Klan that had chased me away from my home. I never told Mr. Johnstone that his resounding, gentle voice and warm manner were gifts to me from God. I had indeed traveled a long, long road and although the path was steep and the load sometimes heavy, I was always given strength and protection.

I had first wanted to be a news reporter at age fifteen when I saw reporters' role in the Little Rock integration story. I especially remember deciding to be a reporter in the federal courtroom, Friday, September 20, 1957, when the judge decreed that we nine black students had the right to enter Central High. I could dare to dream whatever I desired and count on God to help me achieve it. I was now closer to being equal and seeing equal than I had ever been in my life.

Epilogue

THE BIBLE SAYS THAT MAN PROGRESSES not by sight, but by insight. Now at age fifty-six, as I complete this book, I can see that Grandmother India was so right when she urged me to keep this verse always in my mind.

We often receive new and challenging gifts from the universe in our early years when we neither understand nor appreciate them. I believe life is like a gigantic puzzle. We are handed one piece at a time — some we don't recognize, others we grumble about because we don't know where they fit. But what we are asked to do is to trust that God will send instructions. No matter how misshapen or distorted the piece may seem at the time, it will contribute to the overall picture of our whole life.

That spring day when Kellie and I last saw her father would be the only time either of us would ever see him again. He never paid child support, nor did he make any effort to write or call or visit his daughter or me.

Kellie called her father a couple of times over the years. He appeared to have absolutely no remorse and was unwilling to discuss his abandonment of her. She found it strange, however, that he seemed to have kept an eye on my journalistic career. He told her he had collected magazine and newspaper clippings about me, and recited chapter and verse of my news reporting career, knowing when and where I appeared on the airwaves, and asking detailed questions.

At the time, Kellie was struck by his meticulous interest in me, but wondered why, knowing where we were all that time, he never tried to contact us. She was haunted by the question. Now, when I ask myself that same question, I feel gratitude that he abandoned us. It was truly a gift. I am certain that had I remained with Matt, neither Kellie nor I would be the same people we have grown to be today. And I really adore who we have become. We have come a long, long way and enjoyed every step.

Kellie has grown up somewhat in the public eye, not realizing during her early years that all her little friends' mothers weren't broadcasting the evening news or being written about in newspapers or magazines. One of my major goals was accomplished for a time, at least in that I didn't want her to ever experience the same racial prejudice in school that I experienced. Kellie was in the seventh grade the first time one of her schoolmates called her "nigger" and wanted to exclude her because she wasn't white. I was jolted back to my terror at Central High, realizing once more that the prejudices I had suffered in Little Rock were always just around the corner.

However, I could only allow myself to linger in that pity pot for a short time. I had to get over my rage and sadness that yet another generation was enduring the sting of hatred because of the color of our skin. I had to show Kellie how to always move toward the light of understanding and to know that, as Grandma said, just because somebody calls you "rich" it doesn't mean coins jingle in your pocket. Sticks and stones . . .

Together, we got through that seventh-grade experience and grew because of it. Kellie remains the light of my life, always inspiring me to do and be my personal best. Today we are good friends as well as loving mother and daughter. She has been the most valuable part of my life's puzzle, always.

I have to admit that God has a sense of humor, however, and

even plays practical jokes as he hands out the puzzle pieces. Of all the people I first met at Mary Elizabeth Inn, I am still in touch with two women. The one I call Teddy is the biggest surprise. She grew up to become a wonderful mother and wife. It took three marriages to settle her down into monogamous domesticity, but she has been a loyal and loving friend, showing herself to be genuine and caring. Renee, who was there for me when Matt took flight, is also still a friend. Every now and again, since I am in the news, I get a phone call from someone who identifies herself as one of those other young women from the Inn, and we laugh and reminisce about our times together. Kerry Lynn, my old roommate, has always been in and out of my life, taking off periodically to far-away places on her travels.

Now, I'll share with you my biggest surprise, the piece of my life puzzle that I neither understood nor recognized when it was handed to me. At age fifty, I lamented the fact that I had not fulfilled a promise I had made years before. I had promised God I would adopt a child. My passion for adoption had been developed after my eighteen years on the Board of AASK AMERICA—Aid to Adoption to Special Kids, an organization founded by my dear friends Bob and Dorothy DeBolt. While on the board of their organization, I helped with the adoption of more than ten thousand children into loving families. I watched the DeBolts adopt six children of their own.

So here I was, thinking about how I had broken my promise to God since, now that I was past fifty, adoption was probably out of the question. *Of course,* I said to God, *couldn't we just overlook this promise? You know my age will prevent me from qualifying as an adoptive parent.* Then, four years ago, fate presented me with four-year-old twin boys with huge eyes, dimpled cheeks and the exact look of my daughter at their age. How could I refuse? I took them into my heart and my home and what a joy they have been for me. You've gotta see me on the soccer field at 7:00 A.M. Saturdays, or watch me crawl around the back yard looking for roley poleys, or see the joy in my smile as we go for Sunday morning church.

Although the loss of Christopher, my baby boy, was devastating, when I look at my twin sons I remember the Scripture in the Bible that says, "And I will restore to you the years that the locust hath eaten." (Job 2:25.)

Today, I am twice blessed and oh, my dears, I can't even describe the enormity of this surprise, nor can I tell you how perfectly these puzzle pieces complete my life. My heart melts when I hear the twins call "Mom," or when I bend over their little faces to kiss them good night, or when I find a tiny foot sticking out from beneath the covers and kiss it and tuck it in. Oh, how lucky I feel, at my age, to be tripping over toy trucks and reading Mother Goose or Dr. Seuss and watching Barney and planning Easter egg hunts. What a surprise.

NAMASTE

May all your surprises be the blessings
that mine have turned out to be.